Voir, c'est avoir ! Allons courir !
    Vie errante
    Est chose enivrante ;
Voir, c'est avoir ! Allons courir !
Car tout voir c'est tout conquérir !

—*Béranger.*

ON THE ARLBERG PASS.

ISBN 978-1-333-87491-9
PIBN 10701182

This book is a reproduction of an important historical work. Forgotten Books uses
state-of-the-art technology to digitally reconstruct the work, preserving the original format
whilst repairing imperfections present in the aged copy. In rare cases, an imperfection in
the original, such as a blemish or missing page, may be replicated in our edition. We do,
however, repair the vast majority of imperfections successfully; any imperfections that
remain are intentionally left to preserve the state of such historical works.

1 MONTH OF
FREE
READING

at
www.ForgottenBooks.com

By purchasing this book you are eligible for one month membership to ForgottenBooks.com, giving you unlimited access to our entire collection of over 1,000,000 titles via our web site and mobile apps.

To claim your free month visit:

www.forgottenbooks.com/free701182

English
Français
Deutsche
Italiano
Español
Português

www.forgottenbooks.com

Mythology Photography **Fiction**
Fishing Christianity **Art** Cooking
Essays Buddhism Freemasonry
Medicine **Biology** Music **Ancient**
Egypt Evolution Carpentry Physics
Dance Geology **Mathematics** Fitness
Shakespeare **Folklore** Yoga Marketing
Confidence Immortality Biographies
Poetry **Psychology** Witchcraft
Electronics Chemistry History **Law**
Accounting **Philosophy** Anthropology
Alchemy Drama Quantum Mechanics
Atheism Sexual Health **Ancient History**
Entrepreneurship Languages Sport
Paleontology Needlework Islam
Metaphysics Investment Archaeology
Parenting Statistics Criminology
Motivational

out

$\dfrac{\text{out}}{3^{00}}$
net

70375

✓

THE HIGH-ROADS

OF

THE ALPS.

First Edition, August 1910.
Second Edition, May 1911.

THE HIGH-ROADS

OF

THE ALPS

A MOTORING GUIDE TO ONE HUNDRED

MOUNTAIN PASSES

BY

CHARLES L. FREESTON, F.R.G.S.

SECOND EDITION. REVISED AND ENLARGED

WITH 110 ITINERARIES, 102 PHOTOGRAPHIC ILLUSTRATIONS
AND 11 MAPS AND DIAGRAMS

CHARLES SCRIBNER'S SONS
NEW YORK
1911

PREFACE.

THIS book represents the sum of seventeen years' experience of the Alps, during which period I have made many tours among the mountain roads of France, Switzerland, Italy and the Tyrol.

From the first tour to the last I have felt the need of practical information, in concrete form, of a kind which the road tourist may seek in vain in the standard guide-books. They ignore the road route whenever there is a railway within measurable distance; and, when a Pass must needs be described because it is the sole link between two valleys, the vital questions of width, gradients, corners and surface quality are never vouchsafed a single line.

In a word, then, this volume is designed to meet a want—a want which is the more pressing now that the power and efficiency of the modern car have made England seem small, and all lowland touring grounds only too familiar. If there is one place on earth where the tireless qualities of the motor-car may justify themselves, it is on the long-drawn but glorious ascent of an Alpine Pass. The very fact that horsed locomotion, where rises of ten or twenty miles are concerned,

is so slow has led to the high carriage-roads
being taken of necessity rather than choice; but
there is nothing nowadays to prevent the easy, safe
and systematic exploration of mountain routes by
car, and the amassing of a huge fund of delightful
experiences.

Fascinating as is the theme, however, I have
endeavoured in the descriptions which follow
of some hundred Passes to make practical considerations paramount. Full itineraries are given
throughout, with altitudes reduced to English
feet. The figures in existing guide-books, I may
add, are almost uniformly wrong, but I have
not only taken pains to acquire from official
sources the exact bases of metres, but have
worked these out to four places of decimals. Of
the itineraries themselves I may say that they
have never before been collocated in this form—in
a volume, that is, framed with the definite object
of grouping the most picturesque routes of Central
Europe. Many of the data have been most difficult to obtain, even after personal crossing of the
Passes themselves; and, although the itineraries
do but appropriate one-tenth of the total letter-
press, their preparation has involved more time
and labour than the main portion of the text.

Of the illustrations I may say that the majority
are from my own photographs, and in many cases
are intended to show the practical character of
the mountain high-roads rather than their wealth
of scenic attractiveness. It must be remembered,

too, that in addition to the limitations imposed upon the camera by variations of weather, many of the Passes are fortified—oftener than not at the most picturesque stages of the route; and, as a matter of fact, several of the photographs herein reproduced were taken at some personal risk.

Several sketch-maps are provided, from which the relationship of the various groups of Passes to each other may be readily appreciated, as also their immense importance to the tourist who is planning a long continental journey by road. I would also call particular attention to the map of Alpine territory generally, which I have had prepared in refutation of the widely prevalent idea that " the Alps " is a synonym for Switzerland. Although I have dealt with the Swiss carriage-roads seriatim, well knowing that they are all bound ere long to be thrown open to motor vehicles, my chief purpose has been to emphasise the extent and variety of the mountain roads of France, Italy and the Tyrol, greatly surpassing as they do those of Switzerland in numbers, height and quality alike.

C. L. F.

HASLEMERE, SURREY,
        July, 1910.

PREFACE TO THE SECOND EDITION.

THE gratifying reception accorded to this book by the press and the public alike has already necessitated the issue of a second edition; for, though the first was not published until autumn was at hand, it was sold out during the winter months—a fact which is significant of the great interest now displayed in the subject of road touring in the Alps.

Wherever necessary the information has been revised and brought up to date, and sundry minor errata have been corrected. The opportunity has been taken, moreover, of adding the itineraries, etc., of the Col du Glandon in France, and the Buco di Vela, the Broccon, the Gobera and the Jaufen Passes respectively in the Tyrol. Particular attention may be directed to the last-named route, which eventually will form · an important link in the wonderful array of mountain roads which the Austrian Government, with liberal-minded enterprise, has created.

The map of the passes of the Tyrol, facing page 129, is now reproduced on a larger scale, and also indicates the four additional routes mentioned above. I have also made some slight variations in the "Ideal Route" on page 372.

In the main, however, there has been no
need of substantial alteration of the original
text. Numerous correspondents have been good
enough to pay hearty testimony to its general
accuracy, and have welcomed " The High-Roads
of the Alps " as a standard work. I may point
out, however, that incidental changes of one kind
or another may occur, on any of the roads herein
described, at any time. Custom-houses not infre-
quently shift their site, and two or three trans-
ferences of this kind have had to be noted in the
present volume. Local regulations, moreover, may
be relaxed, or new ones may be imposed, without
any notification thereof being widely circulated.
New bridges may be built, and roads described as
poor may be improved, while hotels, of course,
are always likely to spring up in places at present
without accommodation. Hence I shall be pleased
to receive, from any tourist who may encounter
any new feature of importance, such details as
may usefully be recorded in succeeding editions
of this work.

April 30*th*, 1911.

CONTENTS.

CONTENTS.

PAGE

LIST OF ILLUSTRATIONS.

MAPS AND DIAGRAMS.

CHAPTER I.

INTRODUCTORY.

CAN anything new be written about the Alps? There is not a peak that has not been climbed, nor a path that remains untrodden, and from the mountaineering point of view the tale of conquest is complete.

But there are more ways than one of admiring the Alps at close quarters, and recent developments have brought a new sphere of conquest to the forefront. If there are rocks to be scaled there are also roads to be followed; roads that lead into fastnesses that are far enough above the plains, and near enough to towering summits, to provide an ample feast to the eye, together with that splendid exhilaration which is enjoyed when the air is surcharged with the crispness due to the presence of ice and snow. And if it be asked "Wherein lies the new sphere of conquest?" the answer is two-fold. Alpine roads have increased in number to a degree which has made them worthy of study in themselves; and the motor-car has come as unquestionably the finest means of carrying this study into effect.

For generations the traveller among the Alps, as distinguished from the climber, had to trust to his own legs, or call in the aid of the horse. The one method was slow and fatiguing to himself, the other alike slow and fatiguing to himself and to the animal employed. How tedious the ascent

of a mountain pass behind horses really is may be
gauged when it is stated that a man on foot can
easily overtake a diligence or a post-carriage, and
is only overtaken when the horses are able to
trot on the level or downhill. To cross one or
two passes by horsed carriage may be endurable,
but to make a practice of it is quite another
matter; and, as for walking, life is too short for
systematic excursions over Alpine roads. The
pedestrian has not only the labour of toiling ten
or twenty miles uphill, but can only count upon
a limited rate of travel down the other side.
Mileage to him is formidable in itself, apart from
the question of gradients; and he is also at the
mercy of dull stages of the route.

There is one way, however, in which a man
may make use of his own muscles without being
handicapped by mileage, and that, of course, is
by resorting to the bicycle; and herein lies
another modern factor which makes the Alpine
high-roads worthy of more attention than they
have hitherto received. A cycling tour among
the Alps is a truly fascinating experience, far
surpassing the pleasures of pedestrianism or car-
riage-riding, and only excelled by motoring itself.
The outstanding advantage of the bicycle in pass-
work is that its rider can make such good progress downhill. Going upwards he may move
only a little faster than the carriage, and at the
same pace, perhaps, as the walker with a heavy
rücksack; but once at the summit the whole
aspect of affairs is changed. The walker is left
to his uniform tramp, while the carriage is out-
distanced in a couple of minutes, and the cyclist

may revel in an intoxicating "coast" of anything from ten to forty miles.

Centred in the motor-car, however, are the advantages of all other methods of locomotion with the disadvantages of none; to which must be added its own unique qualities of power and speed. It has absolute independence of movement, and can go slowly over picturesque stages or stop altogether without fear of losing ground; while on uninteresting stretches it can accelerate its pace to a degree which entirely banishes tedium. Gradients, as such, have no terrors; a good car will forge its way with ease up any rise the Alpine carriage-roads can present, while it can descend them all in perfect safety, and at an exhilarating speed whenever and wherever the scenery does not demand a slower rate of progression.

For pure enjoyment there is nothing to compare with pass-climbing in a car; I say this with absolute conviction based upon a long and varied experience of Alpine touring by all available means of progression, and also of motoring itself from the earliest days. Grand as it may be to escape from the tortuous and police-ridden roads of England and bowl at high speed along the broad, straight highways of the French plains, the breath of fullest liberty and delight is not indrawn until one finds one's car pulling strongly up a twenty miles' ascent on an Alpine pass, rising to and then piercing the zone of trees, swinging round corner after corner, and with a final upward sweep reaching a summit of nine thousand feet above the sea. As a test of the car itself pass-climbing puts all other forms of trial into the shade; on your own driving skill it makes demands which confer the supremest degree of sport without being dangerous or exacting; while above every other consideration is the fact that you are a roamer amid the finest scenery in Europe, exploring it without trammels of any kind, and embracing in a few weeks what by any other means would not be accomplished in as many months.

CHAPTER II.

THE NEGLECT OF ROAD TRAVEL.

ALTHOUGH the tide of eastward travel, whether from Great Britain to the Continent, or from America to Europe, has increased greatly during the last few years, there are still vast numbers of · people who know little or nothing about locomotion in the Alps. They harbour merely hazy notions on the subject, and these may be reduced to the following definitions:—Firstly, that the Alps are a Swiss monopoly; secondly, that for the most part they offer a perennial exercise ground for acrobatic Englishmen, who are more than half mad; and, thirdly, that the only alternative to scaling a peak by the aid of a rope, ice axe and crampons, is to build a tunnel and rush through it by train.

This state of things, of course, is due to the dominance of the railway era, which for nearly two generations has led people to forget that there are such things as roads. To look at any railway company's map, in almost any country, would lead people to imagine that there was hardly a square mile of territory to which the train would not carry them; but take up an ordnance map, and for every mile of rail there will be found, in England and France at all events, scores of miles of highway, while even in other countries road predominates over rail.

The growth of cycling first brought this fact home; the rise of motoring has clinched it.

But if people have only in recent years begun to think about the roads as a means of locomotion in flat or merely undulating country, it is not surprising that there should be a lack of knowledge on the subject of the roadways of the Alps. In the first half of the nineteenth century, the Englishman who did the "grand tour" was obliged to know something of Alpine roads for the simple reason that he had perforce to drive everywhere by post-chaise; and even now one may meet elderly people who drove over this or that pass in the days of their youth, and who treasure the recollection of summit scenery on which their own grown-up children have never set eyes. They in their turn have either been attracted to other regions, or, if they have crossed an Alpine chain, it has probably been through the bowels of the earth in the shape of the St. Gotthard, the Mont Cenis, the Simplon, the Bötzberg, or the Arlberg tunnel. There is only one pass of importance on which road and rail meet on terms of equality, and that is the Brenner; but its total height is only 4,495 feet, and its summit is devoid of views.

Let us consider further the definitions which I venture to give above of the non-traveller's ideas as to the Alps. First there is the question of the inevitable association of the Alps with Switzerland alone. Professed mountaineers, of course, know better; but the attention of the general tourist has been focussed upon Switzerland simply because the railway companies have attracted him thither by their advertisements. The French Alps are hardly ever heard of. It is true that Chamonix and the Mont Blanc range are in France, but they are quite close to Switzerland, and are usually approached by way of Geneva. But what of Grenoble, with its magnificent environment of mountains, and the grand series of high-roads of which it is the centre?

For every tourist who proceeds by rail to Grenoble, and alights there, there are tens of thousands who will take a ticket to Basle or Berne. Almost the only occasion, in fact, on which the Alps are associated with France in the minds of railway travellers is when they find themselves in touch with the mountains which fringe the Riviera coast; and, as the journey thither is usually taken in winter, there is no question of road locomotion on high ground, and even the motorist who drives right through France to the Côte d'Azur in the season must of necessity keep to the plains, because any road of appreciable altitude will be buried in snow.

Then, again, there is the Tyrol. Until a few years ago this beautiful territory was practically *terra incognita* to the tourist. The Austrian Government, however, has shown extraordinary enterprise in the way of developing the country from the touring point of view, and of bringing its manifold attractions to the notice of English-speaking people. What is particularly pleasing is that, though a certain amount of railway development has been carried out on legitimate lines, road development has received even more attention. Fine new highways have been made

over even the highest passes, and these are linked
together by effective services of motor diligences,
thus solving the problem of how to avoid on the
one hand the terrors of the cumbrous, crawling
horse-drawn diligence, and, on the other, the spoil-
ing of landscapes by rack and pinion railways,
tunnels, or funiculars.

In a word, the manner in which the Tyrol
has been developed as a touring ground is one
of the most pleasing signs of the times; and
at the present moment this Austrian province
stands absolutely unrivalled in attractiveness. It
is neither a barbarous waste, devoid of the con-
veniences which are necessary for comfortable
travel, nor is it a hotbed of rail-borne tourists all
travelling along a beaten track.

As for the theory that there is no alternative
between scaling a mountain on foot and burrowing
through it by rail, facts tell a different tale.
There were high roads over the Alps even in
Roman times. Then in the beginning of the
nineteenth century the greatest road-builder who
ever lived, Napoleon Bonaparte, conceived and
carried into execution a scheme of road communication by which his name will be remembered
long after his military achievements have been
forgotten, and by which also France will eternally
benefit.

The roads over the Mont Cenis, the Simplon, the
Col du Lautaret, the Mont Genèvre, the Col de
Sestrières, the Corniche and the Col de la Faucille,
were all the direct outcome of Napoleonic genius.
Then followed the construction by the Austrian
Government of the wonderful Splügen Pass and

also of the finest high-road in the world, the famous
Stelvio, which was begun in 1820, and only took
four years to build. The St. Gotthard road was
begun by the Swiss about the same time, and
completed in 1832. After this came, if not the
deluge, the crippling influence of the railway,
which put a stop to Alpine road-building for
forty or fifty years. The feverish enterprise of
railway engineers notwithstanding, however, the
necessity for opening up new means of communication in high altitudes has since been recognised
in France, Switzerland, Austria, and Italy alike,
and there are now more than twice as many high
carriage-roads in the Alps as those which were
known to the post-chaise travellers of the earlier
part of the last century.

And of these roads generally, what have they
to offer in the way of attraction to the tourist?
Are they worth traversing for their own sakes;
or are entrancing views only to be enjoyed by
the climber of experience and skill? There can
be no two opinions upon this subject. Mountain-
climbing is entirely a thing unto itself. It is
mainly athletic, even acrobatic, but, splendid as
it undoubtedly is as a pastime, it is not in the
remotest sense of the word the only means of
appreciating Alpine grandeurs at their true worth.

The most famous climbers, I think, would
themselves admit as much. The late Professor
Forbes, in his classic work, "Travels through the
Alps," remarked that "The most successful
" Alpine travellers will, if disposed to be candid,
" admit that the happiest, if not the proudest
" moments of their experiences, have been spent

" on the summit of some of the more majestic
" passes of the Alps, or on some summits not
" of the highest class." Again, "Even the pro-
" spect is itself more noble if every snow peak
" has not been already sunk beneath the feet
" of the spectator; if the view, in short, com-
" bines the range and precision of the eagle's
" outlook with the contemplation of the still
" higher summits which preserve the grandeur of
" ascending perspective with the detail of rough-
" hewn masses of granite and sparkling diadems
" of snow, brought into illusory proximity by
" the transparency of the upper air."

And if it be rejoined that Professor Forbes's
views are now out of date, let me quote that
redoubtable climber, Sir Martin Conway, who
animadverts in his charming book, "The Alps,"
upon the modern climber's practice of using the
train as much as possible and contenting himself
with mere rock-scrambling when he has reached a
given centre. "The whole of a pass," he writes,
" is the route through a mountain range from
" plain to plain. Few mountaineers nowadays ever
" cross a range in that way except by train, and
" yet it is one of the most delightful experiences.
" Motor-cars will enable us to enjoy such traverses
" by road when the Swiss have learned the wisdom
" of granting free passage across the Alps to any
" kind of vehicle. It is only when a range of
" mountains is approached from the plain that its
" importance and geographical value as a dividing
" whole can be felt." And after describing the
delights of an ascent from plain to summit, and
the descent from summit to plain, Sir Martin

Conway adds: "A long traverse of that kind is
" a real pass, a whole pass; nothing else is more
" than a fragment—a choice fragment it may be,
" but still a part and not the whole. The old
" mountaineers such as John Ball used to take
" their passes in this complete form; so did old
" coach travellers like John Ruskin in his early
" days. Now mountaineers scorn to waste their
" time on so lengthy an experience and to remain
" so long at low levels. It is not their way.
" They have continual business aloft. They leave
" to motorists that kind of expedition. What
" good fortune, then, that motor-cars should have
" been invented in time to provide such possible
" delights for climbers when their days of activity
" are done!"

Thus we have the testimony of one of the
most famous of Alpine climbers that the motor-
car has its place in mountain latitudes, and that
the high roads are not to be regarded with contempt. And touching the reference above quoted
to the Swiss, I shall show later how vast a field
of Alpine exploration is open to the touring
motorist outside Switzerland altogether; such, in
fact, is the main purpose of this volume. Not
only, however, will it be made clear that Switzerland is in the enjoyment of no monopoly in
mountains or mountain roads, but also that there
are picturesque regions in plenty which the railway traveller cannot reach at all, and which are
nevertheless provided with high-roads more suited
to motor-cars than to any other form of locomotion.

Where English people are concerned, however,
the idea is bound to linger for some time to

come that rock-climbing is the be-all and end-all
of Alpine exploration; and this is largely due
to the attitude of the Alpine Club, which has
so severe a qualification for membership. Only
climbers are eligible who have done something
specially difficult or dangerous; and even the
man who prides himself upon having climbed to
the summit of the highest mountain in Europe—
Mont Blanc—would have no chance of election
on the strength of that feat alone. Consequently
the Alpine Club does nothing to foster a knowledge of Alpine territory; a man must have
gained his knowledge before he can gain election.
Altogether different, however, are the bases on
which the Continental Alpine Clubs are founded.
A love of the Alps is a sufficient qualification
for membership, and thus we find that the
German-Austrian Club has some 80,000 members,
while even the French Alpine Club has nearly
6,000. The English Club has barely 700.

Even if climbing the loftiest summits invariably afforded the grandest of views—and very
often it does nothing of the kind—it would still
be open to consider what measure of satisfaction
were to be derived from travelling over mountain
roads. The answer is sufficiently emphatic. In
the matter of latitude and longitude the passes
over which there are carriage-roads bring one
within at least measurable distance of all, and in
close contact with the majority, of the chief
mountain groups. In many cases, too, the scenery
actually bordering the road itself is picturesque,
and from no other point can be seen to better
advantage.

For example, the Furka Pass brings one so close to the famous Rhone Glacier that one can actually touch the ice. The Bernina Pass, on the Pontresina side, affords a noble prospect of the Morteratsch Glacier, while the Madatsch Glacier, as seen above Trafoi on the Stelvio Pass, is one of the most impressive sights in the Alps, as also is the view of the Meije from the Col du Lautaret in France.

The finest waterfalls, moreover, adjoin the road on one pass or another; as witness the Handegg and Reichenbach Falls on the Grimsel, the Madesimo on the Splügen, and the Kalt-wasser on the Simplon, not to mention many others. Then again, a river is almost an invari-able accompaniment of a pass, and if Alpine roads had nothing more to offer than the sight of the foaming impetuosity of the Reuss on the St. Gotthard, of the Aare on the Grimsel, or of the Maira on the Maloja, they would still be worth the crossing.

Other items of picturesqueness are gorges and ravines, and these in the nature of things are numerous, nor are the latter by any means confined to the lower portions of the passes; and the same remark may be applied to the frequent galleries or arches, rough-hewn out of the solid rock. Let it be added, too, in passing, that while man has laid a desecrating hand on the face of Nature where railways are concerned, the effect of his handiwork as seen in the construction of mountain roads is almost uniformly to the good. It is no exaggeration to say that the windings of a ribbon road are beautiful in themselves and marvellously

effective in their sinuous curves, while the boldness of construction of the Stelvio, the Splügen,
and others, is a source of unfailing admiration
for human skill without any of the disfiguring
accompaniments which are inseparable from the
railway system.

Lakes, it need hardly be stated, are everywhere regarded as one of the chief features in the
beauty of a landscape. In the case of not a few
passes there is a lake at the actual summit; sometimes there are two or three. Numerous passes,
moreover, lead from one quarter or another to
the lakes of Lucerne, Thun, Brienz, Annecy, the
famous Lombardy group, and the brilliant series
of the Upper Engadine.

Wild flowers, so essential an item in the in-
ventory of Alpine attractions, are found in great
profusion on or near the great carriage-roads,
while at the summit of the new Pordoi Pass, in
the Tyrol, edelweiss itself may be gathered as
easily as cowslips in an English meadow. Pines
and firs the passes can show in myriads, while
the lower slopes are often of great pastoral beauty.

Above all else, however, though I mention it
last, is the snow itself. Up to July it is present
on all the higher peaks, and often covers the
bare rocks right down to the zone of trees; and
on the Stilfserjoch, or Stelvio, great walls of
snow flank the road for some distance below
the summit. In fact, everything that combines
to give the Alps their amazing prodigality of
charm is spread before the enchanted gaze of
the traveller by road; and not the least interesting
factor in the crossing of a mountain road is the

gradual transition from fertile plain to rolling hill-side, from hill-side to fragrant pine woods, from woods to grassy slopes and crisper air, and, finally, in many cases, to an environment of snow-capped peaks.

All the varying sensations, too, of which the mind receives the imprint on the upward journey are intensified anew as they are experienced in inverse ratio on the descent to the plains on the other side of the pass, while yet further variety is added by the contrast between the pastoral charms of the Swiss or Tyrolese valleys on the one side and the smiling opulence of the Lombardy plains. When it is remembered that the Stelvio road attains a height of 9,041 feet, that there are several carriage-roads of over 8,000 feet, and that quite an appreciable number are over 7,000 feet, it is obvious that the variety of intimate feature and distant prospect alike is immense. The mountaineer is welcome to his extra thousands of feet; but no one can truthfully aver that nature as viewed from the roads themselves is not wondrously impressive and magnificently beautiful.

CHAPTER III.

THE GROUPING OF THE PASSES.

WE have seen how a great climber like Sir Martin Conway condemns the practice of rock scrambling to the exclusion of exploration among the passes generally; while railway tourists, on the other hand, are reminded that though they, unlike the climber pure and simple, may pass from valley to valley, they do so in a comparatively useless manner. Even before motor-cars were in general use the late Grant Allen, when describing the main routes to Italy, animadverted on the unsatisfactory method of crossing the Alps by the "mean modern subterfuge of a tunnel."

Until recently, of course, the perfectly valid excuse could have been put forward that none but those possessed of unlimited means and leisure could have betaken themselves to the roads to any appreciable extent; at the same time it was always open to them to cross a pass or two in a horsed carriage, or afoot, in preference to resorting to the train and the inevitable tunnel. The motorist, however, may cross with ease, and without loss of time, not one pass alone but many; and not merely does he avoid the railway tunnel, but he has access to routes and districts in which the railway is absolutely unknown.

And one of the most gratifying features of the situation is the fact that, where the crossing

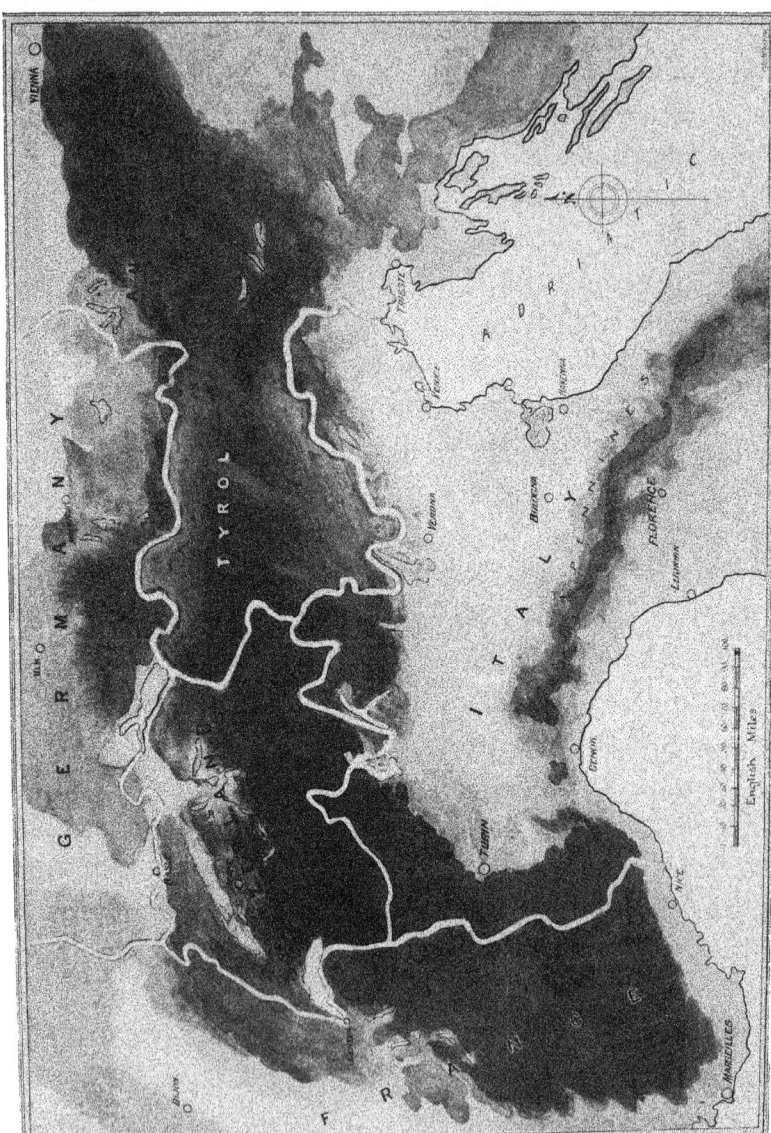

THE ALPS FROM END TO END.

(The Map shows the wide extent of the Alpine ranges, 630 miles in all, of which Switzerland can claim less than one-third.)

of passes is concerned, a man does not inevitably need to possess a motor-car of his own. On many of the Alpine carriage-roads—outside Switzerland, of course—the horse-drawn diligence, as I predicted several years ago would be the case, has been entirely superseded, and regular services of motor diligences are now in operation all over the Tyrol and on many of the chief high-roads of the French Alps.

The non-motorist, therefore, though unable to emulate the car-owner by roaming at will all over Central Europe, may nevertheless use the train to carry him over level ground, and then explore the mountains by means of motor diligences. The number of these is constantly on the increase, and before long it will be just as feasible for the ordinary tourist to enjoy the delights of road travelling among the Alps by a less tedious method than that of sitting behind a team of horses, as it is for the man who is rich enough to employ his own car for the purpose.

It remains, therefore, to consider what is practicable in the way of touring among the Alpine high-roads, such consideration, of course, being the main object of this book. Before entering into details, however, it is necessary that the reader should endeavour to appreciate the extent of the Alpine ranges themselves. He may, for example, be one of those who have regarded the Alps as the monopoly of the Swiss; he may further have supposed that roads over the Alps are very limited in number; and if he escape these errors he may nevertheless have heard—and correctly—that for the most part motoring in Switzerland on

B

high ground is forbidden. Fortunately, however, Switzerland is only a link in the Alpine chain. Fortunately, too, the number of Alpine high-roads outside Switzerland is very great; nor has any other nation but the Swiss adopted an embargo against motor vehicles—an embargo so absurd that Switzerland itself will have to remove it at no distant date.

As a matter of fact the Alps extend the whole way from Nice to Vienna, a distance of no less than 630 miles. Not only is their length formidable but their breadth also. In the extreme east they measure over 185 miles between Linz in the north and Trieste in the south. Now the distance across Switzerland from Geneva to the eastern frontier is only 217 miles as the crow flies, while the country only measures 138 miles from north to south—figures which speak for themselves where the question of exclusive possession is concerned.

The Alps generally are usually divided into three main groups—namely, the Central, the Western, and the Eastern. Their sub-divisions are numerous, and authorities are by no means agreed on the questions of nomenclature or boundary lines. The following, however, may be regarded as the more important groups:—

In the Western Alps there are the Maritime, Cottian, Dauphiné, Graian, Western Pennine, Central Pennine, and Eastern Pennine.

In the Central Alps the chief groups are the Bernese, Lepontine, Tödi, North-East Switzerland, Bernina, Albula, and Silvretta.

In the Eastern Alps there are the Bavarian, Ortler, Lombard, Central Tyrolese, Dolomite, and South-Eastern groups.

It is impossible to claim for any one of these divisions or sub-divisions a monopoly of either picturesqueness or good roads; practically every range has its claims upon the traveller. The Alps are beautiful from end to end, to use the mildest possible expression ; and as for high-roads, ancient and modern, there are scores which surmount altitudes of over 4,000 feet.

Now these roads may be considered from three points of view. In the first place the Alps are Nature's barrier between the West and sunny Italy, and the average English tourist has merely addressed himself hitherto to the problem of how to reach Italy in the simplest manner. Even the automobilist who has no desire, however, to embark upon a campaign of pass climbing must face the question of ascending high ground at least once on the outward journey, and similarly on his return, assuming, of course, that he is not disposed to make extraordinarily long detours.

The problem, however, is in no sense complex. The railway traveller must take his choice between the Mont Cenis (falsely so-called), the St. Gotthard, or the Arlberg and Brenner railways, unless he prefers the fourth option of a hot journey along the Rhone Valley, and passing into Italy by means of the comparatively new Simplon tunnel. Similarly the automobilist may cross the Mont Cenis Pass—that is to say, the real Mont Cenis— to Turin, the St. Gotthard to Como and Milan, or the Arlberg to Innsbruck and thence over the

Brenner, with the option of many delightful routes to Italy through the Tyrol; or he, too, may choose an easy route to Geneva, and reach the Italian lakes by way of the Simplon road.

At the outset the automobilist may approach the question of pass-climbing from the utilitarian point of view alone. I can safely promise that he will find the experience of crossing his first pass so delightful and inspiriting that he will be imbued with the desire to gain a much more extended acquaintance with mountain roads. Though it may be too late to alter his itinerary for that particular journey, he will certainly address himself to the task of finding out what other passes there may be to conquer, and how many of them he can bring within the scope of his next Continental tour.

He will find that the number of lofty carriage-roads is very much larger than he had for a moment imagined, and that of the bulk of them he had never even heard the names; indeed it would be difficult for him to compile a list of what is and what is not available. The guide-books pay scant attention to the carriage-roads if there is a railway within measurable distance, or if this or that pass is off the beaten track, and does not lead from one place of importance to another. In this respect guide-book writers do but share the ingrained habit of the public generally of regarding the railway as inevitable; but now that we are coming back to the roads it is essential that the subject should be approached from a totally different point of view.

I should prefer to divide the Alpine carriage-roads into three classes. In the first place, there are the main routes which must be followed of necessity by the road traveller if making a direct journey to some point in Italy, the Tyrol, or the south-east of France. Secondly, there are many passes which are encountered when roaming in picturesque centres; and, thirdly, there are passes which may be assailed solely for the sake of sport, as a means of testing alike the powers of one's car and the nerve and skill of the driver. The first category is soon exhausted; the second is amazingly full; while the third is small, but large enough to be sufficing.

In other words, the man with a good car who goes roaming about Europe may sample every species of sensation that driving can confer, whether from the artistic or the sporting point of view. He will find means of testing his car of which he had never previously dreamed, and yet of a kind from which it will emerge triumphantly, and cause him to think more highly of it than before. Ere he has finished an Alpine tour, moreover, he will have good reason to pride himself upon his own driving powers to a degree which lack of opportunity had made impossible at home; and he will have witnessed a wealth of beauty, whether panoramic or intimate, such as British landscapes could not even suggest, nor even foreign ones if his journeyings were confined to the railway alone.

But there is one thing above all others which from the very first he should understand, and that is that though, as I have said, his car and his driving skill will be tested in new fashions, and therefore enlarge the variety of his experiences, there is absolutely nothing which he need fear, either for his car or for himself—nothing which a good car cannot surmount, and nothing to which his own physical and mental powers will be unequal.

In no sense of the term will his adventures be of the break-neck order. Strange though it may sound, the gradients will be found to be less steep than those to which he is accustomed at home, though, of course, very much longer-drawn; and, as for personal skill, the "hairpin" corners on the graduated ascents are the only things which will call for special dexterity; a dexterity, moreover, which is soon acquired and speedily becomes second nature.

Even the tackling of "hairpin" corners, however, is as nothing compared with ordinary driving on a narrow, tortuous, and traffic-ridden English highway; and it is possible to sit back in the driving seat and let the car take its own course — generally speaking — to a degree which is altogether impossible on any journey which one may take on any day of the week in any part of England.

CHAPTER IV.

WHAT CROSSING A PASS MEANS.

THE crossing of an Alpine pass is, beyond all fear of contradiction, the most interesting, the most sporting, and the most exhilarating purpose to which an automobilist can devote his car. The word "pass" is here used, of course, and hereafter almost uniformly throughout this book, as implying one which is also a first-class carriage-road. Strictly speaking, a pass is the lowest depression, in a range of mountains, enabling travellers to pass from one valley to another. This depression may be such as only the mountaineer can utilise; or it may be a mule-path; or it may be a narrow apology for a road suitable for small and light vehicles; or, finally, it may be a grandly engineered high-road of wondrous and costly construction. It is with this last-named type that we have mainly to deal.

Now a pass obviously suggests ascents and descents of a formidable character; but so unaccustomed is the non-Alpinist to excessive heights that in all probability the first, if not the only, idea which the mention of a pass conveys to his mind is that of steepness of gradient. If he happens to know that the highest road in Great Britain—namely, Cairnwell, in Scotland—has an altitude of 2,200 feet, and he is then told that one may rise by road

to a height of 9,041 feet—namely, on the Stelvio
Pass—he is altogether unlikely, so far as my
experience has shown, after conversations with
many who have not travelled in the Alps, to
picture this extraordinary elevation as a matter
of unusual mileage, but will at once begin to
think about gradients of extraordinary severity.
His mind cannot conceive how such a height
can be obtained without terrific effort; and if he
has tackled Porlock Hill, in Somerset, or any
other monstrosities of British road-building, he
will probably imagine that to compass a height
of several thousand feet, to say nothing of the
Stelvio itself, is merely a case of Porlock magnified a good many times, and therefore altogether
unfit for sane mortals to attempt.

There is no fact, however, in connection with
Alpine motoring which needs to be more forcibly
iterated and reiterated than that of the entire
simplicity of an ascent so far as mere gradient
is concerned. There are gradients on hundreds, if
not thousands of English roads, which are never
seen on Alpine carriage-roads of the first order.
The necessities of the case have involved skilful
surveys and most scientific construction, and it
would be impossible to find a solitary hundred
yards of road on the main Alpine passes which a
6-h.p. voiturette could not surmount.

On English main roads one may find gradients
of one in six, while on by-roads the figures are
often considerably worse. One in six, in round
figures, is 17 per cent.; and incidentally I may
mention that gradients on the Continent are
usually referred to in terms of percentage, and

not according to our English method.   And what is the average gradient of an Alpine pass?   To the English motorist it may sound incredible, but the fact remains that a gradient of 8 per cent. is rarely exceeded; that is to say, what we should call 1 in 12½.   Their average, however, is considerably lower; and, without further labouring the point, I can only say once more that in this respect there is absolutely nothing to fear.   If a car were to be stopped on an Alpine road it would be from causes which might just as readily occur on Salisbury Plain, such as failure of the engine or of other portions of the mechanism.

Then there is the question of the width of the roads.   Is there anywhere, it may be asked, where the available space is so narrow that the driver has to steer to a hair's breadth to avoid a rock on the one hand and a precipice on the other?   The answer is emphatically in the negative.   On nearly all the passes described in detail in this volume there is not only room for a man to drive in comfort but even to pass another vehicle.   The Mont Cenis road is broader than many an English highway; the Stelvio itself is 19 feet wide; and, though it would be absurd to say that driving on an Alpine pass is almost as simple a matter as driving along an English road, there is nevertheless, generally speaking, nothing whatever to dread in respect of width.

Another question to consider is the degree to which unforeseen dangers are absent or present. Here again my experience leads me to speak in the most reassuring terms.   The concealed corner, so ubiquitous a feature of English roads, is virtually an unknown factor on the Alpine passes, inasmuch as they represent, as I have said, no haphazard thoroughfares, but definitely engineered achievements. I do not say that there are no corners which prevent one from seeing an approaching vehicle, but I do say that there are no corners which cannot themselves be seen in advance, and in the approaching of which ordinary caution is necessary, just as would be taken at any other corner on an ordinary road.

Abrupt alterations of gradient, too, it should be mentioned in passing, are rarities; as a matter of fact, I cannot recall the existence of any whatsoever. The element of surprise, in short, which is the chief and almost only source of road accidents all the world over, is less to be reckoned with on the skilfully designed roads in high altitudes than anywhere else. Such surprises as greet one are of a totally different kind—namely, the sudden unfolding of some wondrous panorama or complete change of scene.

As to surfaces, these are often surprisingly good, and the higher one goes the better they become. Villages, of course, and habitations of any kind grow fewer and fewer as one rises; concurrently, therefore, the amount of vehicular traffic is reduced. On certain passes there may be special causes of road obstruction on the lower slopes in the shape of the presence of saw-mills; and carts bearing huge logs of timber to the mills, or bringing down heavy loads of sawn planks, will effectually disintegrate the road between the mill and some big town in the valley below. Apart from local conditions, however, the maintenance of the majority of the roads is not only good but vastly better than the tourist would ever have thought possible when he reflects upon the heights at which the road repairers have to work, and the extremes of weather which are experienced at such altitudes. Of course, one may strike patches of newly laid stones, especially at the beginning of the summer season; but one cannot expect steam-rollers at heights of 6,000 or 7,000 feet. The stones, moreover, are not flinty in character, and there is less risk of having one's tyres gashed than when touring at home.

As for avalanches and landslides, these are, of course, inseparable accompaniments to Alpine altitudes, but it is seldom that they interfere with freedom of locomotion during the summer months. For one reason, the places where avalanches usually fall are well known, and provision is made accordingly. The road may be conducted through a tunnel of masonry at that spot, as on the Simplon, the Bernina, the Splügen, or the Fluela. There may be both a tunnel and a road outside it; ordinarily the latter is employed, but if an avalanche occurs the tunnel is available.

Horses are now thoroughly accustomed to motor vehicles on all the Alpine roads where cars are allowed to be used; that is to say, everywhere outside Switzerland. I may add that I have never yet encountered a frightened horse on a mountain road, though I began touring among the Alps years before cars came into general use. The Swiss are afraid to permit motor-cars on their passes lest the diligences

should be upset; but no trouble of this kind
has been experienced on the French or Tyrolese
roads, while in many cases, as has been observed
in a previous chapter, the horsed diligence has —
already been superseded, and the motor diligence
is regularly employed all over the Tyrol.

On some of the passes, however, one meets
ox-carts, the drivers of which are totally careless
as to the rule of the road. Sometimes, moreover, they will deliberately choose the side
furthest away from the precipice edge, if there
be one, and in that case it is policy for the
driver of a car to disregard the rule of the road
on his own part, and take the precipice side.
Lumbering of gait as these oxen are in the ordinary way, and slow-moving when it comes to
moving aside at the instigation of the driver's
rod, it does not do to assume that they are incapable of taking fright. I have known them
to shy at bicycles and cars alike, and when they
do make up their mind to do so it is done with
surprising celerity, and in a way which may
even mean the overturning of the wagon or cart
which they may be drawing.

Turning now from these practical considerations, we may review certain physical features
which are common to most, if not all, of the
high-roads, with a view to avoiding superfluous
repetition in the descriptions which follow in
subsequent chapters. We will assume that the
tourist's first journey over a pass is begun at
a low altitude, and not, as is often the case,
after having already crossed a summit, say, of
seven thousand feet, and descended to about

four thousand feet, and there beginning another ascent.

For a good many miles, in all probability, the road will proceed along a broad plain, in close companionship with a river, and will rise quite imperceptibly until a height of perhaps two thousand feet is reached, during which one may have travelled twenty miles or more. The road will then begin to ascend perceptibly, but not steeply, for several miles, until it comes to a point, oftener than not about four thousand feet high, at which the gradient becomes much steeper. On this stage it frequently happens that the broad valley has contracted into a narrow ravine, so narrow, indeed, that the road can no longer run alongside the river, and has therefore to be cut on the side of a hill, usually at a height of two or three hundred feet above the water. It is equally probable that the road cannot be cut absolutely on the edge of the slope, but has to be hewn through the solid rock. In other places it has to be buttressed up with masonry, while sometimes a bridge is thrown across a deep depression formed by a tributary stream.

From start to finish, however, everything is done on a definitely planned scale, and there is nothing akin to the stupid and extremely dangerous style of thing which is so often encountered in Great Britain, particularly in Scotland, where a narrow bridge is built across a stream at the foot of a deep descent, immediately followed by another steep rise, which is also entered upon by another abrupt turn. In ninety-nine cases out of a hundred, moreover, the driver on an Alpine road can see with perfect clearness what he has before him, and can gauge at a glance what is necessary in the way of reduction of speed, the application of brake-power, or the skilful rounding of a curve. On English roads, as any tourist knows, there are countless occasions on which a driver or rider imagines, and legitimately imagines, that all is plain-sailing, but is suddenly confronted with a wholly unexpected emergency, and so suddenly that he has barely time to rise to the occasion and come through the ordeal with entire success.

The approximate level of four thousand feet which I have mentioned above usually marks the beginning of the pass proper, and according to the height of the summit there will be a definite ascent to be faced of two or three thousand feet—and much more in two or three exceptional cases—on any part of which one may encounter zigzags. There are roads, it is true, which themselves may not be much higher than four thousand feet, and which are cut in zigzags from as low an altitude as two thousand feet; but on the long passes the ascent is generally very gradual until more than half the altitude has been attained.

At any point between the plain and a height of about five thousand feet a zone of trees may be expected, and oftener than not the road is cut through the belt. At length one emerges into the open again, and with varying results as regards the prospects to be enjoyed. There may be far-reaching vistas on every side, or the environment

may be more or less confined. Whether the
scenery itself be picturesque or barren, however,
there is still plenty of grass on the hill-sides,
and it is these which constitute the veritable
" alps " themselves.

The Alps, to the native mind, are not the lofty
snow-capped peaks which we usually associate
with the name, but the upper slopes which are
used as pastures, and to which cattle, sheep, and
goats are sent at stated periods of the year from
French, Swiss, Italian, and Tyrolese valleys alike.
The slopes gradually become more and more
bare, however, the higher one goes, until the last
stunted tree has disappeared from view, though
wild flowers are still encountered at unexpected
heights, while often the far-famed edelweiss, which
causes the loss of so many lives among luck-
less swains who climb precipices in tourist-ridden
haunts in the hope of finding a solitary flower,
may be gathered without any risk whatever.

On a car, of course, one may halt at any
point that may suit one's fancy, whether to cull
flowers, admire a superb view, or indulge in
the more prosaic satisfaction of taking refresh-
ment. But there is a peculiar satisfaction in the
tackling of these upper slopes *en automobile* which
nothing in the world but a car can confer. While
horses are toiling painfully upwards, so slowly
as to bore the passengers behind them, and at
the same time with inflexible continuity, so that
they cannot halt when they have a mind, the car
forges its triumphant way to its own supreme enjoyment and that of its passengers alike. Except
in the case of a low-powered engine the gradients

are such that the vehicle is equal to a far greater speed than the corners themselves make possible; and, so far from there being cause for entertaining any anxiety as to reaching the top, the sensation of climbing is so exhilarating, and the power of the motor so all-conquering, that the summit is attained all too quickly and with a feeling of real regret.

Hand in hand, moreover, with the magnificent consciousness of mounting, ever mounting without a falter, doubling one's pride in one's car with every minute, one experiences the delights due to a constant and kaleidoscopic change of view on swinging round the corners of the *lacets*, or zigzags, of the winding road—now to the north, then to the east, now to the south, and then to the east, and back to the north again, and so on until the last "hairpin" has been turned. Some of the passes, in the variety and amplitude of range of their upper slopes, repay this splendid mode of progression even more than others; but on not a single one does it lapse into monotony.

The summit is seldom abruptly reached, and quite frequently it is centred in a plain of appreciable extent, with perhaps a lake, or even two. As regards the prospect to be enjoyed, it should be said at once that too much is not to be expected, for the simple reason that a pass, as has already been said, is the lowest opening in a range, and, naturally, therefore, it does not overlook an extensive panorama, and may even be hemmed in at comparatively close quarters. Nevertheless it cannot be said that any of the summits are unpicturesque, while many of them command a certain amplitude of view; and even where the outlook is restricted the rugged wildness of the scene is itself impressive. Some summits there are, moreover, which are really beautiful, and well repay a long halt.

After having taken one's fill of the scenery, refreshed the inner man at the hospice or inn which is nearly always to be found at the top of a pass, and probably despatched a sheaf of picture postcards, it behoves one to embrace the opportunity of casting an eye over the car generally, replenishing the radiator if the day has been very hot and the ascent particularly prolonged, and carefully examining the brakes before embarking on the descent.

Very often the latter is virtually a duplicate of the ascent, structurally considered, where the first two thousand feet or so of fall are concerned. There may be rather more or rather fewer "hairpin" corners, as the case may be, but the same skilful engineering and uniformity in the design of the road are to be observed. The scenery itself, however, may be very different on one side of the summit from the other, especially when the descent leads into Italy, whether one has crossed over from France, Switzerland, or the Austrian Tyrol.

Wherever the pass may be, however, variety and its resultant reward for the journey may be counted upon as a certainty. No matter how many passes you may ascend and descend in a motor-car, you will never tire of the game until you have traversed the last that is available; and even then you will be only too ready and anxious to renew the experience on any or all of them, both for the sake of the scenery and the pure enjoyment of the driving.

Inasmuch as the ascents are not terrific in the way of gradients, it follows that the same adjective would be out of place if applied to the descents. Though in no sense dangerous, however, they naturally require a certain amount of care, at the corners at any rate ; but the degree of skill which is necessary to the occasion is very quickly realised. It is simply a matter of " hanging fire " at the corner, avoiding the temptation to cut it too fine on the inside, swinging well outwards, and then bringing the front wheels round with a nimbleness that is soon acquired.

Of the part which the brakes have to play in this respect I shall speak more fully in the next chapter, on " The Equipment of the Car," and merely refer to mechanical matters in passing in so far as they affect the question of one's experiences and enjoyment of pass-climbing. Long-drawn, however, as the descents may be, there is no excessive fatigue as regards the application of brake-power, inasmuch as the changes can be rung from one brake to another, while at any time the current can be switched off, and the car allowed to run down against the compression of the engine.

Except in the few cases where an actual "gridiron" is encountered of zigzag after zigzag, the road-winding in almost parallel strata, one beneath the other, it is possible to let the car run freely along the straights, merely taking care to slow up gradually and in good time before a corner comes into view. Reasonable caution, care, and skill are demanded throughout the descent, but no more; nothing of the super-human or acrobatic is required.

Practically the only difference that an English driver will experience after crossing a lofty pass is that his arms may be somewhat tired—at any rate at the first attempt; for the "negotiation," to use a colloquialism, of the "hairpin" corners undoubtedly throws more work upon the arms than ordinary driving. The fatigue, however, is of the type which quickly passes away, and is not akin to that which is induced by a long drive on an English journey, when the mind is perpetually on the *qui vive* as regards traffic, sudden corners, the passing through towns and villages, the changing of gears on hills owing to their abrupt variations of gradient, etc., etc.

And here let me mention what is, in point of fact, the most curious and interesting sensation which is to be derived from motoring on Alpine high-roads. Novel enough, it is true, is the experience of rising, rising, ever rising apparently, to a stupendous height such as seven thousand feet—leaving aside the exceptional case of the Stelvio, which is over nine thousand; and the degree to which it becomes formidable is depen-dent on the power of the individual car.

But grand and glorious as the ascent has been, and great as is the degree to which the automobilist has been imbued with the altered scale of things as compared with his puny alti-tudes at home, the really astonishing and entirely new sensation is that of falling, everlastingly falling from a great height to the plains. If on a small or medium-powered car he may possibly have thought while ascending that he was never going to reach the top; but whatever vehicle he be on he will undoubtedly feel, until habituated to the sensation by frequent road journeys over the Alps, that he is never going to reach the bottom. This feeling is paramount despite the fact that the descent is relatively so easy compared with the ascent; but for some reason or other it takes the eye and brain much longer to accustom itself to the immensities of space when going downwards than when on the previous climb.

Every time, moreover, that one reaches a point in the descent which marks the disappearance of all intermediate hills or other obstructions to the view, and opens up a clear prospect of a distant valley below, the untrained eye seems quite unable for a time to project itself so far as to focus itself upon a winding river or cluster of houses many miles away. I do not know what mountaineers themselves have to say upon the subject, but certainly I have never found ascents of any kind convey so complete an idea of what an Alpine height really means as is conferred by the subsequent descent.

I think this is largely due to the fact that one leaves the summit with the idea that there is no more work to be done, and that the down journey will soon be over. The descent may mean anything from eight to forty miles, during which one passes in quick succession from barren rocks to pine wood, from pine wood to ravine, from ravine to open pastures, and thence to

opulently fertile plains, together with rapid variations of temperature which are felt more forcibly
than on the ascent. The zigzag corners, too, are
easier to manage on the up grade than on the
down, and, if they happen to be of an acute
kind, the length of the descent is emphasised by
the constantly recurring necessity for caution.

After a quick run down, moreover, of say
3,000 feet, the amount of falls appears so
tremendous that it seems impossible that one
can now be far from the bottom; but there
may still be three or four thousand more feet
to descend, or proportionately increased mileage
as the gradient itself is lessened. Whatever the
true explanation may be, however, I can only
state the fact, and that is that it takes longer
to get accustomed to the sensations associated
with the descent of an Alpine pass than those
which concerned the more protracted ascent.

CHAPTER V.

THE EQUIPMENT OF THE CAR.

IT is somewhat difficult, I must confess, to define the precise difference, if any, between the degree of preparation necessary for an ordinary tour and for a journey which incidentally embraces Alpine territory. If one especially impresses the desirability of overhauling the whole car when starting for the Alps, the experienced tourist will reply that he always takes that measure of precaution in the ordinary course. If one expatiate on the special need for good brakes, in perfect order, again it may be replied that no sensible owner of a car ever embarks upon a journey of any magnitude without ensuring his own peace of mind in that respect.

Then, again, it is difficult to suggest in print the difference between the risks of an Alpine and a lowland tour respectively. If the former be over-emphasised the would-be climber of passes may be frightened off an eminently delightful experience, or series of experiences; and, on the other hand, if I were to lead a man to think that he could set off to-morrow and steer straight for the summit of the Stelvio with no more premeditation than if he were taking a week-end run to Brighton and back, he would have very good reason to complain that he had by no means been posted up as to the special requirements of the case.

Whatever I may say, therefore, in the way of counsel as to sundry measures of precaution must be taken in conjunction with the distinct and definite premise that there is nothing in the climbing of an Alpine carriage-road of the first class—and nearly everything described in this volume comes within that category—which need affright the ordinary able-bodied driver possessed of an ordinarily sound car. It is futile to say anything about nerve and skill; these qualities are essential even for a run from Piccadilly Circus to Putney Bridge. As for the car itself, who would suggest that a man should venture out at any time or place on a vehicle in which he had no confidence?

Nevertheless there are one or two features which require to be taken specially into account as regards the equipment of a car for Alpine work; but let it be said in a word that they chiefly concern certain physiographical and atmospheric conditions. What we have to consider is whether a man may find himself in any way out of his reckoning, even if he be an experienced tourist in ordinary latitudes and the possessor of a thoroughly sound car in which he has, and legitimately, every confidence.

In the first place there is the question of the width of the steering lock. Nine cars out of every ten are not wholly satisfactory in this respect even for ordinary driving; in other words, the radius of the smallest circle which they can describe is far too great for convenience, as anyone who has tried to turn round in a narrow street knows only too well. The only self-propelled vehicle that is adequate is the motor-cab, which must conform to the official requirements of Scotland Yard before being licensed; that is to say, it must turn within a circle of 26 feet.

Now this is an ideal to which the touring car cannot possibly conform. It must have a longer wheel-base than the motor-cab, or it would neither be comfortable on rough roads nor capable of being steered easily at high speeds. As far, however, as is practicable in conjunction with the long wheel-base, the touring car should be made to approach an ideal which, though less exacting than that of the motor-cab, is too rarely encountered. If the ordinary car-owner will take the trouble to describe a circle with the steering wheel hard over, on any road wide enough for the purpose, and then measure his wheel-tracks, he will probably be astounded at the difference between the figures and those of the London motor-cab. To show, however, how even touring cars vary in this respect, I may mention that I have seen a six-cylinder touring car turn round quite comfortably in a London street, with eight feet to spare, while a four-cylinder car with a shorter wheel-base could do no better than cross to the other side, its front wheels ending up at right angles to the kerb.

Cars with locks good enough for the tackling of "hairpin" corners do exist, and I am not suggesting any impossible standard; as a matter of fact, I have only to mention that I have made journeys over the Alps and Apennines on three different English cars, two of which were of the six-cylinder type, without having any trouble whatever at the "hairpin" bends.   But I will go so far as to say that a man who contemplates a tour among the Alps with a car that has not a good lock had much better stay at home.   If he cannot get round the first "hairpin" without having to stop and reverse, he will probably have to repeat the process at every subsequent corner; and this will make all the difference as to the enjoyment or otherwise of his tour.   There are eighty "hairpin" corners on the Stelvio Pass alone; there are sixty on the Pordoi.   On the Simplon there are scarcely any, but, generally speaking, if there is any considerable height to be attained, there will be a good many *tourniquets*, or zigzags.

To the driver of a car with a good lock the nicety of skill required for the rounding of these without material loss of speed affords a degree of zest which cannot be experienced elsewhere, and is itself one of the charms of motor mountaineering.   On the other hand, to have to reverse —perhaps not once or twice, but even thrice— at every corner is simply purgatory; in extreme cases, indeed, it is possible to get the car wedged in such a position that it will move neither backwards nor forwards.

I have elaborated this item because motor-car makers have such widely differing ideas as to what the turning radius of their standard patterns should be.   It is not a question of one car turning merely in a foot or two more space than another; there may be a difference of as much as twenty feet, and really some makers appear to think that a car has never to do aught else in the way of steering than to take a right-angled corner with a wide sweep; the doubling back of a road upon itself is a consideration which they have never contemplated, and perhaps never even seen.

To the Alpine tourist, however, the matter is one of such supreme importance that I can only recommend any automobilist who is about to invest in a new car, with a contingent probability of using it at the first opportunity in Alpine territory, to make the steering lock his first consideration, and not on any account to purchase a chassis the steering wheels of which have very little lateral movement.

The owner, on the other hand, who is satisfied in every other respect with his existing car, and proposes to take it abroad, should first test its turning capabilities in a road of moderate width; and if he cannot turn completely round with ease, he will only be looking for trouble if he goes to the Alps. Occasional reversing, of course, does not matter; but what I am anxious that he should avoid is the discovery that all his enjoyment is being marred by the possession of a really bad example of steering lock, such as is to be found on far too many cars professing to be up to date in all respects.

Scarcely less important is the question of radiation. It is quite possible to have a car which in England has never given its owner the smallest anxiety or trouble in respect of overheating, and he may even think at times that the engine is over-cooled; but when he reaches the Alps, and embarks upon a continuous climb, perhaps, of ten or fifteen miles, he may have cause to regard the engine with different feelings.

The difficulty of the situation is that there is nowhere in England where an engine can be fully tested in this respect, for really long stretches of collar-work are quite unknown. The only expedient that I can suggest is to find the longest hill within measurable distance and drive up it on a lower speed than the engine can comfortably take; if, in spite of a racing engine, the radiator still seems adequate, there need be no fear of setting off for the Alps. Possibly the radiation may not prove everything that could be desired on the higher passes, but a little boiling does no harm, and the car can always be stopped in order that the engine may be allowed to cool down, and there is generally water to be had on the road-side; even were it otherwise it is easy to carry a spare *bidon* or two filled with water instead of petrol.

As with the steering lock, however, so with the radiator; the thing to be avoided is the extreme case. If an owner has had trouble with his radiation under ordinary conditions in England, that car should not on any account be taken to the Alps, as there will not be by any means sufficient margin for error. Matters are certainly cut very fine on some cars, quite apart from Alpine requirements, and the delays and annoyances due to constant overheating and refilling of the radiator with a car of this type on the high carriage-roads would be frequent and vexatious. There is one special circumstance, moreover, apart from the long climbs, which conduces to overheating with an under-cooled engine, and that is the fact that, at the time of year when the loftiest passes are free from snow, the weather may be unbearably hot, and one cannot count upon any material degree of coolness in the surrounding atmosphere to assist the engine.

I have mentioned two items in which a car may be found somewhat wanting on Alpine roads to the surprise of a thoroughly practical owner who has never found his vehicle fail him when touring in England, though a hill like that of Amulree, in Scotland, might prove a rude awakening in respect of "hairpin" corners, while one or two other Scottish hills are also long and steep enough to find out the weak spots in its radiation. There is yet another feature, however, which is peculiar to motoring in high altitudes, and that is the carburation. There is a substantial difference between the composition of the atmosphere at the level of the plains and when the car has risen, say, 6,000 feet, and has still another thousand, or even three thousand in the case of the Stelvio, to ascend; and it is quite possible that the carburetter may not be fully equal to the occasion.

The adaptability to varying atmospheres is much greater in some carburetters than others, and it is impossible, of course, to lay down any law of guidance by which a man may know in advance whether his engine will run as well at several thousand feet above the sea as at sea level. I do not think, however, that there is any abiding cause for anxiety in this respect, where the average carburetter is concerned, though I have seen one or two cars in difficulties near the summits as a result of faulty carburation; but there are two measures of precaution which may easily be taken on the chance of their being needed. Some means should be adopted, in the shape of a supplementary lever or otherwise, of giving the carburetter more air than it normally requires; and, secondly, three or four spare jets should be obtained, of different sizes. A change of jet, in fact, is often desirable abroad, as compared with England, even in low altitudes, simply because the petrol is usually much lighter than the brands that are sold in England.

The necessity for good brakes is paramount under all conditions of automobile travel, and it is almost superfluous to remind the tourist of so obvious a fact where the Alps are concerned. At the same time he should bear in mind that, whereas brakes are mostly used at home merely as occasional checks upon the pace of a car in traffic or at corners, or as a sudden and severe check in an actual emergency, they have to be used at times on the higher carriage-roads as a drag for considerable periods.

Power, therefore, is not the only quality that is required; equally important is the capacity to remain on for a long distance without over-heating. I do not think that water-cooling is of much value, as a gallon or so of water is soon evaporated The main essentials are that the brakes should be soundly made and well fitted, and, if possible, there should be three instead of the conventional two. Many cars of continental manufacture are now provided with three brakes as a normal·accompaniment. On a long descent the changes could be rung from one brake to another, for the sake of coolness, but with a general preference in favour of the hand-brake, assuming that it acts on the rear wheels ; and these, by the way, should be watched by the rear passengers, with a view to detecting smoke or the smell of burning oil as indications of over-heating.

The foot-brake, or, if there are two, the one which is most readily applied, should be kept pretty tightly adjusted, as quick and certain action is sometimes required at a "hairpin" corner. The driver, for example, may think that he has got well round the bend, but the front passenger may note that the near side wheel will not quite clear one of the stone "sugar-loaves" which usually border the road, and at his demand the driver may have to pull up *instanter*. A quick-acting foot-brake, moreover, is desirable on a zigzag road if the car fails to get round an acute bend and has to be reversed ; while manœuvring, the driver must know almost to an inch the degree to which he can count upon his foot-brake to stop the road-wheels dead.

The weight of the car, the number of passengers, and the amount of luggage are also factors which have to be borne in mind on long-drawn descents, and the pace should be regulated accordingly, with an ample margin for error. Spare brake-shoes may advantageously be carried, and spare cables if these and not rods are used. Particular attention should be paid to the adjustments before leaving home, as nothing can well be more inconvenient when on a tour than the discovery that the last thread has been reached and that no more tightening up can be done. Even if a town of good size be near at hand, and a local repairer be found, he cannot be counted upon to save the situation if the car be of English make, as he may not have the necessary tools for cutting an English thread.

A good deal of brake wear may be saved by utilising the compression of the engine on long descents with a comparatively regular gradient; the flow of oil to the cylinders, of course, should meanwhile be reduced.

CHAPTER VI.

THE COL DU LAUTARET.

IN dealing with the Alpine passes *seriatim* the difficulty confronts one at the outset of determining the best system of classification. By whatever method the subject be approached, it is entirely impossible to avoid jumping about, as it were, from pillar to post. At first sight it would seem as though it would be a simple matter to classify the roads by countries, and describe the French, Swiss, Austrian, and Italian passes in turn.

The summit of a mountain, however, often presents a natural frontier, and there are many passes which are half in one country and half in another; consequently, to the four groups already indicated we should have to add the French-Italian, the French-Swiss, the Swiss-Italian, the Swiss-Austrian, and the Austrian-Italian respectively. These joint passes, as a matter of fact, are as a rule more important than those which are self-contained. It would be equally impossible to avoid overlapping if the various Alpine groups were described in turn. Another method of classification would be to consider the passes in relation to their altitudes; but height *per se* is not an indication of importance, and in any case the confusion thus created would be considerable. The same objection would apply to an alphabetical arrangement.

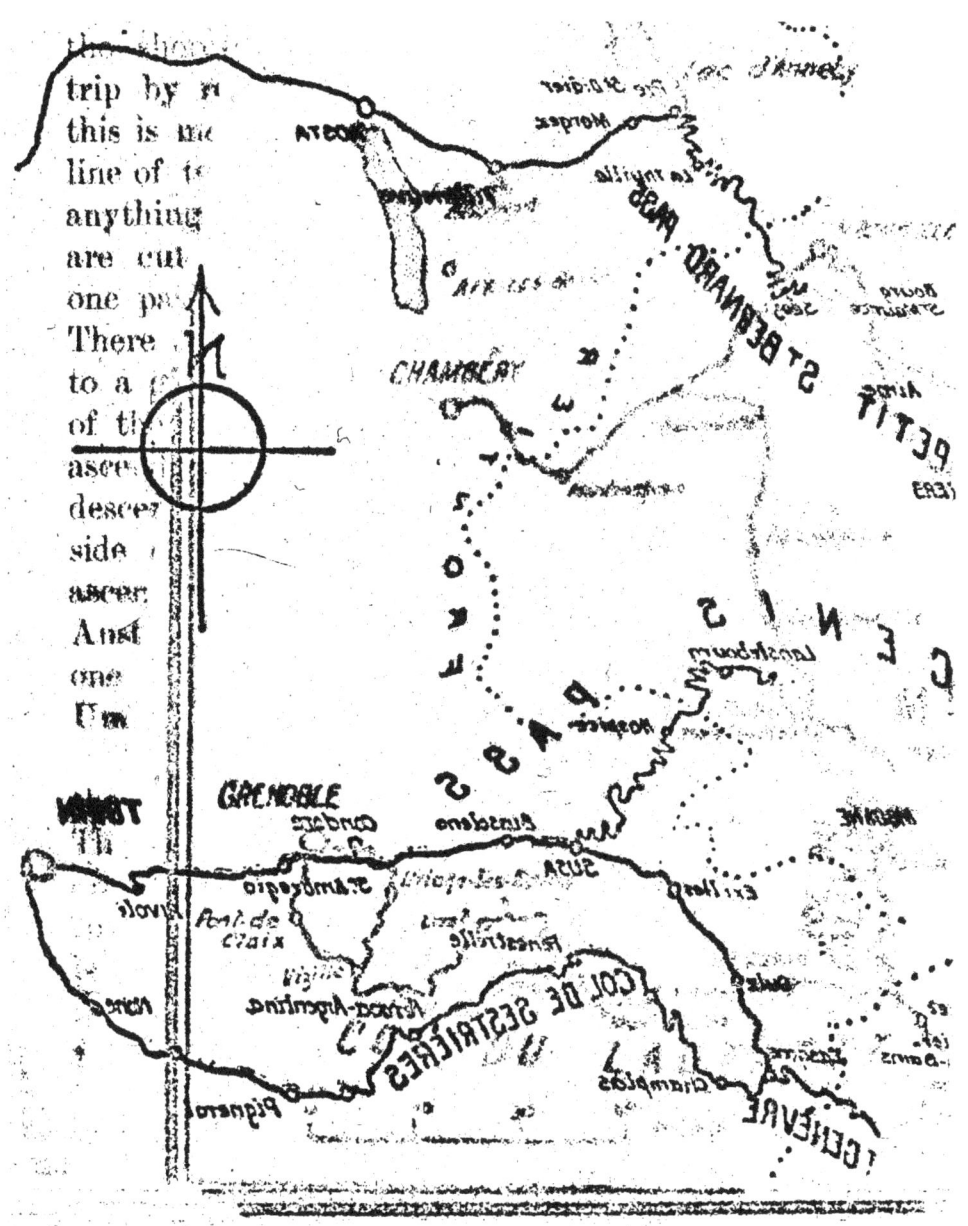

Were it possible, the best method would be to take the passes in the order in which they would be encountered by a traveller landing on the shores of France and making an extensive trip by road in Alpine territory. Unfortunately, this is more or less impracticable. No continuous line of tour could be devised which would include anything like all the Alpine carriage-roads. They are cut in all directions, and the selection of one pass often means the avoidance of another. There are cases, too, where three roads converge to a given point, and to take more than two out of the three is impossible. If, for example, one ascends the Austrian side of the Stelvio, and descends the Umbrail into Switzerland, the Italian side of the Stelvio must be ignored. If one ascends the Umbrail, and descends into Italy, the Austrian side of the Stelvio is missed; and if one drives over the Stelvio from end to end the Umbrail is passed aside.

Again, let us take the case of the Mont Cenis, the Col du Lautaret, and the Col du Galibier. The first two converge to Turin, but they are crossed midway by the Col du Galibier, the three, roughly speaking, forming the letter "A." It is obvious, therefore, that these three passes could not be traversed in their entirety without covering some portions of the road twice. In certain cases it is not possible to cover everything even if one were willing to retrace one's steps to a considerable extent; the disposition of the mountainous roads is such that when a choice has been made of two given routes, and one of them is followed to the end, an enormous detour would have to

would be encountered by a traveller landi
the shores of France and making an ext
trip by road in Alpine territory. Unfortun
this is more or less impracticable. No conti
line of tour could be devised which would i
anything like all the Alpine carriage-roads.
are cut in all directions, and the selecti
one pass often means the avoidance of an
There are cases, too, where three roads cor
to a given point, and to take more than t
of the three is impossible. If, for exampl
ascends the Austrian side of the Stelvi
descends the Umbrail into Switzerland, the
side of the Stelvio must be ignored.
ascends the Umbrail, and descends into Ital
Austrian side of the Stelvio is missed; :
one drives over the Stelvio from end to e
Umbrail is passed aside.

Again, let us take the case of the Mont
the Col du Lautaret, and the Col du Ga
The first two converge to Turin, but th
crossed midway by the Col du Galibier, the
roughly speaking, forming the letter "A
is obvious, therefore, that these three passes
not be traversed in their entirety without co
some portions of the road twice. In certain
it is not possible to cover everything even
were willing to retrace one's steps to a co
able extent; the disposition of the mount
roads is such that when a choice has been
of two given routes, and one of them is fo
to the end, an enormous detour would h

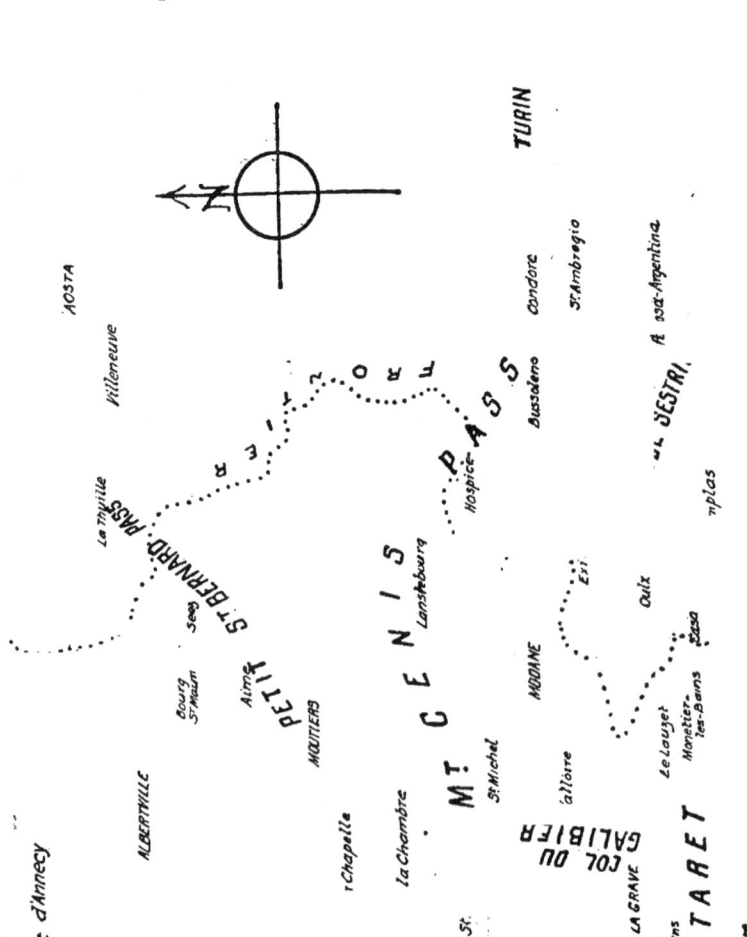

THE MAIN ROUTES FROM FRANCE TO ITALY.

Were it possible, the best method would be to take the passes in the order in which they would be encountered by a traveller landing on the shores of France and making an extensive trip by road in Alpine territory. Unfortunately, this is more or less impracticable. No continuous line of tour could be devised which would include anything like all the Alpine carriage-roads. They are cut in all directions, and the selection of one pass often means the avoidance of another. There are cases, too, where three roads converge to a given point, and to take more than two out of the three is impossible. If, for example, one ascends the Austrian side of the Stelvio, and descends the Umbrail into Switzerland, the Italian side of the Stelvio must be ignored. If one ascends the Umbrail, and descends into Italy, the Austrian side of the Stelvio is missed; and if one drives over the Stelvio from end to end the Umbrail is passed aside.

Again, let us take the case of the Mont Cenis, the Col du Lautaret, and the Col du Galibier. The first two converge to Turin, but they are crossed midway by the Col du Galibier, the three, roughly speaking, forming the letter "A." It is obvious, therefore, that these three passes could not be traversed in their entirety without covering some portions of the road twice. In certain cases it is not possible to cover everything even if one were willing to retrace one's steps to a considerable extent; the disposition of the mountainous roads is such that when a choice has been made of two given routes, and one of them is followed to the end, an enormous detour would have to

D

be followed before one could hark back to the alternative.

Taking all things into consideration, however, I have decided to approach the matter in the first instance from the point of view of the tourist who is not disposed to cruise among the Alps in wholesale fashion, but knows that he cannot tour on the Continent for long without having to cross the Alps at one point or another. Of options he has not a few, and it is with these that I propose to deal in individual chapters, leaving to later chapters the consideration of the many passes which are worth exploring for their own sakes, but which are not inevitable accompaniments to a through journey.

There are three main routes to Italy by way of France—the Col du Lautaret (in conjunction with Mont Genèvre), the Mont Cenis, and the Petit St. Bernard. The first-named is wholly in France, and connects with the road over Mont Genèvre, the summit of which is near the frontier line, as is also the case with the Mont Cenis and the Petit St. Bernard. The Lautaret road is one of Napoleon's masterpieces, and is an excellent example of the type of highway which begins practically on the plains, ascends very gradually at first, and then rises more steeply until it attains a considerable height.

The starting point is Grenoble, a fine town situated amid a magnificent environment, and an admirable centre for a lengthy sojourn, during which interesting out-and-home radiations may be made from day to day before embarking on a definite through journey. The town is strongly fortified, and has some 70,000 inhabitants, being, in fact, the largest in the department of the Isère. Though surrounded by peaks rising to 10,000 feet its own level is only 689 feet above the sea. The ascent of the Col du Lautaret may be made either by way of Uriage-les-Bains or Pont de Claix, the alternative roads converging at Vizille. On the whole the former route is to be preferred.

As this is the first pass to be described in this volume, let me lay down here the fundamental principle which has to be applied to the question of ascending or descending any mountain road. In ordinary touring one regards an itinerary as complete which gives the names of the towns and villages *en route*, with all intermediate and progressive distances. Height, however, is the essential factor in the situation when tackling an Alpine pass; and instead of looking in the ordinary way at the distances to be covered, one must first consider the height which has to be climbed and then the number of kilometres in which the altitude has to be attained. From one point of view, of course, the more the better, for the gradient is reduced in direct ratio to the distance travelled.

For an adequate appreciation, therefore, of the task which has to be performed, an itinerary is necessary which includes the heights as well as the mere kilometric records; and such an itinerary, when provided, should be systematically and minutely analysed in advance. A stage of 20 kilometres, for example, which makes a rise of 1,200 feet will obviously take less time to traverse than one in which the road ascends, say, 3,000 feet in the same distance; and it is only by gauging the general features of the journey at the outset that an estimate can be made of its probable duration, or the best places for luncheon halts and stoppages for the night be predetermined.

For the first pass or two this analysis may prove irksome, but the process then becomes instinctive, experience enabling the tourist to realise practically at a glance not only the exact nature of the undertaking itself, but also the time in which his car will normally accomplish it. Over and above this, of course, he will allow an ample margin for variations of weather, for halts which the attractiveness of the scenery may demand, for photographing if he carries a camera, and for possible need of attention to the car.

The science of touring in any country, but pre-eminently in Alpine regions, is to know as much as may be in advance where practical data are concerned, and to leave as little as possible to chance in that respect; the scenery will provide the elements of novelty and surprise, to say nothing of any adventures that may be encountered by the way. Happy-go-lucky methods never pay in touring, and, when mountains have to be crossed, are even dangerous; the man who thoroughly enjoys himself awheel is the one who masters his available facts beforehand, and; so far from this policy interfering with his freedom of action, it enlarges it to the greatest possible degree. He it is who knows at any given stage whether he may safely make this or that diversion from his original plan, or enjoy a longer halt than he had intended at some particularly tempting spot. In no sense is he hidebound by his itinerary; the whole object of his foreknowledge is to secure the fullest measure of elasticity whenever and wherever opportunity will permit.

In the case of every pass, therefore, described in any detail in this book, the plan will be followed of giving the complete itinerary at the outset, with heights and distances set forth in tabular fashion, so that they may be appreciated at a glance and save the reader the trouble of picking them out one by one from the text. The data have not by any means been easy to obtain, and occasionally the finding of a single altitude or intermediate distance has involved more trouble than the writing of whole chapters.

Distances, of course, are given in kilometres, not miles, as the roadside stones on the Continent are all marked on the metric system. As figures are not inscribed, however, on mountain slopes, and English-speaking persons are accustomed to think of altitudes in feet, the metric heights have been converted accordingly. The figures will rarely be found to coincide with those of standard guide-books, where these condescend to describe a road with any detail, partly because rough-and-ready means are often adopted therein to arrive at the English measurements, and partly because unanimity does not invariably exist as to the original bases of metres themselves.

I have endeavoured, however, in all cases to obtain the latter in correct form from official

continental sources, and have carried out the
figures to four places of decimals when converting
them to feet. At the same time it may be mentioned that the discrepancies between one statement of altitude and another are seldom serious,
merely concerning, as a rule, the tens and units;
none the less I have made passing acquaintance
with an error of 2,000 feet in respect of an intermediate point on a French pass, and one of no
less than 3,500 feet in the stated height of a
village on a Tyrolese route!

With this digression we may return to the
Col du Lautaret road, the itinerary of which is
as follows:—

Place.	Altitude. (Feet.)	Intermediate Distances. (Kils.)	Progressive Totals. (Kils.)
Grenoble - - -	689	—	—
Gières - - -	—	6	6
Uriage-les-Bains - -	1,360	6	12
Vaulnaveys - -	1,131	3	15
Vizille - - -	919	6	21
Séchilienne - -	—	8	29
Livet - - -	2,173	11	40
Les Grandes Sables -	2,330	6	46
La Paute - - -	—	4½	50½
Bourg d'Oisans - -	2,360	2½	53
Le Clapier - - -	—	5	58
Le Freney d'Oisans -	3,090	6½	64½
Le Dauphin - -	3,280	3½	68
Les Freaux - -	4,561	10	78
La Grave - - -	4,888	2	80
Villard d'Arène - -	5,415	3	83
Summit - - -	*6,790*	8	91
Galibier road junction -	—	2	93
Monêtier-les-Bains -	4,890	12	105
Villeneuve - - -	—	6	111
Chantemerle - -	—	2½	113½
St. Chaffrey - -	—	1½	115
Briançon - - -	4,330	4	119

(*Hotels all along the line of route.*)

As is often the case when a large town has to be left behind, it is a little difficult to find the right exit from Grenoble for the Uriage road, and I may therefore mention that the Porte Très-Cloîtres is the gate to be inquired for. The road is level until within half a kilometre of Gières, and then ascends steadily to Uriage-les-Bains, a pleasant little town centred in wooded surroundings. The road then passes through a

BOURG D'OISANS AND THE BELLEDONNE RANGE.

picturesque valley to Vaulnaveys, and descends gradually to Vizille, a town of between four and five thousand inhabitants. At Séchilienne the upward gradient becomes perceptible, and varies from two to five per cent. over the next dozen kilometres, having meanwhile entered the Gorge du Livet and crossed and recrossed the River Romanche. Beyond Livet the road becomes a shade steeper, but after two kilometres crosses the river and continues on the level for some 16 kilometres. At Les Grandes Sables it turns due south, and at La Paute passes the entrance to the road over the Col d'Ornon.

At Bourg d'Oisans one encounters a pleasing sign of the times in the shape of a motor diligence, which plies regularly in the summer from this ancient little town to the Lautaret summit, a fact which of itself should reassure the motorist that he has nothing to fear in the way of difficult driving where an ordinary car is concerned. Just outside Bourg d'Oisans the road crosses to the left bank of the Romanche once more, and recrosses the river at Le Clapier. About a kilometre from the bridge a tunnel is passed through, and the scenery becomes more impressive. At the fourth kilometre from Le Clapier, or the 62nd from Grenoble, the road descends to Le Freney, passes through the tunnel of the Infernet, some 600 feet long, and goes down to the level of the river, but soon begins to rise again, and, passing through the Chambon tunnel, enters a rocky defile. It then descends anew to the level of the river, and crosses it for the last time beyond Le Dauphin.

Though hemmed in by rocks, amidst scenery of awe-inspiring grandeur, the road itself is finely engineered, with a first-class surface, and presents no difficulty to the man at the wheel. On the left is seen the Cascade de la Pisse, with a total fall of 650 feet, while on the right is the first glacier encountered, that of Mont de Lans. The boundary line between the department of the Isère and that of the Hautes Alpes is crossed

THE GORGE OF THE INFERNET.
(*The Lautaret road is high up on the right.*)

two kilometres later, and after three and a half more kilometres another tunnel is encountered, beyond which the first glimpse of La Meije is obtained. After passing the village of Les Freaux, three kilometres higher up, another waterfall, the Saut de la Pucelle, is seen on the left, and the well-known village of La Grave is reached in a couple of kilometres. There is nothing steeper than 7 per cent. between the gorge of the Infernet and La Grave, and the ascent is one which can be made by any decent car with perfect ease.

Of La Grave it may be said that it occupies the most attractive position of any French village outside the region of the Mont Blanc range. It stands at the five thousand or so feet altitude, which, if I may proffer an opinion, offers in almost every Alpine district the finest combination of picturesqueness, pure air that is not too rarified, beautiful wild flowers, and an amplitude of excursions. It may only be personal preference, but looking back upon the hundreds of towns and villages which I have visited in one district or another of the Alps, I find that nearly all the places for which I have a special fondness are somewhere in the neighbourhood of the height named—speaking, of course, from the summer point of view; and La Grave, though far less known to English tourists than the more popular Swiss resorts, is well qualified to occupy a place in one's list of specially memorable spots. At present, however, it is comparatively undeveloped, and has only a couple of hotels, which are much frequented by climbers, pedestrians, and tourists brought by the motor diligence.

THE GRAND PINNACLE OF LA MEIJE (13,080 FEET HIGH)
AS SEEN FROM THE LAUTARET ROAD.

Though centred amid a plethora of mountain
excursions, the chief pride of La Grave is its pro-
pinquity to La Meije, a mountain with no small
claims to distinction.   In the first place it is
undeniably beautiful, and may challenge comparison with any rival in the whole range of the
Alps.   In the second place it is seen to great
advantage from the road itself; in fact, among
the famous road views of the Alps that of La
Meije is only second to the views of the Ortler
and its attendant glaciers from the Stelvio.   I
do not put this forward simply as an opinion of
my own; it is one which has been voiced by
Mr. Whymper and Mr. Coolidge alike, than
whom none are better qualified to speak.   La
Meije is also interesting from the fact that it
remained unconquered long after every Swiss
summit had been attained, and was absolutely
the last peak of any note to be scaled by the
foot of man.

If Grenoble has been left in the morning
La Grave will form a suitable halting place for
lunch; but I may mention that there is a garage
with petrol and oil on sale in connection with
the Hotel de la Meije, and it is the best place
for spending the night if the start from Grenoble
be deferred until the early afternoon.

The region of ravines and overhanging rocks
has now been left behind, and from La Grave to
the Lautaret summit the road ascends eastwards
with a good surface, and only one pair of "hairpin" bends.   Between La Grave and the village
of Villard d'Arène, two long tunnels have to be
passed through, one of them being no less than

600 yards in length. Both are lighted by electricity, but only dimly. Incidentally, however,
I may mention that, for Alpine touring, it is
desirable to dispense with paraffin lamps and fit
an electric equipment instead; the ability to
switch on the lights when entering a long tunnel
will be found a great convenience.

While speaking of tunnels I may also mention
that they are usually constructed in places where

THE CHAIN OF LA MEIJE.

avalanches in winter and landslides in summer are
of frequent occurrence, but there is just an occasional possibility of a landslide on unprotected
portions of a given road. As an instance I may
mention that when I crossed the Col du Lautaret,
in the early part of July, 1908, on the 45-h.p.
Sheffield-Simplex car illustrated on another page,
and stayed the night at La Grave, I heard next

morning that there had been a landslide between
the village and the summit, and that the road
would probably be blocked. Matters were not
so black, however, as they were painted, for on
reaching the spot in question I simply found some
loose boulders over the road, through which it was
possible to drive the car without anything worse
than sundry bumps. And lest any reader may be
unduly alarmed in advance, I may state that
on only one other occasion, out of the scores of
passes I have crossed in one district or another
of the Alps, and at times varying from May to
September, have I encountered anything of the
kind, and that was on the Arlberg.

So well graded are the upper stages of the
Lautaret road that, in spite of the absence of any
series of *lacets*, or zigzags, the gradient nowhere
exceeds 7 per cent., while, as the rise from La
Grave to the summit is only one of 1,902 feet in
11 kilometres, it follows that the average is
considerably less. The grassy meadows through
which the road passes are treasure haunts for
the botanist, inasmuch as they are rich in flora
not readily encountered elsewhere. On arrival at
the summit we find, on a little plateau, both the
hospice and an hotel, on opposite sides of the
road, and the tourist will probably be surprised
at the amount of activity they display in the
summer season. While the actual views from
the summit are somewhat circumscribed, the
backward outlook, as one begins the descent,
is by no means unimpressive.

A fine run down may now be looked forward
to from the Col to Briançon, a distance of 25 kilo-

metres, with a fall of 2,460 feet. It may be said
in advance that, though for the first 10 kilometres
the road is steeper than in its later stages, there
is nothing more formidable in the way of abrupt
descent than two or three sections of 6 per cent.
Two kilometres from the summit a narrow road
on the left will be noticed; it is the entrance to
the Col du Galibier, the second highest mountain
road in France. This, however, is a cross road

THE LAUTARET SUMMIT.

which must be dealt with later, and meanwhile
we will continue the descent to the valley of
the River Guisane, the Romanche, which kept
us company all the way to the summit, having
now disappeared for good.

The road describes several curves, but none
of a difficult character, and passes through two
tunnels, one of which is 660 metres in length.
Naturally they are damp, both above and below,
and slippery to a degree necessitating careful

steering. A little further along one takes a last glimpse of La Meije, and, after several small villages have been passed on the road, we reach the little town of Monêtier-les-Bains. The road continues excellent in character, and descends very gradually, and without any sharp bends, to Briançon, with nothing to mar the enjoyment of the run but an occasional *dos d'âne* or *caniveau*.

Of this run generally of 119 kilometres, or 73½ miles, from Grenoble to Briançon, it may be said that, while not to be accounted of absolutely the first rank from the point of view of picturesqueness, it has no small claims to the tourist's attention in this respect, especially as regards the views of La Meije; and, all things considered, I know of no road which could so usefully be chosen to serve as an initiation into the glories of crossing a lofty pass.

CHAPTER VII.

MONT GENÈVRE.

BRIANÇON lies off the main road, at the foot of a steep hill, and is a fortified town of some 7,000 inhabitants. Not only has it a triple wall round its central fortress, but there are ten forts placed as outposts on neighbouring heights. The town is the terminus of a

BRIANÇON.

branch line from Nice, and by road is within easy reach of Gap, Embrun, Digne, and other well-known haunts in the Basses Alpes. As a matter of fact it is perhaps mostly visited by motorists from the southerly towns, for travellers by the Col du Lautaret road who are proceeding

E

straight over the Mont Genèvre are not obliged
to descend into the town unless for supplies, and
may proceed straight on to Italy. It is the only
town of importance, however, west of Turin in
case a repairer is wanted, and I may also add
that the Grand Hotel, half way down the hill,
has a good garage, if Briançon is reached at a
time of day when it is inadvisable to push on
further ere nightfall.

The erstwhile somewhat sleepy town has lately
been galvanised into new life by the large numbers of automobilists who drive through daily.
Arriving there one day for lunch I was informed
by a petrol-seller that no fewer than sixty-four
cars had passed through that morning, and these
were all vehicles on the way to Gap, and did not
take into account those crossing above the town
from east to west, or *vice versâ*, on the Lautaret
and Mont Genèvre route. It does not pay, by
the way, to lay in too large a store of petrol
here, as duty has to be paid on every litre in
the tank, or on board the car, when entering
Italy beyond the summit of Mont Genèvre.

Assuming that the town has been visited we
must ascend the hill and rejoin the Lautaret
road. From the junction the itinerary is as
follows :—

Place.	Altitude. (Feet.)	Intermediate Distances. (Kils.)	Progressive Totals. (Kils.)
Briançon - - -	4,396	—	—
La Vachette (French Customs) - -	4,363	3	3
Summit - - -	*6,100*	8	11
Frontier - - -	—	1½	12½
Clavières (Italian Customs) - - -	—	1½	14

ON THE SUMMIT OF MONT GENÈVRE.

E 2

Place.	Altitude. (Feet.)	Intermediate Distances (Kils.)	Progressive Totals. (Kils.)
Césanne - - -	4,455	6	20
Oulx - - - -	2,544	11	31
Salbertrand - -	—	6	37
Exilles - - -	—	5	42
Chaumont - - -	—	6	48
Gravère - - -	2,493	3	51
Susa - - - -	1,706	4	55

(*Hotels at Briançon, the summit, Clavières, Cesanne, and Susa.*)

For a couple of kilometres the road is practically level, and then rises and falls another kilometre to the village of La Vachette, where there is a French custom-house. After one's papers have been stamped therein one may proceed with cheerfulness to tackle an uninterrupted ascent of 1,637 feet in eight kilometres, in which, however, there is nothing to the least degree affrighting. The road is 18 feet wide, and has a fine surface throughout. A series of six "hairpin" corners is encountered, but not only are the bends of wide radius, but the road itself is widened on the outer curve in each case, leaving plenty of room in which to manœuvre even a car with a short lock. The gradients range from 4 to 8 per cent. There is nothing in the way of villages on the ascent, but the views, without being very striking, are certainly attractive, while the summit commands an open prospect. On the left is a hospice, which is practically used as a depôt for the gendarmes who figure in my photographs, and also as an hotel.

The road is level for a short distance, and, before the descent is begun, an obelisk will be seen on the left in memory of Napoleon, who

THE SUMMIT OF THE MONT GENÈVRE PASS, LOOKING TOWARDS THE FRENCH SIDE.

built the road in its present form, in 1802, at a
cost of over five million francs. The monument
has an inscription in French, Latin, and Italian,
and is over 60 feet in height. The pass itself,
however, has been used from Roman days, and
the balance of evidence is in favour of its having
been the road by which Hannibal effected his
memorable crossing of the Alps, while it has
been traversed by other armies at various times.
In another kilometre the frontier is crossed, but
the Italian custom-house is at the village of
Clavières, three kilometres from the summit.

If Italian does not come trippingly to the
tongue of anyone on the car, it is only necessary
to make one's enquiries in French, and an officer
will be brought forward who speaks that language
with facility. The formalities at this frontier do
not by any means end, however, with the mere
stamping of one's triptyque, or, failing the
possession of that document, with the payment
of duty on the car. The officer will ask how
much petrol is in the tank, or in cans, and may or
may not accept your statement as to the amount;
whether he does so, or takes the measurement
himself, duty, as has already been observed, will
have to be paid on every litre. A receipt for
the amount will be given, and theoretically it is
recoverable when leaving the country for good;
but, as a matter of fact, the sum is hardly worth
the trouble of attempting to get it back.

More important, however, is the consideration
of photography. Any camera or cameras on the
car must be produced, and will be tied with a
string and sealed, as the Mont Genèvre road

itself and the subsequent alternative routes to Turin are fortified. It is not necessary to present the camera at any point for the removal of the seal, but it is as well to enquire where and when the owner may himself sever the string.

Shortly after leaving the custom-house one runs through Italian fortifications, and then follows a glorious descent to · Césanne, the five kilometres to which prove all too brief. The road surface is excellent, and there is only one pair of " hairpin " corners, while the gradient averages from 7 to 9 per cent. A magnificent prospect unfolds itself immediately after leaving the fortress behind, and the view downwards into the deep valley of the Doire is wonderfully impressive,- while the road can be viewed ahead for almost the whole way to Césanne. When part way down the pass it is worth while to turn round and take a backward look up the valley, dominated at the summit by a sugarloaf mountain, with the finely posted fortress commanding the road from an unassailable position, while for some distance the road is pleasantly bordered by trees.

Gradually the red-roofed houses of Césanne draw nearer and nearer at the foot of the valley, and a snow-capped peak is seen on the north-east. The " hairpins " already referred to are of the same easy type as those on the French side of the pass, but on the outskirts of Césanne itself there are two sharp turns which must be taken with care, as they are bounded by a stone wall. The tiny little town of Césanne is prettily situated amid fertile pastures, and surrounded on every side by wooded hills. Strictly speaking, the

Mont Genèvre road ends here, as Césanne marks the entrance upon the Col de Sestrieres road to Turin, which the great Napoleon built as the final stage of his through route to Italy from Grenoble. This road will be described, however, in a later chapter, but for the sake of convenience I will deal here with the connecting link which joins Césanne with Susa and the Mont Cenis pass.

We turn to the left, therefore, in Césanne and descend by a gentle gradient over a broad road, of good surface, running alongside the River Dora Riparia, and bordered on the right by rocks. After four kilometres there is a short level stretch, and then a moderately steep descent of two kilometres. · Passing through the gorge of Soubras the road descends gently to Oulx, through pastures and walnut groves. Oulx is interesting as marking the southern terminus of the so-called Mont Cenis tunnel, and is a town of about 2,000 inhabitants. As far as Salbertrand the road is fairly level. Salbertrand, by the way, is one of the quaintest villages to be found in Italy. As every traveller knows, the main street in even an Italian town is curiously narrow, but at Salbertrand there is hardly room for a car to squeeze between the houses.

Beyond the village the road becomes of the type known in France as *accidentée*, being undulating throughout, with several steep pitches and awkward corners. The descent into Exilles is as steep in parts as 14 per cent. Two forts are passed midway, one on the left and one on the right. A little way beyond Exilles the road

ON THE ROAD TO OULX.

again descends steeply with a gradient of 10 to 14 per cent., and passes another fortress. A series of undulations follow to Chaumont, and then the road rises slightly to Gravère, after which there is a steep run down of four kilometres to Susa on the Mont Cenis road. On the whole of the journey of 18 kilometres from Salbertrand to Susa it is necessary to have the car well in hand; but this does not mean that the road presents serious difficulties, while for the most part it is eminently picturesque.

CHAPTER VIII.

THE MONT CENIS.

TO the driver of a motor-car the journey over the Mont Cenis pass is one of sheer delight. There are passes that are more lofty in themselves, and passes that are surrounded by peaks of more ruggedness and grandeur; many there are which make more demands upon the driving skill, and therefore give the driver more food for self-congratulation; but there is no pass which presents so magnificent a *parcours* from end to end. Spaciousness is the dominant characteristic of the road throughout; and, though it rises to a height of nearly 7,000 feet, its gradients are mostly easy, and its zigzag corners of the amplest kind. There is steepness enough to try the mettle of the car, and there are corners enough to provide the element of sport; but in neither case does the test become an ordeal. The car is on the swing throughout, and save for the majestic scenery, and the height to which one rises, it were easy to imagine one's self speeding along an ordinary French highway of the finest kind. When Napoleon built the Mont Cenis road, at a cost of twenty millions of francs, he made it as broad as possible with a view to the sweeping of an army with the utmost swiftness on to Italian soil; and the highway which once resounded with the tramp of armed men now provides the most glorious run for the automobile that could be found in any part of the world, if we compare like with like in respect of altitude.

As a through route the Mont Cenis road may be said to begin at Chambéry and end at Turin, a distance of 216½ kilometres, though the actual pass, of course, is considerably shorter. It would be absurd to assume, however, that the tourist will in every case cross the passes described in this volume in one set direction; and, as we have just seen how Italy can be entered from France by way of the Col du Lautaret and Mont Genèvre, we may as well imagine that the traveller is returning westwards over the Mont Cenis, by the following itinerary:—

Place.	Altitude. (Feet.)	Intermediate Distances. (Kils.)	Progressive Totals. (Kils.)
Turin (Torino) - -	787	—	—
Rivoli - - -	1,132	13	13
San Ambrogio - -	—	13	26
San Antonino - -	—	8	34
Borgone - - -	—	4	38
Bussoleno - - -	1,427	7	45
Susa - - - -	1,624	8	53
Giaglione - - -	—	4½	57½
Molaretto (Italian Customs) - - -	—	6½	64
Bard - - - -	4,839	2½	66½
La Grande Croix -	6,069	7	73½
Hospice · - -	6,332	2½	76
Summit and Frontier -	*6,834*	5	81
Lanslebourg (French Customs) - -	4,587	11	92
Termignon - · -	4,199	5½	97½
Sollières - - -	—	2	99½
Le Verney de Bramans . —		4½	104
Villarodin - - -	4,068	7½	111½
Modane - - -	3,524	3½	115
Le Freney - - -	—	3½	118½
La Praz - - .	—	3½	122
Orelle - - -	—	3½	125½
St. Michel - - -	2,336	6½	132

A BACKWARD VIEW INTO ITALY, ON THE ASCENT FROM SUSA.

Place.	Altitude. (Feet.)	Intermediate Distances. (Kils.)	Progressive Totals. (Kils.)
Torrent of St. Martin -	2,247	5	137
Torrent of St. Julieu -	2,034	3½	140½
St. Jean de Maurienne	1,857	5½	146
Pontamafrey - -	—	4	150
La Chambre - -	1,509	7	157
Epierre - - -	1,207	12	169
Aiguebelle - - -	1,066	10	179
Pont. Royal - -	—	10	189
Montmelian - -	935	13	202
Station des Marches -	—	5	207
St. Jeoire - - -	—	2½	209½
Challes-les-Eaux -	—	1½	211
Chambéry - - -	886	6	217

(*Hotels along the line of route too numerous for mention.*)

It is a particularly exhilarating prospect which
lies before the motorist as he leaves Turin; the
city is only 780 feet above sea level, and there is
therefore a rise to be faced of 6,218 feet, which
should amply suffice to show what a car can do,
and at the same time confer all the delightful
sensations of changes of atmosphere and scene
which so protracted an ascent involves. With
respect to Turin itself, however, let it be mentioned that the rule of the road is the same there
as in England, while in any case particular care
has to be observed in some of the streets owing
to the presence of tramcars. How far beyond the
outskirts of the city this local rule prevails it is
impossible to say, as the drivers of carts appear
to do just as they please; but the road is broad,
and, by keeping one's weather eye open, trouble
can easily be avoided.

There is a perfectly straight run of 13 kilometres to Rivoli, practically on the flat. The
road then turns to the right and left, and the

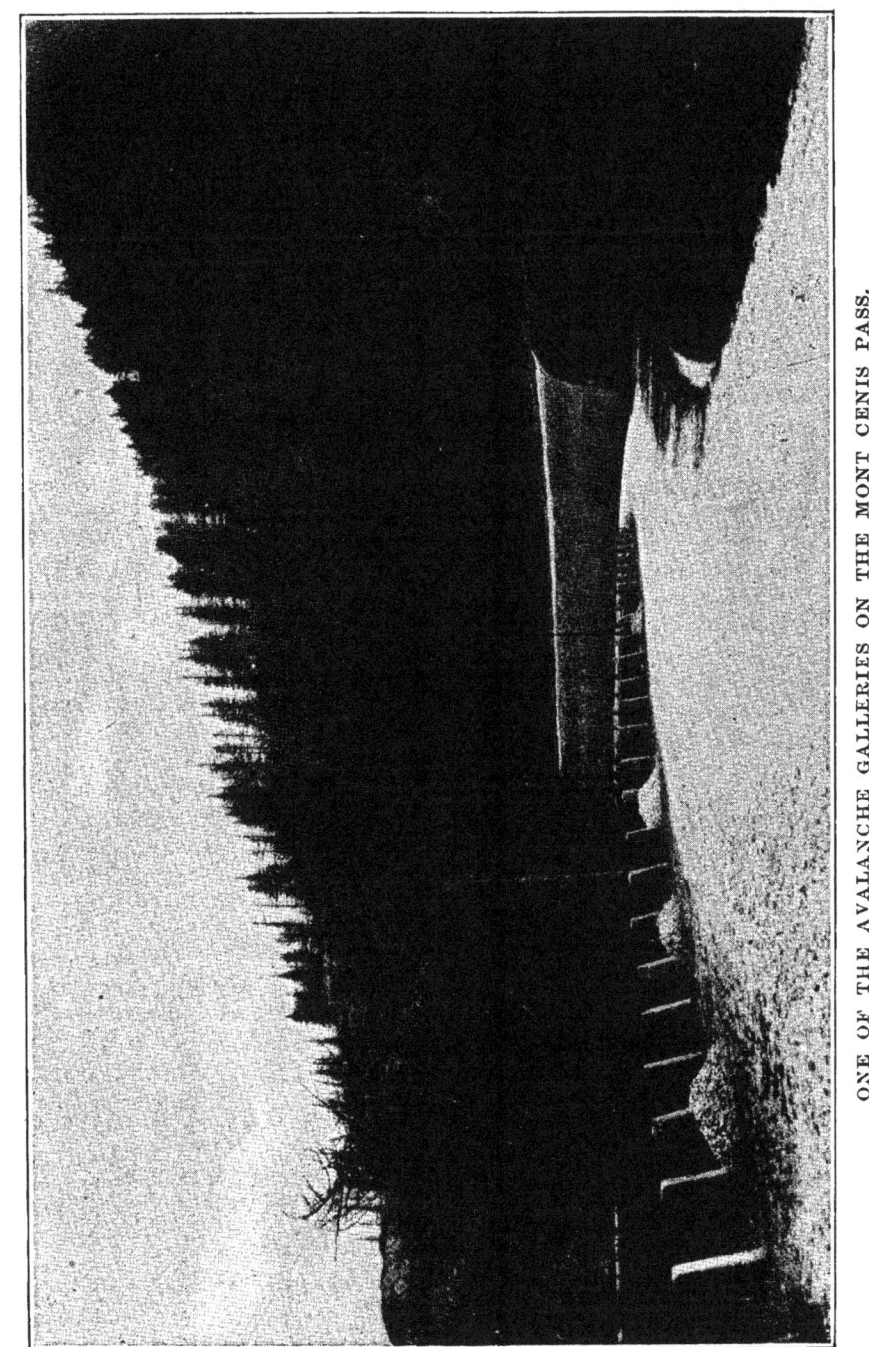

ONE OF THE AVALANCHE GALLERIES ON THE MONT CENIS PASS.

first snow-capped peak comes into view, although
many miles away; and after a slight descent there
is more level running for a long distance, while
the road is again practically straight, and one ·
bowls merrily along at any speed of which a car
is capable, the distant mountains already growing
impressive, while on a hill to the left, near the
village of San Ambrogio is a finely posted castle.
The village must be taken slowly, as it is paved
with cobbles, and there is also a sharp turn to
the right, and another to the left, before settling
down to straight running again.

Once round the corner, however, a new range
of snow-capped peaks comes into sight, flanked
by the two lateral ranges which have been followed
up to now.   Eleven kilometres further on the
River Dora is crossed near Borgone, and at the
end of the next three kilometres a ruined castle
is seen on the right.   Bussoleno, the next village,
is paved, and has two level crossings, but more
grand running follows right up to Susa, which
marks the junction of the Mont Cenis and Mont
Genèvre routes.   In 53 kilometres we have only
risen 840 feet, which means, of course, that to the
eye the road across the broad plain of Piedmont
has been absolutely flat.

Susa is a picturesque little town containing
Roman remains of importance; one of these, in
fact, a triumphal arch in white marble, is declared
to be one of the most precious Roman monuments
in Italy.   It was erected to Augustus, A.D. 7.
The Porta Savoia, a curious old gateway close
by the church of San Giusto, is also worth
inspection.   Susa is known to train travellers, of

THE DENT PARRACHÉE, AS SEEN FROM THE MONT CENIS PASS.

F

course, as a station on the Mont Cenis railway, but, as a matter of fact, this railway has no kinship with the Mont Cenis road save at Susa itself, which is at the foot of the pass, and at Modane, also at a low altitude on the French side.

The falsely called Mont Cenis tunnel is pierced through the Col de Fréjus, 17 miles from the pass; in fact, the tunnel itself and the continuation of the line to Susa form two sides of a rhomboid, of which the Mont Cenis pass from Susa to the summit and the run down to Modane form the other two. It may be interesting to recall, however, that there was once actually a railway on the Mont Cenis road itself. This was on the Fell, or rack and pinion, system, and was opened in 1868, following practically the line of the road from Susa to the summit and down to San Michele. It was only kept in use, however, for three years, being discontinued, and the line being uprooted, when the Fréjus tunnel was opened in 1871.

At Susa the ascent of the Mont Cenis Pass begins in earnest, and represents a rise of 5,268 feet in 28 kilometres, which gives an average of 188 feet per kilometre, or 301 feet per mile. At no point is the gradient steeper than 8 per cent., while for the most part it ranges from 6 to 8. Between three and four kilometres from Susa three "hair-pin" corners are encountered of wide radius, and just beyond Giaglione are four more of like character. Soon afterwards a winter gallery of masonry is passed, and the gradient moderates slightly for a short distance, and then even seems to descend; but this is one of the many instances where appearances are deceptive.

THE ZIGZAGS OF "LA GRANDE CROIX."
(On the left is the cascade of the Cenise river.)

Beyond the 9th kilometre the gradient increases anew, and at Molaretto (11½ kilometres) it is necessary to call a halt to have one's triptyque stamped. Be it noted here that all the guide-books, maps, etc., in existence name Bard, two kilometres higher up the pass, as the seat of the Italian customs; either, therefore, the site has recently been changed, or the customs examination is made at Molaretto on the ascent and at Bard on the descent. Triptyques do not take long to stamp if everything is in order, but one may arrive at an hour when the office is closed; in many cases, in fact, this is invariably so between twelve o'clock and two. It was at a much earlier hour, however, that I happened to arrive at Molaretto when crossing the Mont Cenis in 1908, and found that there was only one officer nominally in charge, and he was out to lunch. In such circumstances one must either pass the time by casting an eye over the lubricators, security bolts, etc. of the car, or imitate the officer's example. After your triptyque has been stamped, by the way, at Molaretto, the *doganiero* gives you a small slip of paper, and states that it will be asked for higher up the pass.

Somewhere on the road, according to the time of day, the wailing notes of a siren will probably be heard echoing from rock to rock, and a Rapid motor-car will be seen descending in fine style. It carries the Government mails, and plies regularly up and down the pass. A fine commentary this on the intelligence of the Swiss, who ban automobiles from nearly all their passes!

Above Bard—where, by the way, no signs of a custom-house are visible—four winter galleries are passed in turn. They are substantially built structures of masonry, through which, however, it is not necessary to drive in fine weather, as they are mere alternatives to the wide road outside. Just beyond the fourth gallery a customs official steps into the middle of the road, and you present him with the slip of paper which you received at Molaretto. At a point $3\frac{1}{2}$ kilometres from Bard the road descends slightly for a short

THE PLATEAU AND LAKE (6,350 FEET HIGH).

stage, and then crosses the Cenise, or Cenischia river; but soon the climb begins once more, and one is faced by a sort of rampart on which the road is clearly outlined in five zigzags, with the tumbling cascade of the Cenise river on the left.

For a moment the sudden series of "hairpins" suggests a formidable task, but the bends are wide and the car swings round them in style. Beyond the last corner is a little plateau known as La Grande Croix, on which there are an inn and other buildings. Soon a large lake comes into sight on the left, with blue-green water, and set in the midst of a spacious prairie which presents one of the most pleasing prospects in the Franco-Italian Alps.

Nowhere else even in the Alps generally is so broad a plateau to be found at so great a height as 6,350 feet, or one with so many habitations; and in some senses it can be compared to the Upper Engadine itself, although the latter has loftier peaks and several lakes instead of one. The chief building is the Mont Cenis Hospice, which is of considerable size, and serves a variety of purposes. One part is used as an hotel, and it is interesting to note that, notwithstanding its altitude, it is open all the year round; another portion is the hospice proper, and admits only travellers of the poorer class; but there is also extensive accommodation for Italian carabineers and *bersaglieri*, together with large stables. In the summer months the hotel is much frequented by naturalists and botanists, as the region is famous for the richness of its Alpine flora. Several rooms contain historic relics, among which are to be found the bed, chair, and desk used by Napoleon when he crossed the pass. Another room has an inscription to the effect that Pope Pius VII. slept there, while in the chapel are still preserved some pictures which are said to have been left by the French army over 100 years ago. The plateau, by the way, is strongly guarded, and perched on the neighbouring hills are no fewer than seven forts.

Just beyond the hospice the road begins to rise, and in another kilometre passes the Hotel de la Poste. Still running alongside the lake—which is two kilometres long, a kilometre broad, and 100 feet deep, and famous for its trout—we come to a final steep ascent of two kilometres, and attain the summit, having risen a distance from Susa which would be represented by a vertical mile, but graded over a distance of $17\frac{1}{2}$ miles.

The frontier line between Italy and Savoy is actually at the summit, and immediately after crossing it an officer steps forward and asks your name, where you have come from, your destination, and also the number of your car. It will save time if you ask him in return to pass over his paper and pencil, so that you may inscribe the details yourself—a procedure to which he will offer no objection. A few yards further along, near refuge No. 19—there are twenty-three of these road-menders' huts on the Mont Cenis road between Molaretto and Lanslebourg—there is a French gendarmerie station, but one's progress is not in any way challenged.

On the French side of the summit, of course, an entirely different prospect opens out, of considerable amplitude, and one may look forward to an uninterrupted descent of many, many miles. There is a particularly grand run down of 11 kilometres to Lanslebourg, with a gradient nowhere exceeding $8\frac{1}{2}$ per cent., and with only five *lacets*, the curves of which are so liberal as to offer little or no check to the car. Here, as on the whole of the ascent on the Italian side, the road is wide and the surface perfect; anything better at such an altitude it would be impossible to conceive, and there are thousands of English roads which can show nothing so excellent. Deep down on the right flows the River Arc, while straight ahead are the noble outlines of the Dent Parrachée, which is no less than 12,180 feet in height.

Mile after mile one reels off in effortless progression until the town of Lanslebourg is reached, 2,308 feet below the summit, and here one must halt at the French custom-house. Lanslebourg, of course, has not the importance that it once held, when a thriving trade was done in carriage and mule transport to the summit, before the Mont Cenis railway was built, but is none the less an interesting old place.

For three kilometres the downward gradient is inappreciable; the road then rises moderately for a kilometre, after which there is a steep drop of $1\frac{1}{2}$ kilometres to Termignon. To this succeeds a very gradual descent of eight kilometres, passing through the village of Le Verney. Where the road crosses the Arc, a rise of from 2 to 3 per cent. is entered upon for three kilometres, and on the right are seen the massive forts of Esseillon. The whole of this stretch of roadway runs through a picturesque ravine, with fine tumbling cascades both to right and left.

Once more the road falls · slightly for three kilometres, through the village of Villarodin, and then descends with a gradient of from 4 to 8 per cent. to Modane, associated in the minds of the railway traveller with the famous tunnel. The entrance to this, however, is really $4\frac{1}{2}$ kilometres beyond the town. It is impossible to pass its yawning mouth without reflecting on the enormous superiority of the road journey, from Susa to the summit and from the summit to Modane, to that of the train-borne traveller. And the comparison is particularly marked in this case because at Modane the train leaves the Mont Cenis route just where it begins to be most interesting, and goes through another mountain altogether, whereas on the St. Gotthard route the train tourist does gain some idea, if incomplete, of the St. Gotthard scenery.

Modane itself is a kilometre from the station of that name—the latter being really situated at the village of Fourneaux—and is only a small town of fewer than 3,000 inhabitants, but nestles amid an environment of mountains. Above Fourneaux two fortresses may be observed on the right bank of the Arc, the Fort du Replaton and the Fort du Sappey respectively, the latter being posted at a considerable height. Communication between the two is maintained by aerial cables.

The road is almost level to the next village, Le Freney, and then descends with a gradient of from 3 to 5 per cent. through La Praz to the Pont des Chèvres, and then drops to Orelle after a short fall of 6 per cent. The gradient moderates for a couple of kilometres or so, and then falls more steeply to St. Michel de Maurienne. This, be it noted, is the northern terminal of the pass over the Galibier from the Lautaret road. The general picturesqueness of the journey from Modane to St. Michel is spoilt at intervals by over-much evidence of the hand of man. There is a paper mill at Le Freney, and at La Praz are the works of an electro-metallurgic company, who have installed a series of huge turbines for the conveyance of water-power, while near St. Michel there are some anthracite mines.

Two physical features of the route may also be mentioned here. A strong wind usually sweeps up the valley, cooling the air even in hot weather. Ere the plain is reached, moreover, it will have been realised that the difficulties of building an Alpine road are not necessarily confined to the highest slopes, for one has occasionally to turn aside owing to the effects of inundations—which usually occur in the spring. Sometimes the diversion may be brief, along a temporarily constructed side road, while a bridge that has been washed away is being reconstructed; but it may happen that the road has been flooded for a considerable distance and covered with *débris* left by the receding waters, with the result that an alternative road has to be followed for several kilometres. The added distance is not great, but the by-road is inferior in width and quality to that of the splendid Mont Cenis road itself.

The descent from St. Michel to St. Jean de Maurienne is very gradual, with occasional undulations at no point exceeding 6 per cent. The road runs through a defile, and, provided it is not impassable at that point, it should cross the Arc three kilometres from St. Jean. It is here, however, that the effects of the spring floods are most likely to be felt, and it may happen that, in lieu of crossing the river, a turn to the right may be enjoined and a narrow winding road followed until it emerges just above St. Jean itself.

The main road now strikes northwards and soon crosses to the right bank of the Arc, and then bends slightly to the north-west in the direction of La Chambre. Whatever gradient may now exist is infinitesimal, as St. Jean is but 1,880 feet in height, and there are still 72 kilometres between it and Chambéry (886 feet), with no intervening hills. As far as La Chambre the road runs between the river and the rail, but in the neighbourhood of that village the line is crossed twice, after which the road once more steers a middle course all the way to Aiguebelle, and offers splendid going for 22 kilometres. It then turns westwards and brings other peaks into view, which grow more and more prominent as one draws nearer and nearer to Chambéry.

For long stretches at a time the road is straight as a die, and both wide and of good quality alike; in fact it is possible to put forward the maximum of speed if there is any occasion for hurry. Care should be taken, however, to note at a distance of ten kilometres from Aiguebelle the road fork at Pont Royal, as this marks the divergence of the Petit St. Bernard route, and may be required on a subsequent occasion. Turning to the left, however, at Pont Royal we reach Chambéry after 28 kilometres of fast running, and conclude an end-to-end journey from Turin which, save for the slight amount of incidental trouble which may have been caused by the possible effects of the inundations above described, will have proved

one of the finest experiences to which the heart
of the road-traveller could aspire.

Even allowing for frontier stoppages and a
reasonable number of halts by the way for meals,
fine view-points, etc., the whole route can be
traversed with entire comfort in one day, while,
if it be taken in the direction here described,
one gains an hour, of course, *en route*, owing
to the difference between French and European
time. It may be as well, however, to take this
opportunity of reminding readers that when proceeding from France to Switzerland or Italy one
must bear in mind that an hour has been lost
midway, or one may arrive at one's hotel too
late for dinner, or at a frontier after the custom-
house has been closed. Somehow or other on a
railway train one never •fails to think of mid-
European time, but on the road one is apt to
ignore it altogether. I must plead guilty to
having arrived late on two occasions, at Geneva
and Turin respectively, through sheer forgetfulness
of this fact.

CHAPTER IX.

THE PETIT ST. BERNARD.

INASMUCH as the Petit St. Bernard Pass attains a height of 7,178 feet, it is obvious that it is " Little " only in name. As a matter of fact the adjective is only used by way of contradistinction from the Grand St. Bernard, which is 932 feet higher. As a route the Petit St. Bernard was known to the Romans and was crossed by Cæsar; but as a modern carriage-road it dates only from 1871. In general character it is more like the Col du Lautaret than the Mont Cenis, but it is not quite so excellent as either in respect of quality. Its average width is the least of the three, but the road surface is normally good. Latterly, however, it has deteriorated over a certain section, owing to the railway extension now in progress, just as the Simplon road was in a bad state while the new tunnel was being built. When I crossed the Simplon, in 1909, however, I found that the ill-effects of the traffic due to the railway operations had partially disappeared; and in due course, no doubt, the portion of the Petit St. Bernard which is for the present similarly affected will revert to its former state.

From the engineering point of view the Petit St. Bernard road has either presented more difficulties than the passes already described, or the difficulties have been less successfully

surmounted ; at all events, the road is much more
tortuous than the others, and has numerous
zigzags. The corners, notwithstanding, are not
over-difficult, and there is no reason why the
road should not be taken by anyone who desires
to travel in that direction; but, to anyone proceeding through France to Italy for the first time,
the other routes, all things considered, are to be
preferred.

With Chambéry as a starting-point the itinerary
is as follows :—

Place.	Altitude. (Feet.)	Intermediate Distances. (Kils.)	Progressive Totals. (Kils.)
Chambéry - -	886	—	—
Challes-les-Eaux -	—	6	6
St. Jeoire - -	—	$1\frac{1}{2}$	$7\frac{1}{2}$
Station des Marches	—	$2\frac{1}{2}$	10
Montmélian - -	—	5	15
Pont Royal - -	920	13	28
Albertville - -	1,132	21	49
Tours - - -	—	5	54
La Bathie - -	1,263	4	58
Arbine - - -	—	1	59
Cevins - - -	1,322	3	62
Feissons - - -	1,368	5	67
Notre Dame de Briançon - -	1,476	2	69
Grand Coeur - -	—	4	73
Aigueblanche - -	—	1	74
Moutiers - - -	1,575	3	77
St. Marcel - -	1,952	5	82
Sieix Tunnels - -	—	$2\frac{1}{2}$	$84\frac{1}{2}$
Villette - - -	—	$2\frac{1}{2}$	87
Aime - - -	2,264	4	91
Bellentre - - -	2,477	$5\frac{1}{2}$	$96\frac{1}{2}$
Bon-Conseil - -	2,657	3	$99\frac{1}{2}$
Bridge over the Arbonne - -	2,802	4	$103\frac{1}{2}$
Bourg St. Maurice -	2,674	$\frac{1}{2}$	104
Séez (French Cus- toms) - - -	2,966	3	107
Belvedere Hotel -	4,659	12	119

Place.	Altitude. (Feet.)	Intermediate Distances. (Kils.)	Progressive Totals. (Kils.)
La Froide - -	—	7	126
Hospice and Frontier	7,077	8	134
Summit - - -	*7,178*	$1\frac{1}{2}$	$135\frac{1}{2}$
Pont Serrand - -	5,331	10	$145\frac{1}{2}$
Gollettaz - -	—	$2\frac{1}{2}$	148
La Thuile (Italian Customs) - -	4,728	1	149
Balme - - -	4,304	3	152
Elleva - - -	—	1	153
Tunnel - - -	3,809	$2\frac{1}{2}$	$155\frac{1}{2}$
Pré St. Didier - -	3,248	$3\frac{1}{2}$	159
Morgex - - -	3,018	4	163
Le Pont-de-la-Salle -	—	3	166
Ruinaz - - -	—	$6\frac{1}{2}$	$172\frac{1}{2}$
Liverogne - -	2,359	$2\frac{1}{2}$	175
Arvier - - -	2,546	1	176
Villeneuve d'Aosta -	2,133	4	180
St. Pierre - -	—	2	182
Sarre - - -	—	3	185
Aosta - - -	1,913	5	190

(There are numerous hotels along the route.)

We follow as far as Pont Royal the magnificent stretch of road already referred to at the conclusion of the chapter on the Mont Cenis route. Instead, however, of turning to the south-east at Pont Royal, we go straight forward in a north-easterly direction along the left bank of the River Isère, the road from Montmélian, on the other side of the town and rail, to the first bend after Pont Royal, offering a straight stretch of no less than 22 kilometres. With merely slight bends there is a straight run for another 15 kilometres to Albertville, one of the brightest little towns in Savoy. The town is divided into two parts, separated by the River Arly, the one on the left constituting the old town, while the buildings on the right are of recent development.

It will be easy to miss the road and take that to Engines, which continues in the same direction as the road from Pont Royal; but, almost as soon as the new town has been entered, one must swing to the right across the Arly and then turn to the left, following the north bank of the Isère to the village of Tours, and there, turning southwards, still following the river, through La Bathie and other villages, to Moutiers. Between Albertville and Tours, by the way, a fine castle will be noted, perched high up on the left. This is the Château Rouge, a 12th century edifice which was formerly the residence of the Princes of Savoy. Above La Bathie are seen on the left the ruins of another old castle, once the home of the Archbishops of the Tarentaise.

The road continues practically level, but winds somewhat, and is crossed no fewer than seven times by the railway. The earlier crossings are indicated well in advance, but those nearer Moutiers are unexpectedly encountered, and are also placed at awkward angles. Here, as in England, and, in fact, all over Europe, the railway builders appear to have had *carte blanche* to do what they liked, and to cross the high-road without any consideration for road travellers. Road, rail, and river continue in close contiguity all the way to Moutiers, where, for the present, the railway is left behind; the extension to which reference has already been made, however, is being carried to Bourg St. Maurice. Moutiers, though a cathedral city, has fewer than 3,000 inhabitants, and is chiefly known by the fact that the neighbouring village of Salins is a thermal station, and the

railway terminus itself is known as Moutiers-
Salins.

With an entire change of direction we swing
round to the north-east, and enter upon a gradual
rise, still following, however, the left bank of the
Isère. The road is picturesque, but, as I have
said, is at present much cut about by heavy traffic.
I found it bad enough in 1908, but a friend of

ONE OF THE ROCK TUNNELS OF SIEIX.

mine who passed that way a year later produced
photographic evidence of still further deterioration.
Numerous heavy wagons are encountered, drawn
by teams of three, and sometimes four, in almost
continuous procession. At the same time, the road
is not so bad but that a motor diligence service
plies over the whole pass.

After passing through the Gorge de la Saulcette
to St. Marcel one reaches the most picturesque

portion of the lower route at the Sieix defile, which is a typical example of the way in which a road has to be bored through the rocks at a considerable distance above the river. Three rock tunnels are passed in succession, and the views here, both backwards and forwards, are very striking. After another six kilometres it is necessary to keep a look-out for a somewhat abrupt entrance to the village of Aime. Still travelling northwards to the village of Bellentre, we obtain a first glimpse of the snow-capped Mont Pourri, which is one of the chief features of the panorama to be enjoyed later from the summit of the pass.

A bridge over the Arbonne torrent is crossed seven kilometres further on, and the road then descends to Bourg St. Maurice, the main street of which is narrow and drops steeply through the town. Rising again, after Bourg St. Maurice is left behind, the road in two kilometres reaches the French custom-house at Séez. Save for the steep pitch in Bourg St. Maurice, there has been no gradient along the whole route up to now which has exceeded 6 per cent., while for the most part the rise has been quite imperceptible.

At Séez, however, we enter upon steady work, the ascent being continuous all the way to the summit. For the first 18 kilometres the gradient is from 5 to 6 per cent., for several kilometres more it is between 3 and 5, while over the last kilometre up to the hospice it is from 6 to 7. The zigzags, however, are very numerous; in fact there is a continuous series of them all the way from Séez to La Froide, a distance of 19 kilometres, by which time fourteen corners have been rounded. From Séez the road winds through a wood, and in 12 kilometres reaches the Belvedere Hotel, which possesses a garage and pit, and is kept open from the 1st of July to the end of September. There are five more corners to round between the hotel and La Froide, but at longer intervals, and after one more "hairpin" the road is carried without further interruption to the hospice. Just after this unpretentious building is reached the frontier is crossed, marked by a stone on the left bearing the word "France," while on the right is the word "Italia" on a board painted in the Italian colours of green, white, and red. Also adjoining the road is a tall monument to St. Bernard de Menthon, erected so recently as 1902.

Those who have occasion to call a halt at the hospice may find amusement in testing the properties of a remarkable echo about a hundred yards away; while botanists may find ample food for study in the garden of Alpine flora which Canon Chanoux, who is in charge of the hospice, has laid out in the vicinity. The summit is then reached, after an almost level stretch, in another kilometre, and affords a fine view of Mont Blanc. A Roman column of rough marble will be seen at the roadside a little further on, and is known as the Colonne de Jupiter. It is over 60 feet in height, and has received within the last generation an addition in the shape of a statue of St. Bernard. Hard by is seen a circle of forty-six stones, of large size, and known as the Cirque d'Annibal, tradition stating that Hannibal once held here a council of war.

Cameras, by the way, have to be presented at the frontier for sealing, and photography is forbidden over the whole of the route to Aosta.

A descent may now be looked forward to of 13½ kilometres, with a fall of 2,450 feet, the maximum gradient of which is 8 per cent., though the average is much less. On the left the small Lac Verney is passed, and soon four zigzags are encountered, followed two or three kilometres lower down by three more. A little further running brings into view a continuous series of a dozen more "hairpins," passing in turn the hamlets of Pont Serrand and Golletaz, and opening up a distant view of the picturesque little town of La Thuile, where the Italian customs have to be dealt with, both as regards the triptyque and the demand for duty on the amount of petrol on board the car. A short level stage leads to a tunnel, at the exit from which is unfolded a splendid view of Mont Blanc, Mont Maudit, and other peaks. There are nine more kilometres of fairly steep descent to Pré St. Didier, with a maximum gradient of 7 per cent. Near La Balme there are four more corners, and after Elleva, a little further on, one passes through another tunnel, reaching shortly afterwards a series of a dozen corners which lead down to the ancient little Roman town of Pré St. Didier, on the right bank of the River Doire. It is charmingly situated, and much frequented as a thermal station, while it is also in close touch with the well-known resort of Courmayeur, five kilometres away up a good winding road on the left.

From Pré St. Didier the road undulates for four kilometres to Morgex, and from there to Aosta is an imperceptible descent, on a good but dusty road, of 1,105 feet in 27 kilometres. Beyond Le Pont de la Salle the fine Derby waterfall is passed, and the road crosses the Doire by the Equiliva bridge, and rises above the striking defile of Pierre Taillée. After leaving the gorge by a small rock tunnel, and passing through Ruinaz,

THE HOSPICE, FRONTIER, AND MENTHON MONUMENT.

one enters another gorge, that of Avise, above which, on the right, are seen three old castles. Beyond the village of Liverogne the road rises to Arvier, and enters yet another gorge, that of L'Enfer d'Arvier, flanked by a huge rock. At Villeneuve, the next village, are seen the ruins of Chatel Argent, and the road again crosses the Doire and runs through a fertile valley, with a fine castle on the right just before reaching

St. Pierre.   At Sarre the road runs close by
another castle, belonging to the King of Italy,
and in five more kilometres reaches Aosta, a town
replete with Roman remains in an excellent state
of preservation.

For the sake of its views of Mont Blanc, its
gorges, its castles, and its pleasant valleys on the
Italian side the Petit St. Bernard route has strong
claims to attention; but considered as a through
route it is not, as I have already said at the
beginning of this chapter, to be recommended in
preference to others which are available.   The
case might be otherwise, however, if one were
permitted to combine the journey with one over
the Grand St. Bernard, which joins the Petit
St. Bernard at Aosta; but here again the question
of Swiss hostility has to be taken into account.

CHAPTER X.

THE SIMPLON.

THIS classic route, the latest to succumb to the feverish energy of the Swiss railway contractor, has much to recommend it as a motorist's gate into or out of Italy, albeit it has attendant drawbacks. Since the great tunnel was built a large amount of traffic has been removed from the road, which should benefit accordingly; and, inasmuch as it was closed entirely to motor-cars up to the time of the completion of the line in 1906, thère is cause for satisfaction, rather than otherwise, that the railway has thus indirectly increased the resources of the road traveller. Whether the cantonal authorities will now neglect the road or not remains to be seen, but in any case it will not be subjected to the amount of wear and tear which the use of diligences involved.

No vehicle is so destructive to a highway as an Alpine diligence, for, in addition to its own enormous weight, and the hammering effect of the twenty iron-shod hoofs of a five-horsed team, there is the brutal action of the skid to be considered. Motor-cars glide smoothly down a pass on rubber tyres, but horsed vehicles are the most unscientific things in the world where brake-power is concerned; and the driver of a diligence, on reaching the summit of a pass, lets down a clumsy shoe, and makes the entire descent with a locked wheel, tearing up the road from start to finish. If the Simplon road henceforth is accorded occasional attention, instead of being entirely neglected on the plea that the railway absorbs the bulk of the traffic, the route should be a popular one for automobilists on tour to Italy or returning thence to Switzerland and France.

It is not in the nature of the Swiss, however, to make concessions gracefully, and though cars are no longer barred from the Simplon Pass they may only cross it under restrictions of the absurdest kind. To some extent custom is already bringing these into contempt, but while they exist they have in the main to be observed, and I append a translation of the official requirements herewith accordingly : —

DECREE OF MAY 1ST, 1909.

Article I.—The circulation of automobiles and motor vehicles on the international road of the Simplon is provisionally authorised.

Article II.—The road will be open every day except on Thursday in each week.

Article III.—Circulation is entirely forbidden at night except in case of actual necessity. No departure can be made from Brigue or from Gondo after five o'clock in the afternoon in the months of June, July, or August, and after four o'clock in the other months of the year.

Article IV.—Circulation is also forbidden to anyone who is not in possession of an official driving licence.

Article V.—All drivers of motor vehicles intending to cross the Simplon must give notification in writing to that effect to the gendarmerie depôts at Brigue or Gondo. This inscription must mention the number of the motor, the names and residences of the driver and the owner, and the date and the hour of departure. A duplicate of this inscription will be handed to the travellers in exchange for a payment of five francs, and will serve as an authorisation to cross the pass. The document must be exhibited on request to all the police agents and road-menders encountered on the road. It must be given up at the gendarmerie depôt on arriving at Brigue or Gondo.

Article VI.—The speed must not exceed ten kilometres per hour, according to the requirements of Article IX of the Federal Act of June 13th, 1904. At corners the speed must not exceed three kilometres per hour. Before arriving at a corner motor vehicles must announce their approach by a horn; all other warnings are forbidden.

Article VII.—Motor vehicles must always, especially when meeting travellers, cattle, or other vehicles, take the outer edge of the road. If cattle or horses are frightened the automobilist must stop his car and also his motor.

Article VIII.—The requirements of the Act of June 13th, 1904, which are not affected by the present decree, must be strictly observed.

Article IX.—Infringements of the preceding regulations will be punished by a fine of from 20 francs to 500 francs, imposed by the Prefect of Brigue, and subject to revision by the Department of Justice and Police.

Article X.—The Prefect of the Brigue district is especially authorised to attend to the carrying out of this order, which comes into force immediately.

Given in Council at Sion, May 1st, 1909, to be published and posted in all the villages of the Canton.

These regulations, however, irksome as they are if literally obeyed, do not include the whole of the conditions to which the automobilist must conform. No car is allowed to enter on a journey over the pass from either side before nine o'clock, or at a later hour than five, and until recently the afternoon limit even for the summer months was even earlier—namely, four o'clock. If all goes well, of course, the journey may be planned so that, save for the ridiculous speed limit, inconvenience may be avoided; but, on the other hand, circumstances may arise which cause considerable delay. It may be impossible to avoid arriving at the pass on the day (Thursday) on which it is closed entirely to cars; and even if that contingency be staved off the embargo as to "closing time" may be fatal.

As an illustration to the point I may describe my own experiences in August, 1909. A downpour of tropical intensity impelled an over-night halt at Stresa, on Lake Maggiore, although I had intended to end the day at Domo d'Ossola or Gondo. Next morning the rain was as bad as ever, but, fearful of losing a whole day, my companion and I left Stresa at nine o'clock. Before we had gone many miles, however, we were soaked to the skin, and had no option but to rush into the first hotel we saw at Domo d'Ossola, demand a room, and effect a complete change.

By the time our clothes had dried the rain had moderated, and shortly afterwards ceased, and but for the official limit we should have pushed on and reached Gondo in time to cross the pass. Even as it was this would have been just possible, as the five o'clock limit had lately come into force; but not only was this extension unknown in England before we left, but even locally we were assured that the barrier still stood at four. Hence we had no option but to stay where we were, condemned to waste a whole day in a spot with no conspicuous attractions of its own. Stress of weather no man can help, and any old-time

THE APPROACH TO THE SIMPLON PASS, NEAR VARZO.

tourist is prepared to accept it with due philosophy; but for one delay to be succeeded by
another which is not the direct consequence of
the weather is less easy to endure.

Of the precise way in which the restrictions
operate against the driver of a car when actually
on the pass I will speak *en passant* while dealing
with the route. The itinerary, detailed from the
Italian side, is as follows:—

Place.	Altitude. (Feet.)	Intermediate Distances. (Kils.)	Progressive Totals. (Kils.)
Domo d'Ossola - -	919	—	—
Preglia - - -	951	$2\frac{1}{2}$	$2\frac{1}{2}$
Crevola - - -	—	$1\frac{1}{2}$	4
Campeglia - - -	1,293	$1\frac{1}{2}$	$5\frac{1}{2}$
Varzo - - -	1,865	6	$11\frac{1}{2}$
Iselle (Italian Customs)	2,155	$5\frac{1}{2}$	17
Paglino - - -	—	$2\frac{1}{2}$	$19\frac{1}{2}$
Frontier - - -	—	1	$20\frac{1}{2}$
Gondo (Swiss Customs)	2,821	1	$21\frac{1}{2}$
Al Gaby (or Gstein) -	4,035	$6\frac{1}{2}$	28
Simplon (Sempione) -	4,878	$3\frac{1}{2}$	$31\frac{1}{2}$
Eggen - - -	5,250	$1\frac{1}{2}$	33
Old Hospice - -	6,140	5	38
Hospice - -	6,562	2	40
Summit (Hotel) - -	*6,594*	1	41
Eggen - - -	—	7	48
Bérisal - - -	5,003	2	50
Ganter Bridge - -	4,616	$1\frac{1}{2}$	$51\frac{1}{2}$
Laueneu - - -	—	7	$58\frac{1}{2}$
Schlucht - - -	2,972	1	$59\frac{1}{2}$
Brigue - - -	2,231	$3\frac{1}{2}$	63

(*Hotels at Domo d'Ossola, Gondo, Simplon, the summit, Berisal, and Brigue.*)

From Domo d'Ossola to the Italian frontier is
a rise of 1,236 feet in 17 kilometres. There are
several undulations, however, which make the
average gradient rather steeper than would appear
from these figures. The road runs due north
for three kilometres, then turns to the right

towards Crevola, where it turns sharply to the left and leads through Campeglia to Varzo, by which time it has begun to veer westwards towards Iselle, through the characteristically Italian valley of Vedro, along which flows the River Diveria. At Iselle one passes the Italian customs. There are fortifications in the vicinity, and cameras, needless to say, must not be used ; but they are not officially demanded and corded

A VIEW NEAR AL GABY.

as in the case of the Mont Genèvre route. The new Simplon tunnel also ends at Iselle, and its yawning mouth may be seen quite close to the road. The Swiss frontier is reached $3\frac{1}{2}$ kilometres further on, but the custom-house is at the village of Gondo, 10 kilometres from Iselle.

Here the motorist has a double purpose to fulfil, not only having to pass the customs, but to conform to the regulations enumerated above as to the crossing of the pass. The gendarmerie station is on the left and the custom-house on the right. It is policy to get the business over with the gendarmes first, as the time of your departure will be marked on the permit. If the custom-house is visited first the time spent there is to one's loss; but if the process of presenting one's triptyque, etc., is gone through after leaving the gendarmerie the time occupied is so much to one's benefit, as it comes out of the ridiculous time limit of four hours which, strictly speaking, one must occupy in passing from Gondo to Brigue.

Within the gendarmerie station one is asked to fill up a document entitled " Autorisation de passage," giving the name, profession, and residence of the bearer. There is no separate entry for the owner, as distinguished from the driver, or *vice versá*, as might have been inferred from Article V; nor, if I recollect aright, has the number of the car or of its engine to be set down. The gendarme fills in the hour of leaving and signs the document, which, by the way, is printed in French and German, and the recipient has also to append his signature.

I may testify to the fact that the gendarme in charge at Gondo is less inclined to stand by the strict letter of the law than might be supposed, and, if he is asked how long one must take to cross the pass, will probably put down something in round figures. In my own case, for example, I left at 9.15, but he wrote down one o'clock as the time for reaching Brigue. Now, the distance from Gondo to Brigue is

42½ kilometres, or 26 miles, and the summit is, practically speaking, midway. It is perfectly well understood that no driver on earth will attempt to regulate his pace to that of the official stipulation of six miles an hour, and even the gendarme himself may remind you that there is an hotel at the summit.

What actually happens, therefore, is that one mounts the pass at a reasonable speed, and the summit will probably be attained in about an hour. A good couple of hours may then be counted upon for admiring the scenery, taking photographs, writing picture post-cards, and lunching at the hotel; in fact, if the regulations had been intended for the enrichment of the buildings at the summit, they could not have been more successfully devised.

Irrespective of halts for the enjoyment of the scenery or photography, the descent can with difficulty be made to extend to the fourth hour, as, so far from there being any particular necessity for the imposition of a particular speed limit, the road is singularly devoid of dangerous factors. There are no long series of *lacets*, and, as a matter of fact, scarcely any corners at all. The road, indeed, is less like a pass, so far as the word suggests the running through ravines and alongside precipices, and the construction of innumerable zigzags, than any other which could be named, and is absolutely the last on which anything in the way of special restriction of speed should be enjoined.

If the Simplon necessitates an amble of six miles an hour on the straight, and of a mile and three quarters (*see* Article VI) at corners, the Petit St. Bernard, with its ever-recurring *lacets*, demands, as a proportionate degree of precaution, a special speed limit of about two miles an hour on the straight, and a dead stop at every corner, with a final proviso as to sending a man in front to wave a red flag. The Simplon regulations, in fact, are wholly farcical, and I would undertake to drive a car from Gondo to Brigue with a cargo of old ladies, delicate invalids, or young babes, taking every precaution which the circumstances would enjoin, and cover the distance in an hour and a half.

The practical issue, however, is this, that though four hours have to be devoted to the journey, continuous travelling during that period is not compulsory, and one may use the time as one pleases. The real awkwardness of the cantonal decree is centred in the fact that one can only cross between certain hours, and that one day in the week is barred; by the perversity of fate it may happen that, however carefully an itinerary has been planned, bad weather or other sources of delay may cause one to arrive at the foot of the pass on Wednesday evening. The ruling out of a given day, moreover, is inconvenient enough apart from the question of anything of an untoward character which may occur either as to weather, the car, or anything else, and Thursday may just be the very day on which one would elect to cross the Simplon, having in view the number of days before one's holiday must come to an end and the distance which has to be traversed before one reaches home. Although, of course, with a good car one has always some margin of elasticity, twenty-four hours is a considerable slice to have to cut out of one's programme; and really, it must be remembered, the embargo is for more than twenty-four hours, being from five o'clock on Wednesday until Friday morning.

Having dealt with the question of the speed regulations peculiar to the Simplon, we may now consider the road from the practical point of view. It is not by any means so wide as the Mont Cenis, but at the same time is broad enough to travel along in comfort, and for the passing of other vehicles. The surface is more or less of the bumpy order, especially on the Gondo side; at the same time it is not so bad as might have been expected, considering the fact that the building of the railway tunnel brought a good deal of heavy traffic over the pass. The ascent from Gondo is one of 3,773 feet in $19\frac{1}{2}$ kilometres; that is about 300 feet per mile. There are short pieces of 9 per cent., and one of 11 per cent., but of *tourniquets*, as I have said, there are none.

The most picturesque feature of this section of the road is that encountered soon after leaving the custom-house behind, for, after swinging round two sharp corners, one enters the Gorge of Gondo, one of the most famous fissures in the Alps. Massive rocks tower perpendicularly above the road on either side to the height of no less than 2,000 feet, and this fact alone is sufficient to render the passage through the gorge at all times impressive; but the degree to which the place is awe-inspiring is largely a matter of atmosphere.

H

and, while on a dull day the contiguity of the
mighty precipices might cause a nervous person
to shiver, they are shorn of their terrors in a
brighter light.

Soon after entering the gorge the Fressinone
waterfall is seen tumbling down at a furious rate
on the right. It dives underneath the road and
drops into a chasm spanned by a bridge. A
long tunnel is then entered, 220 metres in length,
the cutting of which is said to have been both
perilous and costly owing to the hardness of the
rock; the miners had to be suspended from
ropes while making the side orifices through
which light is admitted. Very soon, however,
the gorge is left behind, and we run westwards,
and, after swinging to the south and back again to
the north, reach the village of Al Gaby, or Gstein,
picturesquely situated among wooded pastures.

The first snow-capped peaks now come into
view at Simplon (*Italian*—Sempione), and 3½ kilometres higher up the prospect begins to grow
more ample, though the village itself is insig-
nificant. The road then takes a couple of turns
and enters upon a diversion which is practically
new, the original road lying 30 feet below, buried
in *débris* which was carried down by a landslide
in 1901, from the Rossboden Glacier, with such
dire effect as to sweep away forests and châlets,
and cover with huge boulders an area twice as
large as Hyde Park. At the hamlet of Eggen
the gradient moderates for a kilometre, and then
rises fairly steeply to the summit. The road
runs through a wooded valley, crosses the
Krummbach river, and passes a weather-beaten

THE VERANDAH OF THE HOTEL BELLEVUE, SIMPLON SUMMIT.
(*On the left is a motor garage, one of the highest in the world.*)

H 2

structure, the old hospice, which is now used as a herdsmen's hut. The new hospice is two kilometres higher up the pass, and is a building of considerable size, dating. from 1825 so far as its completion is concerned, though it was founded by Napoleon himself in 1802. It is dominated by the Schönhorn and other peaks. In another kilometre the top of the pass is reached, and on a little plateau stands the Hotel Bellevue, opposite which is a post-office. The building seen just behind in my photograph is a motor garage, and it is, of course, one of the highest in the world. The situation is charming, and is by no means the least attractive of the road summits of the Alps.

The environment of peaks is magnificent, and particularly striking is the view of such famous giants of the Bernese Oberland as the Jungfrau, the Nesthorn, the Aletschhorn, and the Aletsch Glacier, which possesses the distinction of being the largest ice-field in the Alps. Even if the Simplon Pass had not to be crossed of necessity as a portion of a through route from Italy, it would be worth ascending if only for the sake of the panorama which may be enjoyed from the northern side of the summit. One would be quite content to stay here for some time, especially as the hotel is a comfortable one, even if one were not practically compelled to do so by the four hours' limit; at the same time one prefers perfect freedom of choice to arbitrary compulsion. I may mention in passing, however, that the tourist who does not wish to take his luncheon early may find a suitable hotel at Bérisal, nine kilometres down the pass.

RAIN-CLOUDS ON THE BERNESE ALPS : A VIEW JUST BELOW THE SIMPLON SUMMIT.

The descent of 22 kilometres embodies a fall
of 4,363 feet. As far as Bérisal it ranges from
4 to 8 per cent., and just beyond that village
there is a short piece of 9 per cent., followed
by a level stretch of 1½ kilometres. There are
several more kilometres of 4 to 8 per cent., and
then the road becomes more steep, even attaining
12 per cent. at Lauenen, while the run down
into Brigue is from 6 to 9 per cent. The surface, though not first-class, is better than on
the Gondo side, and the road is of pretty good
width.

For some distance from the summit the noble
amplitude of outlook is continued, albeit interrupted by three tunnels in succession. In all
there are four tunnels, but the road winds outside
one of these, as it is only necessary to use it in
winter, but through the others one must pass
perforce. The second tunnel is 130 metres long,
while the third is 50 metres, and has eleven
openings at the side. These galleries are built to
prevent the road being blocked by the movement
of the Kaltwasser Glacier, the avalanches from
which slide over the roofs of the galleries. A
fine cascade, moreover, issuing from the glacier
rushes over the top of the fourth tunnel and
dives down the precipice side, so that in point of
fact one drives beneath the torrent. Incidentally
it may be mentioned that the Simplon road as a
whole has 10 tunnels and 600 bridges, great or
small, while it is frequently buttressed with long
stretches of substantial masonry. It was undoubtedly a difficult road to build, but in that
respect does not impress the eye to the same

extent as the Petit St. Bernard, or many others on which *tourniquets* abound.

After passing a hamlet which, curiously enough, bears the same name as one on the other side of the pass, namely Eggen, and winding through a wood of larches, one soon reaches Bérisal, a pleasant spot with a good hotel, and so far up to date as to run a motor-car of its own to Brigue and back. It is policy, by the way, to bear places of this kind in mind on one's journeys, and not assume that the lowest point of the pass is necessarily the best at which to stay the night. Bérisal, for example, would be more agreeable than Brigue itself if the crossing of the pass has not been begun until late in the day, whereas a natural but delusive instinct would lead the traveller to finish up at Brigue itself.

Below Bérisal the road describes two wide " hairpins," and descends to a bridge over the Ganter, and there, after a turn to the left, runs on the level for a kilometre and a half alongside the river. It then descends anew with a gradient of from 4 to 8 per cent., and with several changes of direction runs down to Lauenen and Schlucht, and then winds downwards into Brigue. The entrance to the town is steep and narrow, and must be taken with care.

The gendarme to whom one should hand the permit may not be visible, and must be sought out accordingly, though one does not very well see how any particular penalty can attach to the non-delivery of the document, as one has already conformed to the regulations by obtaining and paying for it, and, unlike the triptyque, the paper does not require to be stamped. In my own case I stopped at a petrol shop, and, not seeing a gendarme about, despatched a messenger to seek him out. The gendarme hastened up in his shirt sleeves and accepted the permit without demur. By way of banter, however, I asked him if it was quite *en règle;* he merely glanced at the times and politely waved the car onwards. It is abundantly clear, therefore, that the decree of May, 1909, is something which is not to be interpreted too literally, and for all practical purposes it might as well be rescinded forthwith. Inasmuch, moreover, as the railway now diverts passengers from the road, and the posting business is dead, it is obviously to the interest of people living on the pass to cultivate automobile traffic. Already it has been mentioned that there is a garage at the summit, and even at a little *osteria* on the hospice side one may see the notice exposed: " *Auto-benzin.*" Why, therefore, should all this pother be made about motor vehicles?

By way of a postscript it may be added that almost at the very doors of Brigue is an outstanding illustration of Nemesis overtaking the short-sighted selfishness of the Swiss villager. Visp, only five miles away along the Rhone valley, was once the centre of a thriving trade in mule transport between the village and Zermatt. The Government desired to build a carriage-road, but the villagers foresaw that the business in mules would disappear, and vetoed the project accordingly. Subsequently, however, a company obtained a concession from the Government to build the well-known railway line to Zermatt, and this the inhabitants had no power to prevent. As a result they were worse off than ever, for there is neither any trade in mules nor has any new carriage traffic sprung up, as would undoubtedly have been the case if a proper road had been constructed. Visp is now one of the most melancholy places imaginable. It has no particular attractions of its own, while even the fact that it is at the foot of the Zermatt line brings it no prosperity, the railway passengers who come along the Rhone valley from Geneva or Lausanne simply bundling out of their carriages and changing over to the Zermatt train. In the intervals between train times the place is as quiet as the grave.

NOTE TO SECOND EDITION.

Article II. of the regulations quoted on page 104 *has now been amended, and the special restriction as to Thursdays no longer exists. The time of closing has also been extended to six o'clock during the months of May, June, July, and August.*

CHAPTER XI.

THE ARLBERG.

LIKE the Simplon, the Arlberg is a route on which a line of railway runs for some distance and then disappears into the bowels of the earth. None the less, I am happy to say, the road itself is not neglected, and no one need have the slightest hesitation in crossing the pass. It is of good width, with an excellent surface for the most part, while the gradients are in no sense formidable.

I am the more anxious to emphasise these facts because of a brief but ridiculous and wholly false summary of the route which appears in the well-known and in many respects adequate " Guide Taride." M. Taride, it is to be feared, approaches the question of travelling on high ground from the point of view of the plain-dweller, pure and simple, and says of the Arlberg :—

" Route superbe, mais que nous indiquons que pour mémoire, à cause du passage si périlleux de l'Arlberg. Nous ne croyons pas devoir la recommander aux automobiles ni aux cyclistes."

There is only one possible construction to place upon this paragraph, and that is that it was written by a cyclist with a feeble brake equipment, and for whom the Arlberg was the first and only Alpine road he had ever crossed. So far from the Arlberg being a specially dangerous pass it is one of the easiest to surmount, and the man who could be deterred from crossing it by the description quoted above would be wise to stay at home and abandon all thoughts of Alpine touring by road. In no single detail is the Arlberg Pass unsuitable for the ordinary touring motor-car, and the fact may even be re-called that it has been crossed by actual racers; for, inasmuch as it is part and parcel of the main road to the Austrian capital, it was necessarily traversed by the competitors in the famous Paris-Vienna Race in 1902. Scores of cars then drove over it with safety, although they were urged at the highest speeds which the circumstances would allow.

Individual cases of imprudence were, of course, forthcoming, but were the natural accompani-ments of a contest in which the keenness of international rivalry was paramount. Two of the resultant accidents, by the way, had their humorous side, and I cannot refrain from mentioning them here. A motor-cycling competitor whose brakes failed him came tearing down the road, yelling with all his might that he was utterly unable to stop his machine. The driver of a car in front pulled aside, and, as the motor-cycle hurtled by, he managed to seize the rider's collar and literally pull him off the machine, which promptly dis-appeared over the edge of the road. The other accident was that of a voiturette driver, who in his impetuosity took a corner too fast, and allowed the car to leave the road. He jumped off the car as it was falling over the edge, and it promptly rolled over and over into the bottom of the valley, hundreds of feet below. As he himself was climbing back on to the road another car came swooping down, the driver of which, seeing the disabled car at the bottom of the ravine, was overwhelmed with astonishment at the miracle which had taken place, for he inferred that the first driver had rolled down the precipice side with his car, and had climbed back again uninjured!

A race is one thing, however; a tour is quite another. Cars in plenty cross the Arlberg every day in the summer months, and the route is an excellent one for those who wish to approach the Tyrol without taking too much German territory on the one hand, or too much of Switzerland on the other. We may suppose, however, that the tourist has either come by way of Constance, in which case he must descend the valley of the Rhine to Feldkirch, or he may have followed the Lake of Zurich, crossed the ridge to the Walen See and driven to Sargans. Leaving the road to Ragaz and Chur, he must turn to the left at Sargans and follow the Rhine valley to Buchs, where the Swiss and Austrian customs must be passed. From Zurich the journey is enjoyable throughout—much more so, in fact, than most of those which are available in Switzerland; while the roads are above the average in quality, particularly along the Rhine valley.

The itinerary from Buchs is as follows:—

Place.			Altitude. (Feet.)	Intermediate Distances. (Kils.)	Progressive Totals. (Kils.)
Buchs	-	-	-	1,475	—	—
Schaan	-	-	-	—	3	3
Neudel	-	-	-	—	5	8
Feldkirch	-	-	1,500	6	14

ON THE ARLBERG PASS, BETWEEN STUBEN AND THE SUMMIT.

Place.	Altitude. (Feet.)	Intermediate Distances. (Kils.)	Progressive Totals. (Kils.)
Frastanz - - -	1,550	3	17
Nenzing - - -	1,665	9	26
Bludenz - - -	1,905	10	36
Dalaas - - -	3,055	17	53
Langen - - -	3,990	11	64
Stuben - - -	4,600	3	67
Summit - - -	*5,912*	$5\frac{1}{2}$	$72\frac{1}{2}$
Hospice - - -	5,740	$\frac{1}{2}$	73
St. Anton - -	4,222	$7\frac{1}{2}$	$80\frac{1}{2}$
Pettneu - - -	—	$7\frac{1}{2}$	88
Flirsch - - -	3,795	$5\frac{1}{2}$	$93\frac{1}{2}$
Pians - - -	—	12	$105\frac{1}{2}$
Landeck - - -	2,677	6	$111\frac{1}{2}$

(Hotels practically all along the route.)

There is good level running to be enjoyed all
the way from Buchs to Feldkirch, where a turn
to the right must be taken for Frastanz. Keep
to the right also at the next fork, and follow the
River Ill to Nenzing. A few kilometres further on
the river is crossed ere reaching Bludenz. Without
being altogether striking the scenery is by no
means unpicturesque, while the towns have many
attractive buildings. At the fork beyond Bludenz
keep to the left, and follow the Alfenz river to
Dalaas. A gradual rise leads to Langen, where
the railway buries itself in the Arlberg tunnel.

Here the ascent proper may be said to begin,
and is one of 1,920 feet in 8 kilometres. There is
nothing difficult in the way of gradients, and the
only section which makes any demand on either
the driver or the car is at Stuben. There one
comes suddenly upon four " hairpin " corners,
which are not visible in advance. The curves are
fairly wide, but the gradient is somewhat steep,
and one must have the car well in hand; that

is to say, the driver must be prepared to change speed before approaching the first corner, and probably to a still lower gear almost immediately. After the *tourniquet* has been surmounted, however, he may look forward to an enjoyable run up to the summit, through a valley which, if somewhat barren in itself, presents not a few fine outlines, both retrospective and prospective, particularly those of Mt. Scesaplana.

ON THE WAY TO THE ARLBERG SUMMIT.

The going is excellent throughout, and the summit is soon attained. It is devoid of buildings, but just beyond is the hospice of St. Christophe, with a small church. The province of Vorarlberg has now been left behind and the Tyrol is entered—the finest touring ground in the whole of Europe, and the one above all others which it should be the ambition of every automobilist to explore.

About a kilometre below the summit the road swings to the left at Kalteneck, with striking views in every direction, particularly towards Mt. Patteriol on the south. A pleasant descent leads into the Rosanna valley and to St. Anton, where the Arlberg railway emerges from the great tunnel. This village is fast becoming a popular resort in summer and winter alike. It is the centre of many agreeable excursions, while in winter the neighbouring slopes provide ample opportunities for ski-ing and tobogganing. The Post is an excellent hotel, with a very good garage, and I may say that I personally received much kindly assistance there from the proprietor and his son in rather curious circumstances.

I have said that the road generally is a fine one, and perfectly safe so far as the gradients and corners are concerned. But truth compels the admission that landslides are not unknown. When I crossed with a friend in August, 1909, we met a descending car on the Langen side, the driver of which signalled to us to pull up. An exchange of conversation disclosed the fact that there had been a landslip on the Tyrolese side of the pass, as a result of which the other car had turned back. On further enquiry, however, I found that the road was clear for a considerable distance, the block being between St. Anton and Landeck; and, not being disposed to change my route, I decided to push on and resort to the railway at St. Anton.

In the end we did not lose much time, for, bespeaking a truck overnight at St. Anton, I was able to put the car aboard next morning, my friend having meanwhile gone on to Landeck to receive.

A TYPICAL VIEW OF THE ARLBERG ROAD.

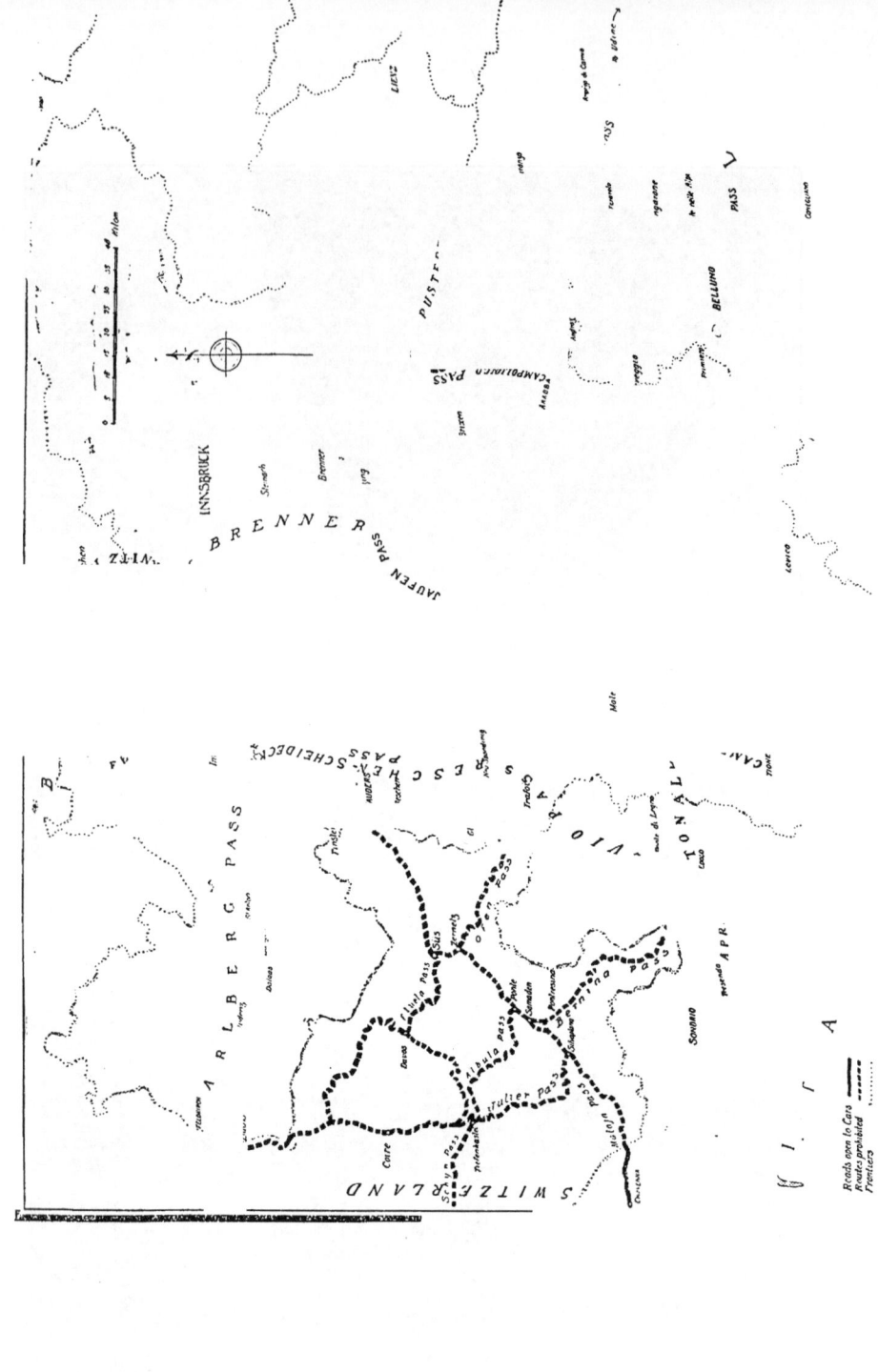

Roads open to Cars
Routes prohibited
Frontiers

A TYPICAL VIEW OF THE ARLBERG ROAD.

it, while I followed on the next passenger train
after the car had left.   At Landeck I was able to
warn several other motorists who were preparing
to ascend the pass.   It will thus be seen that
though the automobile tourist may perchance have
his journey interrupted by an incident of this kind,
there is always the railway to fall back upon; and,
even if not forewarned as I was, and nothing
is known of the obstruction until it is actually

THE ARLBERG SUMMIT.

reached, it is a simple matter for him to turn
back and drive to the nearest station.   The mileage
cannot be great in any case, for even the distance
over the pass from Langen to St. Anton is less
than nine miles, while below the ends of the tunnel
the railway practically adjoins the road.
  Of the stage from St. Anton to Landeck I
am therefore unable to speak from experience;
I am informed by a friend, however, who has
made the journey, that the road continues good and

presents no difficulties. As Landeck is 2,677 feet high, the descent from St. Anton is only one of 1,545 feet in 37 kilometres, and the gradients involved, therefore, are inconsiderable. In Landeck one is sure to meet many automobilists bound either westwards for the Arlberg Pass, eastwards for Innsbruck, or southwards for the Reschen-Scheideck and the Stelvio. As I propose, however, to deal next with the Brenner we will assume that the traveller from St. Anton continues his journey to Innsbruck, along a valley road which is somewhat narrow and rather winding.

The journey is somewhat dull over this stage, and does not merit description in detail. One point requires especial mention, however, and that is that at the village of Imst, 18 kilometres from Landeck, care must be taken to avoid the natural inclination to go straight on, as this will either lead one over an alternative, but longer and hillier, route to Innsbruck, or over the Fern Pass. A sharp turn to the right must be made at Imst, and the road thus found crosses ere long to the south side of the river, but re-crosses it near Telfs and follows the north bank right up to Innsbruck, 72 kilometres from Landeck.

CHAPTER XII.

THE BRENNER.

THE Brenner is the one and only pass of more than 4,000 feet in height on which the ordinary rail traveller may meet the road tourist on fairly equal terms. I do not suggest by this that the train journey is as enjoyable as either walking, cycling, or driving; but the line does manage to reach the same altitude as the summit itself; and, though it runs through twenty-one tunnels of varying length, it does not burrow into the ground beneath the mountain top, as is the case with the Mont Cenis, St. Gotthard, Simplon, and the Arlberg. Such views, therefore, as are available from the pass are virtually common to all methods of locomotion alike.

Unfortunately for the train tourist, however, who has no personal zest in the means by which he progresses, the views are in no sense grandiose; yet it is typical of the limitations which train travelling enjoins that many people may be found ready to declare that the train journey over the Brenner route is "magnificent." I remember, for example, conversing some years ago with a distinguished politician on the charms of road travelling among the Alps; and, while confessing that he had had no experience of such delights, he spoke most eulogistically of the "splendid scenery" to be enjoyed from the Brenner railway.

It is no wish of mine to detract from any

enjoyment which the tourist may derive by taking train from Innsbruck to Franzensfeste; few railway journeys are half so attractive. But the essence of my contention is that anyone who will take the trouble to cross Alpine roads of greater height will enter upon scenes which are infinitely more magnificent, more wondrously majestic in every way; and yet road locomotion is still so uncommon a thing, relatively speaking, that train travellers waste their superlatives on landscapes which, though the best they may have seen, are vastly inferior to those of loftier altitudes.

Compared with the majority of the passes described in this volume the crossing of the Brenner is for the motorist an easy saunter. It is wholly pleasant throughout. Of grandeur it has none, but, provided he starts without high expectations, he will find the journey entirely agreeable, as the road is good and well-graded, and the pastoral scenery decidedly satisfying, while on the Bozen side there are several small towns of typical Tyrolean picturesqueness. To the man who has approached the pass without encountering any previous high ground it will serve as a very useful experience where his car is concerned; for it is just long enough and steep enough to show what steady collar-work means as compared with the undulations and short, steep rises of ordinary touring work. If the car will keep cool after an uninterrupted journey from Innsbruck to Brenner village, it may or may not be equal to the more formidable ascents to be found elsewhere; but if it will not rise to the summit without the water in the radiator boiling, it will most certainly find itself in poor fettle on the upper slopes of the Stelvio and other great passes.

In all probability, however, the motorist who drives southwards from Innsbruck will already have crossed the Arlberg, if nothing else, and will rightly regard the Brenner as a very simple task. The pass is at once the oldest and lowest of the main roads over the Alps; and as Innsbruck, the starting point, is 1,885 feet above the sea, and the summit of the Brenner is but 4,495 feet, the total rise is one of 2,610 feet only, and this is extended over a distance of $38\frac{1}{2}$ kilometres. The itinerary is as follows:—

Place.	Altitude. (Feet.)	Intermediate Distances. (Kils.)	Progressive Totals. (Kils.)
Innsbruck - -	1,885	—	—
Schupfen - -	2,310	8	8
Schonbergerhof -	3,280	7	15
Matrei - - -	3,240	$6\frac{1}{2}$	$21\frac{1}{2}$
Steinach - -	3,430	5	$26\frac{1}{2}$
Gries - - -	3,806	$6\frac{1}{2}$	33
Brenner (*Summit*) -	4,495	$5\frac{1}{2}$	$38\frac{1}{2}$
Brennerbad - -	4,390	4	$42\frac{1}{2}$
Gossensass - -	3,495	5	$47\frac{1}{2}$
Sterzing - - -	3,115	$5\frac{1}{2}$	53
Mauls - - -	3,940	9	62
Mittewald - -	2,625	7	69
Franzensfeste - -	2,451	6	75
Vahrn - - -	—.	$4\frac{1}{2}$	$79\frac{1}{2}$
Brixen - - -	1,835	$3\frac{1}{2}$	83
Klausen - - -	1,715	12	95
Waidbruck - -	1,545	$6\frac{1}{2}$	$101\frac{1}{2}$
Atzwang - - -	1,220	$7\frac{1}{2}$	109
Blumau - - -	1,020	6	115
Bozen - - -	876	8	123

(*Hotels all along the line of route.*)

As Innsbruck, by the way, is an important centre, the automobilist should not leave it before casting his eye over his car in case any "spares"

may be wanted, or repairs need to be effected
which he may not care to do on the road. At
the garage of Richard Holzammer, near the Hotel
Tirol, he will find a skilled mechanic and a good
tool equipment; at the same time it must be
remembered, as has been mentioned in Chapter V,
that British threads cannot be cut on foreign
dies.

A VIEW ON THE BRENNER PASS, LOOKING NORTH.

Leaving almost immediately the plain on
which Innsbruck stands, the Brenner road rises
fairly steeply for three kilometres. It is broad
and of good surface, and winds in sweeping
bends without zigzags. The retrospective view
of Innsbruck and its fine backing of mountains is
the most striking of the whole journey, especially
if the season is not sufficiently far advanced for
the snow to have disappeared. In the valley
below to the left the rail and the river still run

in close companionship. There is then a level
stage of five kilometres to Schupfen, followed by
a further ascent of seven kilometres to Schon-
bergerhof. For a time the surface becomes a
little rough, though not really bad, and, after
slight rises and falls, the road leads to Matrei in
another six kilometres. A steeper rise follows to
within a kilometre of Steinach, with a moderate
descent into that village. The surface has meanwhile improved, and in fact is now super-excellent.
A gentle rise brings us to Gries, and the valley
contracts for a time and loses sight of the railway. Above Gries the gradient increases for a
short stage, and is then level for a kilometre, and
finally rises again to the summit, passing on the
way the green Brenner See.

The run throughout is altogether pleasant,
and the villages *en route* are charmingly situated
and wear a very prosperous appearance; but the
whole road runs between two lines of hills and is
devoid of grandeur. The village of Brenner is at
the summit itself. The railway station adjoins
one side of the road, faced by an hotel and other
buildings. Though the village is 4,495 feet high,
however, the local environment is such as to
suggest neither a summit nor even any altitude.
The most interesting fact connected with the
place is that it was visited by the poet Goethe
in 1786, and on the wall of the Post Hotel
may be seen a recently erected medallion in
commemoration of the event.

An enjoyable descent to Franzensfeste may
now be anticipated of 2,044 feet in 36½ kilometres.
The gradient is not uniform, however, but un-

dulates occasionally; for all practical purposes it
is a continuous fall of a moderate type, save for
a stretch between Brennerbad and Gossensass,
where it is more accentuated. Some care, in
fact, is requisite when entering the latter village,
as the road through it is not only narrow but
takes an acute turn, and accidents of the kind
due to careless chauffeurs are not unknown
here, though there is not the slightest need for

A FÊTE DAY IN BRENNER VILLAGE.

apprehension if prudence and consideration are
observed.

It is interesting to note, by the way, that
the road is here tar-coated, and it is the only
place so far east at which I have seen that
up-to-date treatment adopted. It may be added
that the train is not equal to the task of following
the road at this point, but makes an enormous
detour to Ast, and comes back almost on its

own tracks before entering Gossensass. Just
beyond the village the road crosses the rail and
the River Eisak, and runs west of both to Sterzing, a charming little town with a picturesque
environment.

At the fork care must be taken to follow the
road to the left. The castle of Spreckenstein, on
the east side, and two others—namely, Thumberg
and Reifenstein on the west, with a glimpse of
snow peaks, soon come into view, and about
three kilometres from Sterzing the road again
crosses the river and then the railway itself, and,
keeping to the same side for a considerable distance, passes through Mauls, and swings to the
left before descending to Mittewald.

About four kilometres further on the road
once more crosses the river, and runs between
it and the railway through the Brixener-Klause
defile, the southern end of which is dominated
by the fortress of Franzensfeste, and hard by is
the station of that name. About a kilometre
before this, however, there is a bad *caniveau*
which must be treated with respect. At the
fork at Franzensfeste the right-hand road must
be taken, the road now running between the rail
and the river as far as Brixen, where the Bozen
road is joined by the fine highway from Toblach
through the Pusterthal.

In Brixen itself it is necessary to turn to the
right, then to the left, and then to the right
again ; and, just outside, what seems the proper
course to follow—namely, a broad road, must be
avoided, as it only leads to the railway station,
the main road veering to the left. Just beyond,

three *caniveaux* follow in quick succession,' the road then running under a railway bridge, and keeping henceforward to the right of the railway and the river alike.

The road improves in quality, and shortly afterwards brings into view, magnificently posted on a high hill, a Benedictine nunnery, which remains a conspicuous feature of the landscape for some time, but is seen to the best advantage

THE DESCENT TO KLAUSEN.
(*The building on the hill-top is a Benedictine Nunnery.*)

from the other side of Klausen. The little town, formed of a single street, and centred in a defile, has a situation of unusual picturesqueness, as it nestles at the base of a hill, and is bounded by a river on each side, and the general view afforded by a pause when some distance out of the town is particularly striking (*vide* p. 141).

About five kilometres beyond Klausen there is a very rough place in the road due to the effects

of a torrent on the right; and, though vehicles
have to bump over the road as best they can,
there is a permanent foot-bridge on the left for
the benefit of pedestrians. At Waidbruck, the
next village, the Gröden valley is entered, and
finely posted on the left is the castle of Trostburg.
The road then descends more steeply for over a
kilometre, and afterwards undulates to Atzwang,
still in close touch with the rail and river. Both
of these are crossed, however, just before Blumau
is reached, while, a little further on, the road
harks back over the railway and runs between
the rail and the river.

A hot breath comes up the ravine from Bozen,
which might almost be described as the oven of
the Tyrol, and the good surface suddenly deteriorates as the town comes into view, and one drives
over a kilometre or two of very bumpy road
covered with loose dust. With the exception of
this stage, however, and the spots singled out
above for special mention, the road generally over
the whole descent from the summit of the pass
is excellent; and, with its numerous villages,
alternating with romantic ravines and rushing
streams, it provides a thoroughly interesting drive
throughout.

For the convenience of those proceeding
further southwards I append the continuation of
the Brenner route to Verona:—

Place.	Intermediate Distances. (Kils.)	Progressive Totals. (Kils.)
Bozen - - - - -	—	—
Leifers - - - - -	10	10
Branzoll - - - - -	3	13
Auer (*It.*, Ora) - - - -	7	20

A CHARACTERISTIC TYROLESE TOWN: KLAUSEN, FROM THE
SOUTH SIDE.

Place.	Intermediate Distances. (Kils.)	Progressive Totals. (Kils.)
Neumarkt - - - - -	5	25
Salurn - - - - -	10	35
Fork for Tonale Pass - -	7	42
St. Michele - - - -	2	44
Lavis - - - - -	$8\frac{1}{2}$	$52\frac{1}{2}$
Gardolo - - - - -	3·	$55\frac{1}{2}$
Trient (Trento) - - - -	$5\frac{1}{2}$	61
Matarello - - - - -	7	68
Calliano - - - - -	9	77
Volanó - - - - -	3	80
Rovereto - - - - -	5	85
Lizzano - - - - -	$2\frac{1}{2}$	$87\frac{1}{2}$
Serravalle - - - -	$8\frac{1}{2}$	96
Ala - - - - - -	$6\frac{1}{2}$	$102\frac{1}{2}$
Borghetto (Austrian Customs) -	9	$111\frac{1}{2}$
Frontier - - - - -	2	$113\frac{1}{2}$
Ossenigo - - - - -	2	$115\frac{1}{2}$
Peri (Italian Customs) - -	2	$117\frac{1}{2}$
Dolce - - - - -	$7\frac{1}{2}$	125
Ceraino - - - - -	3	128
Volargne - - - - -	$3\frac{1}{2}$	$131\frac{1}{2}$
Fork for Castelnuovo di Verona -	2	$133\frac{1}{2}$
Domegliara - - - -	$1\frac{1}{2}$	135
Ospedaletto - - - -	2	137
Parona all'Adige - - -	9	146
Borgo Trento - - - -	5	151
Verona - - - - -	1	152

(*Hotels at Bozen, Trient, Rovereto and Verona.*)

It is sufficient to say that the road is virtually
flat from end to end.

CHAPTER XIII.

THROUGH THE DOLOMITES.

A T Bozen we find ourselves in the heart of a district which, more than any other in Europe, is worthy of being called the motorist's Paradise. I have toured in eleven countries, and exhaustively in each, but have no hesitation whatever in saying that the Tyrol should be the objective of every automobilist

THE SAN LUGANO ROAD, NEAR FONTANE FREDDE.

who elects to travel on the Continent at all. The scenery of the Tyrol is no whit behind that of Switzerland in beauty and grandeur, while in the matter of road locomotion there is absolutely no comparison between the two countries.

The Tyrol is not yet over-run with railways; on the other hand, it has many fine roads, magnificently engineered, and free from the anti-automobile restrictions which are so unwelcome a blot on Swiss administration. Certain roads, it is true, in one part or another of the Tyrol are barred to motor-cars, but for individual reasons; that is to say, they are not considered by the authorities to be suitable for the purpose. But there is no wholesale embargo against automobiles as such; indeed, their presence is encouraged rather than otherwise, while motor diligences have everywhere superseded the old and ponderous horsed type.

Touring in the Tyrol, moreover, is a perpetual delight from every point of view. The Tyrolese themselves are a fine race, who enjoy their own existence and are prepared to follow the policy of " live and let live " where others are concerned. They look happy and greet you with a smile when you pass, in marked contrast to the scowls of the Swiss peasantry. The absence of excessive railway accommodation, moreover, means that the country is not crowded with trippers. Of tourists there are sufficient to tax the accommodation of the available hotels, but that is because the Austrian Government is developing the district to the utmost of its power; the travellers, how-ever, if they wish to penetrate into the heart of the Dolomites and other beautiful districts, must come in the main by road, and therefore cannot possibly be so numerous as if they had been dumped down in train-loads.

The most pleasing example of Tyrolean enter-prise is the new Dolomitenstrasse, or Dolomites road. It begins at Bozen and goes over the

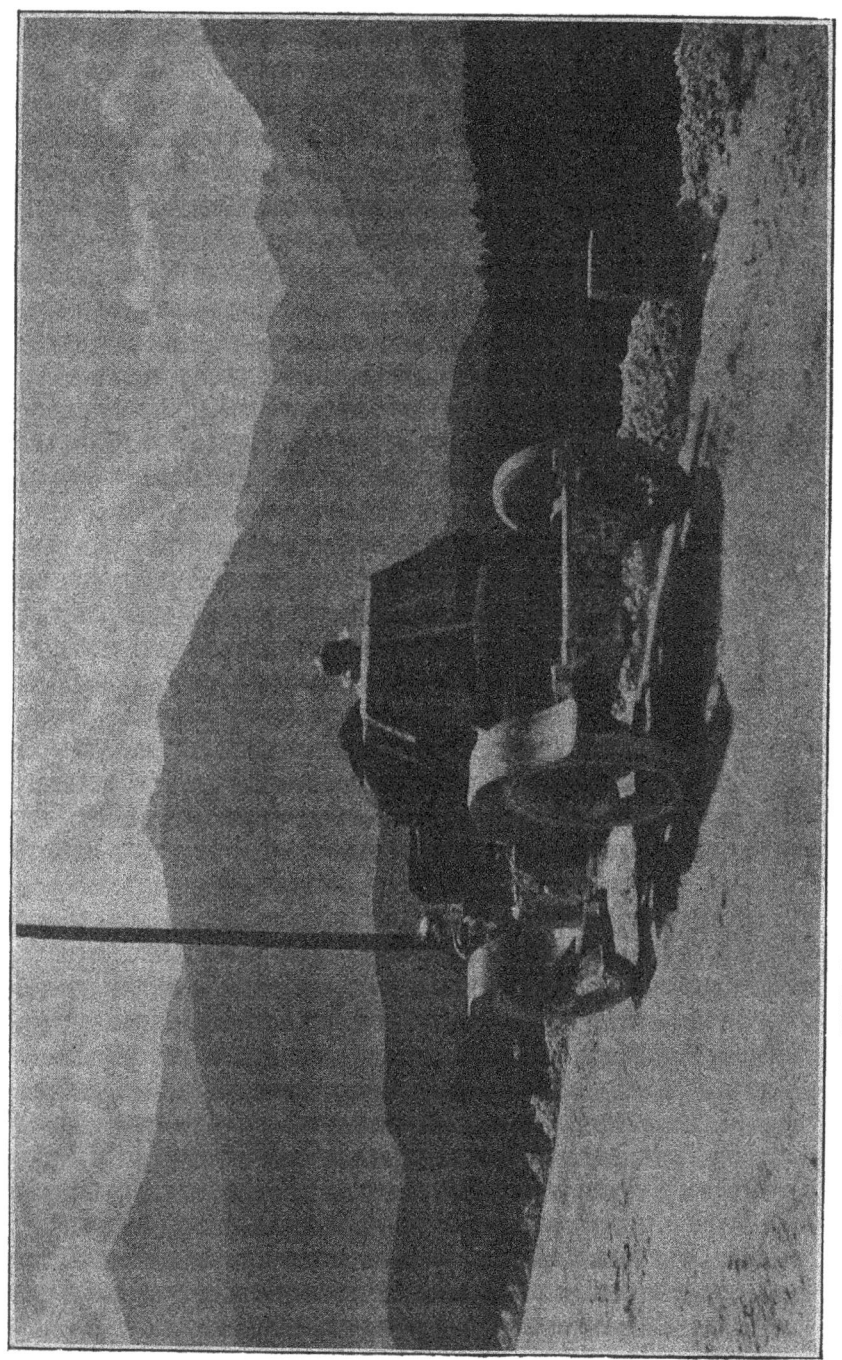

THE FLEIMSER MOUNTAINS ON THE SAN LUGANO PASS.

K

Karer Pass; it then crosses the Pordoi Pass; and, finally, it leads to the summit of the Falzarego Pass and descends to Cortina. The Karer road was completed in 1895; the Pordoi was finished in 1904; while the final stage over the Falzarego was only consummated in August, 1909, and I myself had the pleasure of driving over it a day or two after the actual opening. This linking up of Bozen to Cortina represents the most important instance of road development in Europe for many years, and one does not know which to admire most—the splendid scenery through which the Dolomitenstrasse passes, or the admirable construction of the road itself.

It is to the Pordoi and the Falzarego passes, however, to which the motorist must direct his attention, as the Karer Pass is somewhat narrow in places, and the authorities, though they allow the Government motor diligences to ply thereon, do not as yet consider it altogether desirable for automobiles, merely because of the narrowness of the Eggenthal portion. No particular hardship, however, is thereby involved, as there is an alternative route which does not necessitate any very great detour, and it leads through landscapes of much picturesqueness. Moreover, it is only half of the Karer Pass that is closed to motorcars, and there is nothing to prevent one from running up to the summit and back from the eastern side.

The San Lugano Pass.

To make the acquaintance of the Pordoi and the Falzarego, therefore, the automobilist must first run over the pass of San Lugano, otherwise

THE FIRST VIEW OF THE DOLOMITES, ABOVE MOENA.
(On the left is the Langkofel group; on the right is the Boëspitze, or Sella.)

known as the Cavalese; but he must refrain from drawing wrong conclusions concerning what is to follow. This initial stage of the route to Cortina is dusty along the plain and somewhat rough on the ascent, for reasons which will be explained; but he may comfort himself with the fact that the Pordoi and Falzarego roads are altogether different.

The itinerary of the San Lugano Pass is as follows :—

Place.	Altitude. (Feet.)	Intermediate Distances. (Kils.)	Progressive Totals. (Kils.)
Bozen - - -	876	—	—
Leifers - - -	810	$10\frac{1}{2}$	$10\frac{1}{2}$
Branzoll - - -	—	3	$13\frac{1}{2}$
Auer - - -	781	7	$20\frac{1}{2}$
Montan - - -	1,625	4	$24\frac{1}{2}$
Fontane Fredde - -	3,115	9	$33\frac{1}{2}$
Summit - - -	*3,599*	$2\frac{1}{2}$	36
Cavalese - - -	3,281	$8\frac{1}{2}$	$44\frac{1}{2}$
Tesero - - -	3,451	5	$49\frac{1}{2}$
Predazzo - - -	3,337	$8\frac{1}{2}$	58

(*Hotels at Bozen, Cavalese, and Predazzo, and sundry inns* en route.)

Bozen, the starting place, is a large town with fine hotels, and is pleasant enough to stay in if the weather is cool; but, at the time of year when the uplands are most enjoyable for road travelling, the town itself is insufferably hot. There is much local traffic in the neighbourhood, moreover, and the roads are bumpy in consequence; but, making the best of a bad job, the motorist must steer his car, in the first instance, for the Eisak river, and, crossing the railway, keep due south for Leifers, Branzoll, and Auer. At the last-named village he must be careful not to run past a narrow road to the left, at the foot of which is a notice-board inscribed

ON THE PORDOI PASS: THE MASSIVE BOËSPITZE, OR SELLA GROUP.

with the word " Fleimstal." If, however, he does
happen to miss this, he may as well run on to
the next village, Neumarkt, five kilometres further
along the plain. From either of these villages the
road ascends the San Lugano Pass, the junction
being effected near a ruined castle below Montan.

The ascent is rather steep, and continues so up
to Fontane Fredde, otherwise known as Kaltenbrunn. There are some zigzags, but the bends

THE POEDOI ROAD AND THE SELLA GROUP.

are not difficult, while they afford fine retrospective
views. The surface, however, is rough, and one
soon discovers the reason why. Cart after cart
loaded with laths suggests the presence of a saw-
mill somewhere on the road, and this comes into
view at Kaltenbrunn. By this time we have risen
2,334 feet in 13 kilometres. The road continues
to ascend, through a wood, and at some point or

NEARING THE SUMMIT.
(The road is seen on the right, with the Langkofel peaks in the background.)

other one may meet a sign of Tyrolese up-to-dateness in the shape of a motor diligence.

Once over the summit the mountains of the Fleimser-Thal come into view. A gentle descent now leads to Cavalese, but at a point about midway there is a fork at which the driver would be in doubt as to which turn to choose, as the only indication is a sign-board bearing the words " Per Castello." The correct road to take, however, is the one to the left.

The road now rises again, winding along a hill-side, the Fleimser mountains coming nearer into view until, at Tesero, a point is reached nearly as high as the San Lugano summit itself. A corresponding fall leads to Ziano, whence there is a level run to Predazzo.

The Pordoi.

From a square in the centre of Predazzo village the Rolle Pass branches off to the right, by the church, but for the Pordoi route we take the left-hand corner past the hotel. It is usually a hive of activity, although its accommodation is somewhat primitive. The itinerary is as follows :—

Place.			Altitude. (Feet.)	Intermediate Distances. (Kils.)	Progressive Totals. (Kils.)
Predazzo	-	-	3,337	—	—
Forno	-	-	3,720	5	5
Moena	-	-	3,897	5	10
Soraga	-	-	—	$2\frac{1}{2}$	$12\frac{1}{2}$
San Giovanni	-	-	4,383	3	$15\frac{1}{2}$
Pozza (toll)	-	-	4,314	1	$16\frac{1}{2}$
Perra	-	-	—	1	$17\frac{1}{2}$
Mazzin	-	-	4,534	$2\frac{1}{2}$	20
Campestrin	-	-	4,531	$1\frac{1}{2}$	$21\frac{1}{2}$
Fontanazzo	-	-	4,564	1	$22\frac{1}{2}$

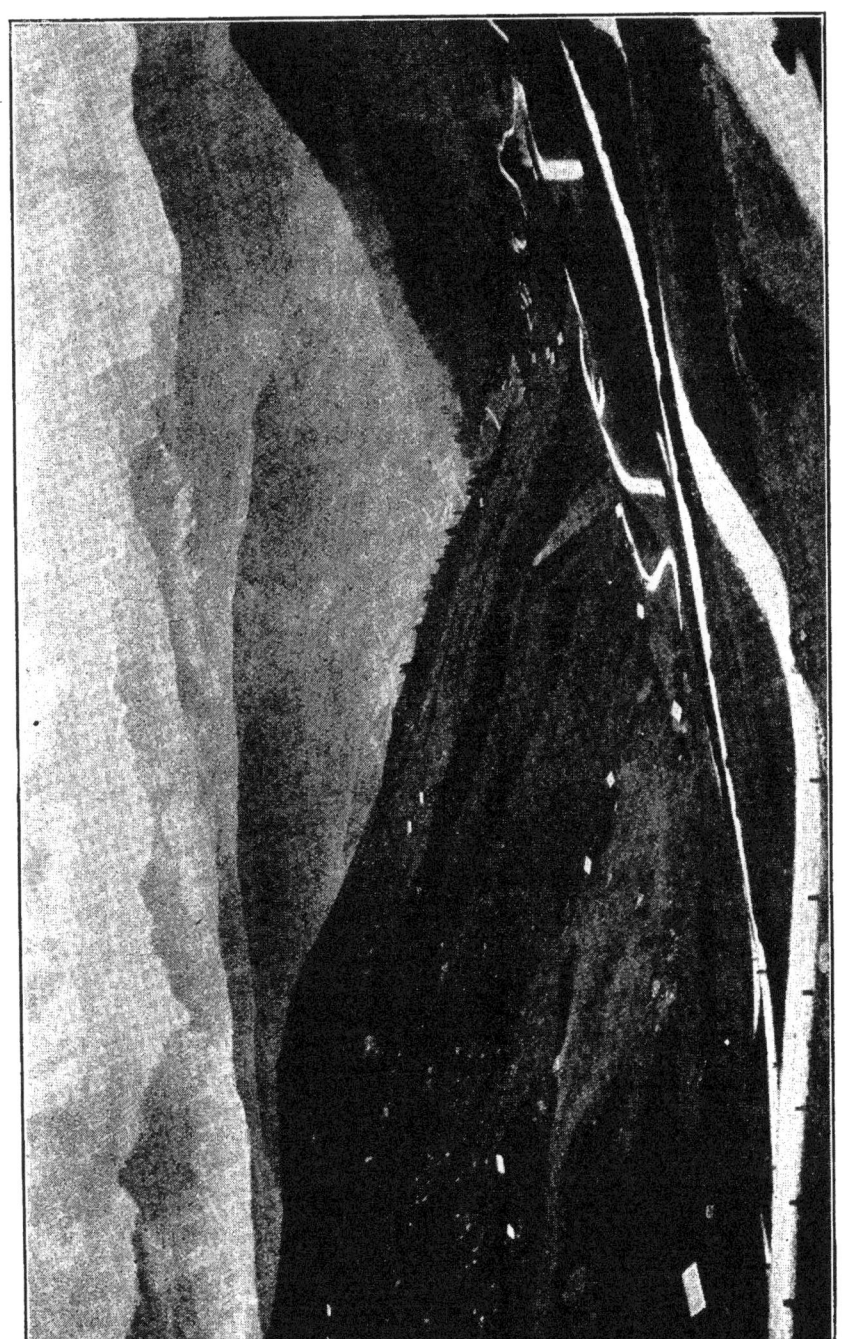

THE WINDINGS OF THE PORDOI ROAD.

Place.			Altitude. (*Feet.*)	*Intermediate* Distances. (*Kils.*)	*Progressive* Totals. (*Kils.*)
Campitello	-	-	4,715	1½	24
Gries	-	-	4,777	2	26
Canazei	-	-	4,823	1	27
Hotel Pordoi	-	-	7,020	10	37
Summit	-	-	*7,382*	2	39
Arabba (toll)	-	-	5,253	10	49

(*Hotels at Predazzo, Moena, Campitello, Gries, Canazei,
37th kilometre, and Arabba, with sundry inns.*) .

For several kilometres the road runs along the
narrow Fleimser valley, rising gradually to Forno,
following the left bank of the Avisio, and still
more gradually to Moena, where the Fassathal
is entered. The road is good and the scenery
inviting, with distant prospects of Dolomitic peaks
soon to be seen at closer quarters. Several small
villages are passed in turn. A few hundred yards
beyond San Giovanni a narrow road will be
noticed on the left, leading up to the village of
Vigo di Fassa, which marks the terminal point
of the Karer Pass.

The Pordoi road, however, continues northwards, and descends slightly to Pozza, where a
toll of six *kronen* is demanded in exchange for a
small orange ticket; and I may anticipate matters
somewhat and state that a similar amount will
have to be paid at Arabba before entering on the
Falzarego Pass.

It must not be assumed, however, that these
exactions are designed for the exploitation of
automobilists; as a matter of fact the toll is
imposed on horse-drawn vehicles as well. The
portion of the Dolomites road from Moena to
Cortina cost some three million *kronen* to-build,

INTERESTED SPECTATORS.

(The picture shows the final discarding of a mudguard which was originally broken on French "pavé.")

and, as the inhabitants of the district are comparatively few in number, it is only fair that tourists, for whom this fine highway has been constructed, should pay their share towards so magnificent an achievement.

All the way to Fontanazzo, six kilometres ahead, the road is virtually level and flanked with several small villages, but to Campitello there is a slight increase in the gradient. A brief descent follows, and there is then a gradual rise to Gries and Canazei. Here the ascent of the Pordoi Pass begins in earnest, and provides one of the most enjoyable drives, from the motorist's point of view, to be found anywhere throughout the Alps.

The road is wide, and of astonishingly good surface, while the way in which it is engineered is wholly admirable. Between Canazei and the summit, a distance of twelve kilometres, there are no fewer than thirty-four corners, of which twenty-eight are of the "hairpin" type, and these figures alone suffice to indicate the formidable task which the road-builders had to face. Right well, however, has it been performed, for none of the turns are difficult, and the average gradient is only 6 to 7 per cent., while at no point does it exceed 7·9 per cent.

Indeed it is almost too easy where the motorcar is concerned; for the joy of breasting a mountain road and swinging round corner after corner is of itself so exhilarating that, for the driver at all events, and even the passengers if they are keen motorists, there is the temptation to avoid the manifold claims of the scenery. It

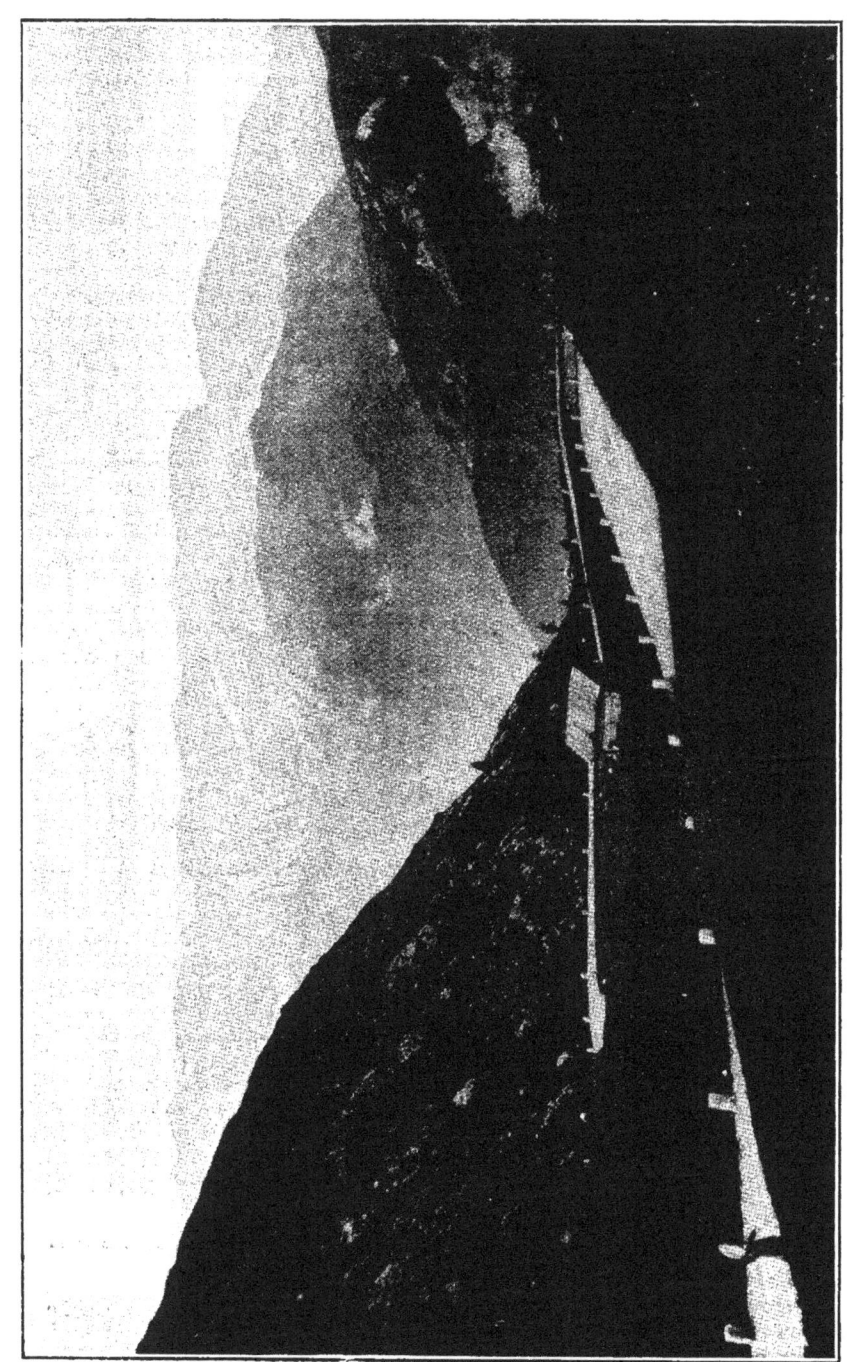

A VIEW NEAR THE PORDOI SUMMIT, LOOKING TOWARDS THE ROSENGARTEN.

is true that for some distance, as may be inferred
from the altitude figures, the road runs through
a zone of trees, but even before these have been
left behind one may enjoy, as my photograph
will show, a fine view of the Langkofel peaks.

But let the driver not harbour any anxiety
to reach the summit. There is absolutely nothing
in the way of gradient that will tax his car, and
he will do well to pause at any point and survey
the glorious landscape. To two points in particular
I venture to draw his attention. The first is
five kilometres from Canazei; the other is a like
distance higher up by the Pordoi Hotel. The
amplitude and majesty of the scenery from here
—the peaks of the Langkofel, the massive Sella
group, and the lovely Rosengarten range—beggar
description; one does not know whether to be
more grateful to the car for having brought one
to such a spot, or annoyed at the fact that,
being on a car, one has embarked on a tour of
more or less magnitude, and that the factor of
time has to be taken into account. Fortunate
indeed are the French, Austrians, and Italians in
having the Alps at their own doors, and scarcely
less fortunate are the Germans, for whom the
highest Alpine roads are within easy reach.

The most splendid view of all, however, is
from the summit itself, just before turning the
last corner. There is a noble expansiveness in
the outlook which has few parallels elsewhere.
There is less snow and ice in the height of
summer than is seen from the summits of certain
Swiss passes, but infinitely more variety of out-
line; while, paramount among the many charms

THE SUMMIT OF THE PORDOI PASS (7,382 feet).

of the Dolomites, is the wonderful effect of the rising or setting sun upon the mountains, which respond to its rays with a vivid glow of marvellous and awe-inspiring effect. It is well worth while to time one's journey so as to arrive at the summit in the afternoon; or, failing that, to halt there until the sun has set. Once seen, the afterglow on the Rosengarten group will never

A CONTRAST IN OUTLINES : THE FIRST VIEW OF THE CRODA DI
LAGO AND THE NUVOLAU ON THE FALZAREGO PASS.

be forgotten. The night can be stayed at the Hotel Pordoi, only two kilometres away, or one may run down to Arabba before dark.

On the summit itself, which is no-less than 7,382 feet in height, there is a small hospice, and hard by is an obelisk which was erected in November, 1904, in commemoration of the

A WILD SPOT ON THE FALZAREGO PASS.

(*The road is seen on the right.*)

A PASSING ENCOUNTER.

completion of the road, and bears the following inscription :—

STRADA DI PORDOI

MOENA —CANAZEI—P. PORDOI—ARÀBA

INAUGURATA NELL'ESTATE 1905.

ALTEZZA DEL VALICO

M. 2250 S.M.

PENDENZA MASSIMA $7 \cdot 9\,^{\circ}/_{\circ}$, MEDIA $6 \cdot 7\,^{\circ}/_{\circ}$

RAGGIO MINIMO 10.0 M.

←——◀◀◀◀ DISTANZE ▶▶▶——→

CANAZEI KM. $12 \cdot 0$ ARÀBA KM. $9 \cdot 7$

(Val di Fassa)   (Livinallongo)

STRADA DI PORDOI

construita in regia propria

negli anni 1901–1904

regnante

S. M. L'Imperatore

FRANCESCO GIUSEPPE I.

Ad incremento del paese contribuirono

Stato Provincia Interessati

Direzione Superiore Consigl. Aul. A. Ritt

Dirigente I lavori Ing. Vitt. Dal Lago.

Without in any way disparaging the next stage of the journey, I may state here that the side of the Pordoi Pass which we have ascended is more picturesque than the descent to Arabba, and it is on the ascent that one should do one's loitering. The wild flowers alone are a feast unto the eye, while edelweiss grows freely. If the day's journey has been started from Bozen, the best halting place for luncheon would be Canazei, or the Pordoi Hotel, the latter being the most important on the pass. I may also mention that

THE FALZAREGO SUMMIT.

(The photograph was taken shortly after the official opening of the road.)

though the opportunity will probably have been taken at Bozen, as it is a big town, to fill the tank with petrol, there are plenty of places on the Pordoi where it may be bought, and the

L 2

number of cars one meets testifies to the growing
popularity of the route among automobilists of
the surrounding countries.   If I could induce
English and American tourists also to steer their
cars thither in greater numbers, I should not
have written this book in vain.

The descent to Arabba is one of 2,129 feet in
ten kilometres, and the average gradient is 6·95
per cent.   The downward run is beautifully

A DISTANT VIEW OF MT. SORAPIS.

graded, and for some distance without zigzags,
although these eventually become almost as
numerous as on the ascending side.   While the
environment is more restricted than on the west,
it is none the less rich in attractiveness.   Retro-
spectively the road is dominated by the Marmolata,
the king of Dolomitic peaks, while forwards the
fine Ampezzo groups come nearer and nearer into

A CURIOSITY IN ROAD CONSTRUCTION: THE "HAIRPIN" TUNNEL ON THE FALZAREGO PASS.

view, and whet the appetite for the panoramas to be enjoyed on the last stage of the journey over the Falzarego Pass. The quality of the road continues unquestionable, and through pleasant pastures the car glides steadily down in all too quick time to the village of Arabba. The whole journey from Predazzo has been ' one of forty-nine kilometres only, or thirty miles; but it has been picturesque at every point, and the motorist who has the good fortune to find himself travelling over this glorious route should adopt *Festina lente* as his motto.

The Falzarego.

A drive over the Falzarego Pass provides all the sensations which are usually associated with a tour on foot away from the beaten track. The road is so new that there has been no time as yet for any villages to grow up around it, and, with the exception of the little hospice at the summit, there is hardly a habitation to be found between Andraz and Cortina.

What is so pleasing to the automobilist is that the road has been built for through traffic, thus reversing the usual order of things. Roads as a rule are constructed from local considerations, and only become linked up so as to form a continuous highway in course of time. If, for example, a big village had grown up a mile or two above Cortina the footpath would have developed into a bridle-path, and the bridle-path into a road of one sort or another. Another village might then have sprung into being still higher up, followed by another piece of road; and,

THE VIEW AFTER PASSING THROUGH THE "HAIRPIN" TUNNEL.

if a similar process of evolution had taken place on the other side of the summit, a further linking up would eventually have been brought about. Save in France this parochial idea is that which has dominated road construction in every country, and is paramount to this day, notwithstanding the magnificent example, which the great Napoleon put forward over a hundred years ago.

All the more credit, therefore, is to be ascribed to the Tyrolese authorities for definitely embarking on the scheme of their Dolomitenstrasse as a continuous route through the very heart of the Dolomites ; or, in other words, providing direct communication between more or less distant points instead of merely following the line of what we may call suburban development. For the present, therefore, there is nothing in the way of detail by the way to be mentioned in connection with the Falzarego Pass; save for the carriage-road itself it is almost virgin ground. The itinerary is as follows :—

Place.	Altitude. (Feet.)	Intermediate Distances. (Kils.)	Progressive Totals. (Kils.)
Arabba - - -	5,253	—	—
Pieve di Livinallongo	4,819	8	8
Andraz - - -	4,662	3	11
Dolomitenziel Inn -	6,360	7	18
Summit - - -	*6,913*	4	22
Pocol - - -	4,990	11	33
Cortina - - -	3,983	6	39

(*Hotels at Arabba, Pieve, and Cortina, and inns at Andraz, Dolomitenziel, the summit, and Pocol.*)

At Arabba the second toll above referred to must be paid before embarking on the Falzarego route. The first stage of this is slightly on the

NEARING CORTINA: MT. SORAPIS (LEFT) AND MT. ANTELAO (RIGHT).

down grade, and, after passing a fortified bridge, the road runs alongside a ravine of impressive depth. A slight rise, after a long fall, leads to the town of Pieve di Livinallongo, picturesquely set on a hillside. Still continuing to descend slightly, the road runs in three kilometres to the village of Andraz, at which point begins the ascent, which continues uninterruptedly to the summit, and represents a rise of 2,260 feet in 11 kilometres.

A comparison with the figures of the Pordoi Pass will show that the gradient of the Falzarego is practically identical with that of its predecessor. The average is 6 per cent., with a maximum of 8 per cent., while the minimum radius of the corners is the same as on the Pordoi, namely, 10 metres, or nearly 33 feet. Variety is the paramount feature of the route. In the first instance the road itself, apart from the windings on the zigzags, takes many directions. Starting due east, it runs to the south-east towards Pieve di Livinallongo, beyond which it veers round to the north-east, and, continuing almost due north to the summit, it addresses every point of the compass on the zigzags. At the summit it turns due east again, but, when a few kilometres above Cortina, it winds northwards once more, then turns east, south, and east again into Cortina itself.

To the frequent change of outlook which the road itself necessarily confers, there is added the amazing variety of the mountains themselves, which display more diversity of shape than in any other district of the Alps—some nobly massive,

The Croda di Lago. *The Cinque Torri.*

THE LAST MILE INTO CORTINA, ON THE FALZAREGO PASS.

some wonderfully symmetrical, and others ruggedly fantastic. The crossing of the pass, in fact, is a liberal education in outlines. In the degree of outlook itself, moreover, there is great variety; at one point the road is almost hemmed in by adjoining hills, while at another a panorama of immense range unfolds itself.

The road surface is good throughout, though at the time of my crossing it was not quite settled at the sides; at the same time there was nothing on the ascent itself which in any way interfered with the freedom of one's progression. In the way of habitations, as I have said, there is little to intercept the gaze, but high above Andraz stands the picturesque ruin of Buchenstein Castle. Four kilometres from the summit is the Dolomitenziel Inn, above which is a curiosity in the shape of a "hairpin" corner which is pierced through a rock tunnel, and it is after passing through this that there comes into view one of the finest prospects of the route.

The inn at the summit has a verandah from which a glorious panorama is revealed of the mountains in the neighbourhood of Cortina, while a saunter round the plateau enables one to take in the varied outlines of the Col di Lana, the Civetta, the Marmolata, the Pala di San Martino, the Sasso di Stria, and other peaks. Close by the road, on the left, is a newly-erected obelisk commemorating the completion of the road.

The descent, which we have now to consider, leads through the Falzarego valley which gives the pass its name, and is one of 2,945 feet in 16 kilometres. It is practically identical as to gradients with the ascent, except that five kilometres from the summit the fall is moderated for the next three kilometres. The road is excellent in the centre, but at the time when it was actually opened, at all events, there were plenty of loose stones at the sides. Before long, however, the road is bound to be perfect in every respect. Splendid views are afforded on the run down of the snowy Marmolata, the Croda da Lago, the Cinque Torri, the Tofana, and the Nuvolau among other mountain groups.

Driving through the wood one swings round several zigzags, and at length enjoys a magnificent view of Cortina, with its fine environment of mountains. There is a glorious run down into this beautiful village, one of the most charming places in the Eastern Alps, and a delightful resting-place. As a summer resort it has been growing in popularity year by year, but the interesting fact may be mentioned that it has recently become a winter station as well, for which it is admirably adapted by reason of its situation, altitude, and climate alike.

CHAPTER XIV.

THE AMPEZZO.

YET another delightful way of entering Italy, provided some town as far east as Venice be the objective, is by the Ampezzo Pass. To the tourist with a small car it confers the advantage of offering practically nothing in the way of serious climbing. It is true that the altitude of the highest point of the journey is as great as 5,066 feet; at the same time, the means by which it is reached are of the easiest possible description, and in point of fact the journey throughout is devoid of anything serious in the way of *tourniquets* or even stiff gradients.

The Ampezzo Pass lies between Toblach and Cortina, and is of especial interest to automobilists from the fact that it was the first road in the Alps on which the horsed diligence was superseded by the power vehicle. It is a road of great attractiveness, and is at all times a popular excursion for visitors to the Tyrol. Incidentally, however, it happens to be on the main line of route to Venice; and as in these opening chapters I am dealing seriatim with the various ways by which the tourist may travel from the west, and enter Italy by one gateway or other through the Alps, I must devote a separate chapter to this road, and indicate the nature of the through journey as a whole.

For the nonce, however, we must hark back to Franzensfeste on the Brenner route, and imagine ourselves confronted with the alternatives of descending south to Bozen and Verona, or of turning eastwards to Toblach, and then veering southwards over the Ampezzo Pass; we will now, therefore, suppose that we have rejected the former route in favour of the road to Venice.

The west to east portion of the route is as follows :—

Place.			Altitude. (Feet.)	Intermediate Distances. (Kils.)	Progressive Totals. (Kils.)
Franzensfeste	-	-	2,450	—	—
Mühlbach	-	-	2,745	7	7
Vintl	-	-	2,495	5	12
Kiens	-	-	2,560	$9\frac{1}{2}$	$21\frac{1}{2}$
St. Lorenzen	-	-	2,665	$6\frac{1}{2}$	28
Bruneck	-	-	2,725	$3\frac{1}{2}$	$31\frac{1}{2}$
Welsberg	-	-	3,555	17	$48\frac{1}{2}$
Niederdorf	-	-	3,790	$5\frac{1}{2}$	54
Toblach	-	-	3,965	$4\frac{1}{2}$	$58\frac{1}{2}$

(*Hotels all along the route.*)

From the altitude figures it will be noticed at once that this is virtually a level road, and, as a matter of fact, it runs through the beautiful Pusterthal and alongside the Rienz river. While it can boast nothing in the way of grandeur, the run is exceedingly pleasant throughout, with a superabundance of grassy slopes, and possesses towns and villages of characteristic Tyrolean charm. The road is marvellously good, and I need only call attention to two *caniveaux*, close together, just beyond Vintl, while there are one or two awkward corners; in the main, however, the highway provides glorious running.

The chief place of importance on the road is Bruneck, and, after this has been passed through, a pause should certainly be made to enjoy a retrospective glance at one of the most harmonious schemes of architecture that could be imagined, set amid an environment of hills. The building embosomed in the centre of the picture is the Bishop of Brixen's castle, and the apparent flaw in the photograph, above the double-towered church on the extreme left, is really a puff of smoke from the guns of a company of soldiers who were firing a salute in honour of the Emperor of Austria's birthday, on which date I happened to be passing through the town.

By the time Niederdorf is reached, the first Dolomitic crags have come into view, though, of course, they are seen to much less advantage than on the Pordoi and Falzarego Passes. At Toblach, $3\frac{1}{2}$ kilometres beyond Niederdorf, a turn to the right must be made, and the road runs over the railway and into Toblach, a beautifully situated little town, the popularity of which is betokened by the number of its hotels.

If the run along the Pusterthal has been charming, that from Toblach to Cortina, by the route subjoined, is even more delightful :—

Place.	Altitude. (Feet.)	Intermediate Distances. (Kils.)	Progressive Totals. (Kils.)
Toblach - - -	3,965	—	—
Landro - - -	4,615	10	10
Schluderbach - -	4,730	3	13
Summit - - -	5,065	4	17
Ospitale - - -	4,835	$2\frac{1}{2}$	$19\frac{1}{2}$
Cortina d'Ampezzo -	3,983	$11\frac{1}{2}$	31

(*Hotels or inns at every stage.*)

BRUNECK, IN THE PUSTERTHAL.

M

The road is wide and of excellent quality, which is the more remarkable when the volume of traffic is considered between the two points during the season. For some distance the road runs due south along the Hohlensteiner valley, which is watered by the Rienz river. The little Toblacher lake is passed on the right, and the road enters a gorge, rising gradually to Landro, with fine views of the Klausenkofel and the

CORTINA D'AMPEZZO, FROM THE WEST.

Dürrenstein. Just before reaching Landro a fortress is seen near to the road.

The little village of Landro is one of the many pleasant resorts of this district, and affords views of the famous peaks known as the Drei Zinnen, and also of Monte Cristallo, one of the most imposing mountains in the Tyrol. Beyond the village, to the left of the road, is the tiny Dürrensee, a green lake which is usually almost

CARS IN CORTINA VILLAGE.

M 2

dry in summer, and is seen at its best after the melting of the snows in spring.

Schluderbach, the next village, is a favourite centre for excursions, and is very attractively situated at the mouth of the Popena valley, which takes its name from the Piz Popena, one of Monte Christallo's principal neighbours. It is very pleasant to sit in front of one or other of the hotels adjoining the roadside, and watch the kaleidoscopic changes of the tourist traffic passing through from Toblach or Cortina by motor-car, motor diligence, horsed carriage, or on foot, while some particularly attractive native costumes may be seen, worn by young women who, in physique and comeliness, are in every way superior to their Swiss sisters.

Our road now swings to the right and runs westwards for three kilometres, and then turns south-westwards and soon reaches the Ampezzo summit. The gradient is almost imperceptible, being one of 333 feet in four kilometres. The pass forms the watershed between the Rienz and Boite rivers, and is also the boundary line of the Ampezzo district. An imposing environment of peaks includes the Croda Rosa (or Rotwand), the Col Freddo, the Croda dell' Ancona, and the Crepa di Zuoghi on the right; the massive Tofana and the Col Rosa in front; and the Punta del Forame on the left, while in the rear are the Monte Pian and the Cadini. Passing the Bianco-lake, we cross the Rufreddo and the Gottresbach in turn, and descend to the hamlet of Ospitale. The road now undulates for a couple of kilometres, and then swings to the north, and, doubling back upon itself to the south, soon enters the Ampezzo valley, along which is a fine straight run over a broad and well-kept road to Cortina d'Ampezzo.

From here the itinerary to Venice is as follows:—

Place.	Altitude. (Feet.)	Intermediate Distances. (Kils.)	Progressive Totals. (Kils.)
Cortina - - -	3,983	—	—
Zuel - - - -	--	4½	4½
Austrian Custom-House	—	4	8½
Italian Custom-House -	3,661	¼	8¾
S. Vito di Cadore -	3,317	4	12¾
Borca - - -	3,091	3	15¾
Cancia - - -	3,107	1	16¾
Vodo - - - -	—	2½	19¼
Venas - - -	2,838	5	24¼
Valle di Cadore di Sotto	2,726	3½	27¾
Tai - - - -	—	3	30¾
Fork to Pieve di Cadore	--	—	—
Perarolo - - -	1,745	6½	37¼
Rivalgo - - -	1,627	6	43¼
Ospitale - - -	1,535	3	46¼
Termine - - -	—	4	50¼
Castello Lavazzo - -	—	2	52¼
Longarone - - -	1,555	2½	54¾
Fae - - - -	—	2½	57¼
Fortogna - - -	—	2½	59¾
Road to Belluno - -	—	4	63¾
Alternative road to Belluno - - -	—	1½	65¼
Ponte Nelle Alpi -	1,276	1	66¼
S. Croce - - -	1,316	11	77¼
Lastra - - -	1,447	½	77¾
Fadalto Pass - -	*1,604*	1½	79¼
Serravalle - - -	528	10½	89¾
Vittorio - - -	410	3½	93¼
S. Giacomo di Veglia -	362	2½	95¾
Fork - - - -	—	7	102¾
Conegliano - - -	203	3	105¾
Susegana - - -	249	5½	111¼
Spresiano - - -	184	8½	119¾
Visnadello - - -	—	2½	122¼
Limbraga - - -	—	7½	129¾
Treviso - - -	49	3	132¾
Preganziol - - -	—	7	139¾
Mogliano - - -	—	5	144¾
Mestre - - -	13	8	152¾

(*Hotels or inns at practically every stage.*)

As far as the village of Zuel the fine highway continues southwards, and then veers to the south-east to the Austrian and Italian custom-houses, which are not far apart, and adjoin the roadside. With a slightly increased gradient it descends to S. Vito di Cadore, and thence through several other villages, turning gradually to the eastwards until, just before Venas, it runs slightly to the north-east. It then describes a wide bend to the left, and swings back again to the south-east, after which it runs north-eastwards through Valle di Cadore, where the gradient becomes more accentuated, to Tai.

Just beyond this village is a fork, where we take the right hand; incidentally it may be mentioned, however, that the left road leads in a couple of kilometres to Pieve di Cadore, which is not only the chief town of the Cadore district, but is famous as the birthplace of the immortal Titian. The actual house in which he was born is still extant, and, as there are many other objects of interest in the town, it is worth while to make this slight digression from our route.

A short distance from Tai the road turns southwards and describes several zigzags to Perarolo, where the Boite and Piave rivers converge. Between Perarolo and Longarone, a distance of $17\frac{1}{2}$ kilometres, the road runs through a wild and narrow ravine, with numerous villages, and a couple of fine waterfalls.

Between Longarone and Ponte Nelle Alpi the valley is much wider, and the river suggests an Amazon in miniature, for it carries a burden of innumerable pine-logs which cover the surface of the water almost from bank to bank. In nine kilometres from Longarone a fork to the right leads in eight kilometres to Belluno, which is off the main road; but, as it is the most important place in the district, there may be occasion to make a passing call there even if the tourist be proceeding to Venice. If the route here described be taken in the opposite direction there is an alternative fork for Belluno much lower down, which, of course, will be encountered first.

At Ponte Nelle Alpi we have descended to a level of 1,275 feet, and it may be imagined that, having long since left the Dolomitic crags behind, and passed through the ravine stages, there is nothing more to expect in the way of picturesqueness over the remainder of the road. Its resources, however, have not yet been exhausted, and the run to Vittorio is decidedly attractive.

The Fadalto.

Indeed we have a small pass yet to cross, that of Fadalto. In height it is inappreciable, but it lies between two lakes which are by no means without charm. As our itinerary will show, the road rises from Ponte Nelle Alpi to the village of Santa Croce, and runs alongside the river of that name, which is about four kilometres in length. Continuing to rise beyond the village and through Lastra, we reach the summit of the Fadalto Pass in two kilometres, and then enjoy a very pleasant run down, on a somewhat narrow and winding road, passing the Lago Morto and two smaller lakes, and descending through a long defile to Serravalle.

Here, it must be conceded, the really picturesque portion of the route comes to an end, and the remainder is over the plains. Vittorio is the terminus of a branch railway which comes up from Venice. For nearly the whole way to the gondola city the road is broad, and in many places shaded by groves of trees. Unless very dusty through drought it affords good running, virtually in a straight line, through Conegliano and Treviso, right down to Mestre.

———◆•●•◆———

CHAPTER XV.

THE ROLLE.

IT is a matter of opinion whether the Rolle Pass should be treated simply as one of the manifold attractions of the Tyrol, or regarded in the light of a through route to Italy. It offers, however, so delightful a drive, and is so supremely beautiful from end to end, that I

A SAMPLE OF THE ROLLE ROAD.

cannot forbear from according it a chapter to itself. Quite legitimately it may be regarded as a through route, if others which are more obvious are avoided; and there is always the possibility that a tourist may have driven southwards over other passes on previous journeys, and may take this means of reaching Italy for the sake of striking new ground. It is the bounden duty, however, of every seeker after the picturesque to visit the Rolle Pass at some time or other; and, if he cannot follow it in its entirety, owing to a justifiable desire to follow the Dolomitenstrasse to Cortina, he should at least break off at Predazzo, run up to the Rolle summit, and hark back again to Predazzo in order to cross the Pordoi and the Falzarego.

THE CIMONE DELLA PALA.

Let it be assumed, however, that not only the Dolomitenstrasse but the Pusterthal have been explored, and that the tourist is free to drive over the Rolle Pass from start to finish. The journey will leave upon his mind an enduring imprint of transcendent loveliness. Nevertheless there is no superfluity of detail to embody in any description of the Rolle, as it has few villages by the way, and is only forty-three

ANOTHER VIEW OF "THE MATTERHORN OF THE DOLOMITES."

kilometres in length. In the appended itinerary, however, I follow the route beyond the actual limits of the pass, and continue it as far as Feltre, from which the options are available of proceeding through Belluno to the Ampezzo Road, or descending southwards to Treviso and to Venice :—

Place.	Altitude. (Feet.)	Intermediate Distances. (Kils.)	Progressive Totals. (Kils.)
Predazzo - - -	3,337	—	—
Bellamonte - -	4,101	$5\frac{1}{2}$	$5\frac{1}{2}$
Paneveggio - -	5,171	8	$13\frac{1}{2}$
Summit - - -	*6,424*	8	$21\frac{1}{2}$
S. Martino di Castrozza	4,911	8	$29\frac{1}{2}$
Fiera di Primiero -	2,346	$13\frac{1}{2}$	43
Imer - - -	2,133	5	48
Pontet (Austrian and Italian Customs) -	1,870	5	53
Fonzaso - - -	1,066	14	67
Arten - - -	1,030	3	70
Feltre - - -	889	$6\frac{1}{2}$	$76\frac{1}{2}$

(*Hotels at Predazzo, Paneveggio, S. Martino, Primiero, and Feltre, and a good inn at the summit.*)

In Predazzo village one should leave the square by the far corner on the right, past the church, and follow the left bank of the river Travignolo. In two or three kilometres a series of four zig-zags is encountered, after which the road ascends gently to the little village of Bellamonte. The surface becomes rather bumpy for a while, but the scenery grows in grandeur, while before the next village, Paneveggio, is reached the surface has greatly improved

Here the first views are obtained of the top-most pinnacles of the Cimone della Pala, generally known as the " Matterhorn of the Dolomites," though the phrase has also been applied to the

A MOTOR DILIGENCE AND AN ENGLISH DAIMLER AT THE SUMMIT OF THE ROLLE PASS (6,424 FEET).

Pala di S. Martino. The Travignolo is shortly afterwards crossed and left behind, and then begins a magnificent drive over a splendid surface, the road winding round several hairpins of wide radius through glorious woods, which bring 100,000 gulden a year to the Austrian Crown. As the summit is 6,424 feet in height the zone of trees gives place eventually to pastures and a

ON THE ROLLE ROAD.

rolling landscape, with impressive views of the Cimone della Pala, and its neighbour the Cima di Vezzana.

The gradients are not steep, and the summit is attained without any manner of difficulty; and, when attained, it unfolds, in a southerly direction, one of the finest prospects that the heart could wish for. I say prospect advisedly, as the effect is not panoramic; but the downward view into Italy, flanked on the left by jagged peaks, is

ON THE ROLLE SUMMIT : THE STRIKING VIEW FROM THE INN.

wondrously attractive. One could sit for hours
on the little plateau in front of the inn, content
to gaze indefinitely upon the glorious scene. As
on the other mountain roads of the Tyrol, a motor
diligence plies on the Rolle Pass, and one of my
photographs shows the vehicle itself just starting
off on the return journey to Predazzo, while on
the right is the 38-h.p. Daimler on which my
fellow voyager and I had just made the ascent.

The drive to S. Martino di Castrozza may be
looked forward to with keen anticipation, as the
downward run is in every sense delightful. The
road surface is good, and the gradients do not
exceed 7 per cent. After comparatively straight
running for a couple of kilometres the zone of
trees is entered, and one winds through woods by
means of a fine series of over a dozen zigzags,
followed, after another straight stretch, by several
more ere S. Martino di Castrozza is reached. It
would be difficult to find a more pleasant halting
place, the beauty of the surrounding landscape
being such that several hotels have already sprung
up here, and the village is earning much popularity with tourists. Dolomitic peaks in every
variety of shape are seen at all points of the
compass, with the usual evening accompaniment
of a brilliant afterglow, while the pastures are a
paradise for the lover of wild flowers.

The resources of the Rolle Pass, however, do
not end here, for a fine run follows along the
right bank of the Cismone river, and through
the famous valley of Primiero. The little village
of Fiera di Primiero is centred amid velvety pastures and slopes richly clothed with chestnuts,

THE DESCENT INTO ITALY.

N

mulberries, and other characteristic features of the
luxuriant vegetation of a sub-Alpine vale on the
borders of Italy.   Immediately above the village
rise the pinnacles of the Sasso Maggiore, behind
which is the curiously shaped Cima di Ball, and
in the further distance is the impressive Rosetta.

The gently descending road follows the right
bank of the Cismone for some three kilometres,
and, at the Ponte San Silvestro, crosses the stream
and runs through the Gorge of Schenero valley
to Pontet, otherwise known as Monte Croce, where
the Austrian and Italian custom-houses are passed
in turn, while just beyond is an Italian fortress
built into the rock.   The   river   is   once . m°re
crossed, and the road runs high above the stream,
and passes the old Castle of Schenero.   Several
kilometres further along, the road crosses back to
the right bank at the Ponte della Serra, where
another fortress is encountered, and leads thence
to the town of Fonzaso.   At Arten, three kilometres further south, a level run of 9½ kilometres
brings us to Feltre, a fine town—like not a few
Italian cities, half ancient and half modern.   From
here there is a quick run over an excellent road,
almost due south, to Treviso of 55 kilometres,
while another twenty brings us to Mestre.

Here we must leave the car behind and sail
across the lagoon to Venice, the incomparable.
The City of the Doges, of course, is not a place to
see in a moment, nor leave in a hurry; and, unless
the traveller has time to make a long stay here,
it is not worth his while to go south of Feltre.
He should either go back into the mountains by
the Ampezzo road, or else turn west at Arten,
and proceed to Trient by way of the Val Sugana.

THE BEAUTIFUL VALE OF PRIMIERO, ON THE ROLLE PASS.

CHAPTER XVI.

THE MENDEL.

NOWHERE in the wide ranges of the Alps is there a town from which so many pass roads radiate as in the case of Bozen.

THE CASTLE OF SIGMUNDSKRON.

We have seen already how the Brenner road comes down from the north; we have dealt with the continuous line of three passes—the San Lugano, the Pordoi, and the Falzarego—on the east, and have also seen how they are linked up with the Ampezzo Pass at Cortina and the Rolle Pass at Predazzo.

But this is far from exhausting the list of Bozen's resources, and, in addition to many fine

routes over the plains to the south, there are yet
further passes to be conquered on the west and
north-west. Between Bozen and Landeck there
is the Reschen-Scheideck Pass, available as an
alternative to the Brenner, while a fine chain of
three passes—namely, the Mendel, the Tonale,
and the Aprica—connects Bozen with the foot of
the Stelvio, and leads thence to the Lake of
Como.

These three passes are not by any means so
well known to the road traveller as they deserve;

A GLIMPSE OF THE MENDEL ROAD.

but, as it is highly probable that the tourist who
has entered the Tyrol by any of the routes I
have already described will find it desirable to
leave it by way of this interesting trio, which
form one continuous route, I will take them next
in turn.

The following are the route figures of the
Mendel :—

Place.	Altitude. (Feet.)	Intermediate Distances. (Kils.)	Progressive Totals. (Kils.)
Bozen - - -	876	—	—
Bridge over the Adige -	—	$4\frac{1}{2}$	$4\frac{1}{2}$
Frangart - - -	—	1	$5\frac{1}{2}$
S. Michele - - -	1,365	$4\frac{1}{2}$	10
Summit - - -	4,475	15	25
Ronzone - -	3,555	$7\frac{1}{2}$	$32\frac{1}{2}$
Fork to Fondo - -	—	1	$33\frac{1}{2}$
Caverone - - -	—	$\frac{1}{2}$	34
San Zeno - - -	—	9	43
Dermullo - - -	—	4	47
Cles - - - -	2,150	5	52
Dres - - - -	—	1	53
Mostizzol Bridge -	2,066	6	59
Bordiana - - -	—	3	62
Caldes - - -	—	4	66
Malé - - - -	2,418	3	69

(*Hotels at Bozen, S. Michele, Mendel Summit, Ronzone,
Caverone, Cles, and Malè, with sundry inns.*)

The Mendel, unfortunately—as to its summit,
at all events—is fast becoming a Tyrolese Rigi,
for it has been connected since 1903 with the
plain below by means of an electric cable railway.
Those who ascend by this line, however, though
their opportunities are by no means to be despised,
miss the delights of winding up the hillside by
road, and the more varied views which this mode
of progression affords.

The Mendel road itself is also modern, having
been completed so recently as ·1885. In one
respect it is almost unique, though the Aprica
Pass has certain points of similarity. Instead of
following the river bed along one side or the other
of an ascending valley, or winding round shoulder
after shoulder, with constant changes of direction
and view, the Mendel is simply cut and carved

out of the face of a single mountain, the whole of which is exposed to view from the plain below. Although, therefore, one winds about on a precipitous slope, enjoying much more variety of outlook than that which the traveller obtains who is simply hauled up in a straight line by the funicular, the fact remains that the road is practically looking down upon the same plain the whole time until the zone of trees is entered.

Were the view less attractive the effect might be monotonous; but, as a matter of fact, the woods are entered with regret. This is due to several factors. The plain itself is unusually ample, and large enough, indeed, to make the town of Bozen itself look tiny when one has risen to the highest point of the pass which is not obscured by trees; there is a splendid backing of mountains to the east, including the massive Rosengarten, the peaks of the Langkofel, and the Marmolata, while a peculiarly attractive feature of the landscape is the deliciously green lake of Kaltern, which remains in view the whole time one is below the belt of trees.

A more agreeable view of its type does not exist within the whole series of Alpine carriage-roads, and, as it is not a lofty pass, the road is one peculiarly adapted to the requirements of the pedestrian. The only things with which I can compare it in effectiveness are the view of the Torno basin at the southern end of Lake Como, as seen when one ascends the marble-cobbled pilgrimage path of Monte Bisbino, and the first view of the lakes of the Upper Engadine as seen when crossing the Julier Pass from Tiefenkastel, and descending a mile or so below the summit. In one respect the latter view is much more beautiful, as the Bernina peaks opposite are always covered with snow and ice; but the Engadine valley itself is very much narrower, and in this respect the two types of view are altogether dissimilar.

It need not take long to describe the journey over the Mendel Pass in detail. We leave the town of Bozen by the Tafelbrücke, and soon pass a fine castle on the left. For several kilometres the surface is bumpy, as all the roads are in the immediate neighbourhood of Bozen. The road rises gradually to the village of San Michele, soon after leaving which the Kaltern lake comes into view. For a time the ascent is fairly steep, but without windings, and then zigzags are encountered, round which one winds up the face of the cliff right up to the summit.

The road surface is excellent, and the gradients are not excessive. As the whole journey from San Michele to the summit is one of 15 kilometres only, and the upper portion is well wooded, it behoves the motorist to take it slowly and enjoy the delightful view as long as possible. Incidentally, however, on a practical issue, I may mention that he should take the precaution, before leaving Bozen, of telephoning from his hotel to one of the hotels on the Mendel summit, as to whether accommodation is available; the hotels are large enough in all conscience, but, on the other hand, the railway brings crowds of visitors in the season, and if no rooms were available the alternatives would have to be faced of a return to Bozen on the one hand, or a very long journey on the

THE MENDEL ROAD, WITH THE DOLOMITES BEYOND

other side of the summit before anything satisfactory could be discovered. This passing reminder,
of course, only applies to the case of travellers
who have left Bozen in the afternoon, with the
intention of staying the night on the summit.

When one enters the woods, by the way,
though the continuous view of the plain and
lake, and of the glorious mountain panorama, is
no longer available, one does obtain recurrent

HOTELS ON THE MENDEL SUMMIT.

glimpses through openings in the trees; while
the most attractive prospect of all is that which
opens out after rising above the woods and
nearing the summit. There is one spot in particular where, from a dizzy height, one gazes
down into the valley, or across to the mountain
chain, the scene being one which will linger long
in the memory of any traveller in the Alps
fortunate enough to behold it.

OVER THE MENDEL SUMMIT: CARS DESCENDING TO RONZONE.

Views into the depths when travelling among the Alps are not a matter of the height which one may attain, but of the conformation of the land; and, though the point from which this magnificent view is obtained is only some four thousand feet in height, I do not think it is possible on any road to find a spot whence one can gaze downwards to such a depth, for the river becomes a mere streak, villages are reduced to dots, and the town of Bozen takes on the semblance of a village.

The summit of the Mendel Pass is almost unique among Alpine roads, for instead of a hospice there are several hotels, two of which have each over two hundred rooms. As I have explained, however, it is not road traffic that makes possible this state of things, but the funicular from the valley. In due time, no doubt, the bulk of the tourist traffic by road will be that of motorists alone, for there is not much sport in toiling up many miles of steep road behind horses.

For the descent towards the foot of the Tonale Pass, at Malè, two options are available from the Mendel summit, one leading through Fondo, and the other by Cles. The fork at which the two roads diverge is beyond Ronzone, where we turn left, the road to the right leading to Fondo. Whether the latter road be preferable I cannot say from personal experience, as I was strongly advised at the Hotel Penegal to take the other road. It has certainly one advantage in that it is easy to follow, inasmuch as a new electric railway has been laid practically along the whole route, and was just ready for opening when I passed that way in August, 1909. Occasionally the railway is lost sight of for a short time, but soon rejoins the road, and practically acts as a landmark throughout. Beyond Dermullo the road crosses a bridge nearly 500 feet above the stream, and thence rises gradually to Cles. Up to now the surface has been excellent, but at Cles it deteriorates and becomes somewhat bumpy. After a short rise to Dres the road descends to the Mostizzol bridge, where a junction is effected with the Fondo route.

For the alternative route between Ronzone and the Mostizzol bridge, by way of Fondo, the itinerary is as follows :—

Place.	Altitude. (Feet.)	Intermediate Distances. (Kils.)	Progressive Totals. (Kils.)
Ronzone - -	3,555	—	—
Sarnonico - -	—	$1\frac{1}{2}$	$1\frac{1}{2}$
Fondo - - -	3,149	2	$3\frac{1}{2}$
Brez - - -	—	6	$9\frac{1}{2}$
Cloz - - -	—	2	$11\frac{1}{2}$
S. Maria - -	—	$\frac{1}{2}$	12
Romeno - - -	—	3	15
Revò - - -	2,375	1	16
Cagnò - - -	—	2	18
Ponte Scanna - -	—	2	20
Mostizzol Bridge -	2,066	$3\frac{1}{2}$	$23\frac{1}{2}$

(*Hotels at Ronzone and Fondo ; inn at Revo.*)

It is quite probable that this route is more picturesque than the other, as local advice is seldom to be trusted.

CHAPTER XVII.

THE TONALE.

I HAVE twice crossed the Tonale Pass, in opposite directions, and each time alike have been impressed with the different points of view from which it would be regarded according to whether one travelled in a horsed vehicle or by some speedier method of locomotion. Its beauties are confined to the upper stages, and a through journey would be found tedious to the ordinary traveller; as a consequence, in fact, the route is little known. Seated behind one's trusty motor, however, one may pass easily over the valley stages, and before very long come into view of striking snow-capped peaks and glaciers of peculiar beauty.

On the Austrian side the road describes few *tourniquets,* but runs alongside a ravine of enormous depth. The line of route, nevertheless, is by no means straight, but, owing to the numerous *couloirs,* or gulleys, which descend into the ravine, the road is constantly swinging outwards to the right in wide bays, with intervening bridges. Of horsed traffic one encounters scarcely a vestige, but each time that I have crossed it has been in August; and, though there was an interval of nine years between the two periods, the same interesting, if inconvenient, feature was displayed —namely, that of the presence of innumerable ox-wagons loaded with hay.

They are encountered with such frequency, and are so erratically driven, that one does not know whether to be amused or annoyed. If not wholly on the wrong side the oxen are probably ambling down the middle of the road, and it is entirely at the option of the individual teamster whether he guides the beasts to the left or right. According to the rule of the road he should do the latter; but he may prefer to put you and your car between his wagon and the precipice.

Other than those above named there are no obstacles to comfortable and enjoyable progression up the Tonale Pass from Malè, where we ended the itinerary of the Mendel Pass. The Tonale itinerary is as follows :—

Place.	Altitude. (Feet.)	Intermediate Distances. (Kils.)	Progressive Totals. (Kils.)
Malé - - - -	2,418	—	—
Croviana - - -	2,379	1	1
Presson - - - -	—	3	4
Fork to Campiglio Pass -	—	1	5
Mastellina - - -	—	2	7
Piano - - - -	—	$1\frac{1}{2}$	$8\frac{1}{2}$
Mezzano - - -	—	$2\frac{1}{2}$	11
Cusiano - - - -	3,090	$4\frac{1}{2}$	$15\frac{1}{2}$
Fucine - - - -	3,135	$1\frac{1}{2}$	17
Cortina - - - -	—	3	20
Pizzano - - -	4,265	2	22
Strino Fort - - -	5,110	4	26
Albergo Locatori (Austrian Customs) - -	6,065	5	31
Summit - - - -	*6,181*	$\frac{1}{2}$	$31\frac{1}{2}$
Ponte di Legno (Italian Customs) - - -	4,140	11	$42\frac{1}{2}$
Pontagna - - -	—	3	$45\frac{1}{2}$
Stadolina - - -	—	4	$49\frac{1}{2}$
Vezza d'Oglio - -	—	3	$52\frac{1}{2}$
Edolo - - - -	2,264	$9\frac{1}{2}$	62

(*Hotels at Malè, Ponte di Legno and Edolo; inns at Mezzano, Fucine, Pizzano, and Austrian custom-house.*)

There is a slight descent to the village of
Croviana, and then a gentle rise to Presson; and
near a bridge over the Noce, a kilometre further
on, the road over the pass of the Madonna di
Campiglio branches off to the left. Continuing
westwards, however, the Tonale road still ascends
very gradually on the right bank of the Noce,
through several villages, until Fucine is reached.
In 17 kilometres the ascent has been one of
1,715 feet; but steeper work has to be entered
upon, as from Fucine to the summit involves a
rise of 3,045 feet in 14½ kilometres.

The road winds through the Vermiglio valley,
passing the village of Cortina—not, of course, to
be confounded with Cortina d'Ampezzo—and that
of Pizzano. Baedeker tells us that the Austrian
custom-house is situated here; as a matter of
fact, when I crossed the pass in 1901, there was
an Austrian custom-house to pass both at Pizzano
and the summit, but in 1909 I searched in vain
for the lower of the two. One may drive, therefore, through Pizzano without endeavouring to
locate a non-existent *dogana*, and enter upon the
most picturesque portion of the journey. The
road runs, as I have said, alongside a deep ravine
with tributary gulleys, and affords magnificent
views on the left of the glorious peaks of the
Presanella. Always above the snow-line, they
offer a splendid vista of glistening ice and snow
even in the hottest of weather, and, though in
a sense the sole attraction of the journey, are
potent enough as such to justify the Tonale Pass
being included in one's itinerary wherever that
can be contrived.

THE PRESANELLA PEAKS, ON THE TONALE PASS.

(The avera e condition of the road is much better than when this ' ' h was taken.

0

One word of caution, however, must be inter-polated here. At the spot on the road where the Presanella glaciers are the most impressive, and one is tempted to unship' one's camera accordingly, it is particularly essential to re-member *Punch's* " advice to those about to marry." There are forts on most of the Tyrolese and Italian passes, but they are usually well within view from a distance; in this particular case, however, the little fort of Strino adjoins the road just round a shoulder, within a few yards of the spot which I have indicated as suitable for the taking of photographs.

The road is in full view of the soldiers on guard, and, if you wield your camera, you will have the mortification of being allowed to ascend to the custom-house, five kilometres higher up, and will there be ordered to return on your tracks, as an officer at the fortress urgently desires your presence. The explanation, of course, is that the fortress and custom-house are con-nected by telephone, and that instructions have been passed over the wire while you have been ascending the upper stages of the pass. The best that you can then hope for is that your camera does not possess a lens of a sufficiently wide angle as to include the fortress in your pictures of the peaks, for the plates or films will be developed on the spot in a dark room with which the fortress is provided.

Assuming, however, that no untoward incident of this kind has occurred, you will clear the Austrian custom-house (in the Albergo Locatori), and in a few hundred yards reach the actual

summit, which is of a fairly open character.
Soon after the border-line is crossed an Italian
infantryman is encountered, who challenges your
progress. He intimates his desire to accompany
you, and you drive with him on the footboard
for a short distance until you reach a *dogana* on
the left of the road. Your papers, however, are
not stamped here, and you are informed that that
operation must be performed at Ponte di Legno,
which is eleven kilometres down the pass. This
is one of several instances where there is a roadside custom-house at or near the summit, and
another and more important one in the nearest
town ; but why both are necessary, or how the
officials divide their duties, I have never been
able to discover.

The soldier again boards the car, and rides
with you all the way down to the little town,
over a descent of 2,040 feet in seven miles.
Ponte di Legno is not attractive in itself, but is
a centre for excursions, and the hotels will probably
be found to be fairly full. One of them, at all
events, is enterprising enough to have a garage,
and petrol is obtainable.

The descent to Edolo represents a fall of
1,875 feet in 19½ kilometres, and, with a gradient
of less than 100 feet a kilometre, should not, if uniform, involve any *tourniquets*. There are sundry
almost level stretches, however, with corresponding
augmentations elsewhere, so that zigzags occur at
intervals. None the less the bends are of a
sweeping kind, and present no difficulty, while
the road is of good surface throughout, and affords
a run down that is in every way pleasing.

For the benefit of those who may be proceeding southwards to Brescia I append the
following itinerary :—

Place.	Altitude. (Feet.)	Intermediate Distances. (Kils.)	Progressive Totals. (Kils.)
Edolo - - -	2,264	—	—
Cedegolo - - -	1,394	15	15
Capo di Ponte -	—	6	21
Breno - - -	—	$9\frac{1}{2}$	$30\frac{1}{2}$
Ospitale - - -	—	$3\frac{1}{2}$	34
Pian Borno - -	—·	6	40
Casino Boario ·	—	4	44
Corna - - -	—	1	45
Darfo - - -	—	$\frac{1}{2}$	$45\frac{1}{2}$
Pisogne - - -	—	11	$56\frac{1}{2}$
Vello - - -	—	8	$64\frac{1}{2}$
Marone - - -	—	2	$66\frac{1}{2}$
Sale Marasino -	—	3	$69\frac{1}{2}$
Sulzano - - -	—	$3\frac{1}{2}$	73
Pilzone - - -	—	2	75
Iseo - - -	—	3	78
Provaglio d'Iseo -	—	3	81
Mandolossa - -	—	14	95
Brescia - - -	479	$4\frac{1}{2}$	$99\frac{1}{2}$

(*Hotels at Edolo, Breno, Casino Boario, and Brescia, with
inns along the lakeside.*)

The road is almost level all the way, and
from Pisogne to Iseo it runs alongside the
charming Lago d'Iseo.

CHAPTER XVIII.

THE APRICA.

W E come now to the third link in the interesting chain of passes between Bozen and Tresenda. The Aprica Pass takes its name from a village on the line of route, and provides as easy a journey as could well be

THE SUBSTANTIAL PARAPET ON THE APRICA PASS.

imagined, particularly if taken from east to west. Leaving the little town of Edolo, where one may buy peaches at 3*d.* per lb., we may look forward to a moderate ascent of 1,610 feet in 15½ kilometres. The road is a little bumpy on its lower stages through the Val di Corteno, but later on the surface is excellent; as a matter of fact, on the Tresenda side it used to be the best I had ever seen, but is now a shade less good, although there is nothing to complain about.

The Aprica road has one distinguishing feature throughout—namely, that it is provided with a stone parapet practically along the entire route, save for occasional breaks. The substantial wall, which is pierced with semi-circular holes to allow the passage of the melting snow in winter, affords a feeling of security to an unusual degree, although there are plenty of other passes on which its provision would be even more welcome. Villages are few and far between, as may be seen from the itinerary subjoined.

Place.	Altitude. (Feet.)	Intermediate Distances. (Kils.)	Progressive Totals. (Kils.)
Edolo - - -	2,264	—	—
Cortenedolo - -	2,975	5	5
Corteno - - -	3,295	2	7
S. Pietro - -	—	8	15
Summit - - -	3,875	$\frac{1}{2}$	$15\frac{1}{2}$
Albergo Negri -	—	.1	$16\frac{1}{2}$
Aprica - - -	—	1	$17\frac{1}{2}$
Belvedere Inn - -	3,010	2	$19\frac{1}{2}$
Roadmenders' Hut -	—	4	$23\frac{1}{2}$
Motta - - -	—	$2\frac{1}{2}$	26
Tresenda - -	1,220	$3\frac{1}{2}$	$29\frac{1}{2}$

(*Hotels at Edolo, S. Pietro, Aprica, and Tresenda.*)

There is no ambiguity about the route, save at one point, a few kilometres from Edolo. A white board, however, will be noticed, bearing the words "Hotel Aprica" and a black hand. A sharp turn to the right must be taken in the direction in which the hand is pointing. The valley then contracts somewhat, and the road rises gently. On the left of the road, just below the summit,

THE VIEW INTO THE VALTELLINA, WITH THE STELVIO AND BERNINA ROUTES BEYOND.

(Note the parapet and road on the right.)

will be noticed the Hotel Cerf, which may serve
as a stand-by in case the Hotel Negri, beyond
the summit, is full, as is frequently the case in
the season.

Driving over an open plain, we soon begin to
descend, and shortly reach the Belvedere, a point
from which an expansive view is unfolded of the
Valtellina, through which winds the Adda river.

ONE OF THE ROCK TUNNELS BELOW MOTTA.

In the distance are seen the peaks of the Bernina
range, with their resplendent glaciers. Ere long,
the road winds down in sweeping zigzags through
groves of chestnuts, over the face of a hill which
strongly resembles the Mendel; in lieu of the
Kaltern lake, however, and velvety pastures, we
have the broad gravelly bed of the Adda, and
more or less waste land due to inundations. To

the north and north-east, however, one may see the windings of the Bernina and Stelvio passes, and the prospects are in every way striking.

To the left of Tresenda lies the level road to Sondrio and Colico, 59 kilometres away, and on a neighbouring hill is seen the ruined castle of Teglio. On the road itself, the only interesting feature beyond its breadth and quality, and the wonderful parapet, are a couple of rock tunnels just below the village of Motta. Finally it may be said that the grading of the road down the hillside is most skilfully effected, and the fall from the Belvedere to Tresenda is one of 1,790 feet in ten kilometres. A turn to the right at the foot of the pass brings one to Tirano and the Stelvio Pass in nine kilometres.

CHAPTER XIX.

THE STELVIO.

SUPERB from every point of view, the Stelvio is the unquestioned king among mountain carriage-roads. It is loftier than any other

A BIRD'S EYE VIEW OF THE STELVIO PASS, SHOWING ABOUT SEVEN MILES OF ROAD.

Alpine highway, and has no rival even in the Himalayas themselves; but mere altitude is very far from being its sole claim to pre-eminence. To climb it should be the ambition of every automobilist who tours, for it possesses every quality which can give zest to the undertaking. As a test of his car he could wish for nothing finer; as a driving feat it is the most amply satisfying that may be obtained without actual severity; while, as for scenery, it is unparalleled in its splendid majesty.

And even if it lacked all these virtues, who is there who could not admire the magnificence of the Stelvio as a triumph of the roadmaker's skill? It is the one road which, in the boldness of its conception, excels anything conceived by the titanic genius of Napoleon himself. I have crossed it twice, and each time one thought was paramount—that the British public in general, and the British surveyor in particular, simply do not know what road-making is. The heights, in the literal and figurative sense alike, to which road-building may attain are as far beyond their

MERAN, THE ANCIENT CAPITAL OF THE TYROL.

ken as the planning of St. Peter's, Rome, would be to the builder of an Irish hovel.

It would have been remarkable enough if when the Austrians decided, nigh a hundred years ago, to construct a road between the Tyrol and the plains of Lombardy, across a barrier of 9,041 feet, they had succeeded in constructing one on which a carriage could be driven at all, without reference to quality; but when I say that the surface of the Stelvio is equal to anything that can be found on English highways, and actually better than that of many, the measure of the Stelvio's super-excellence may be better understood. Without steam-rollers and every other modern appliance the making of such a highway might well have been deemed impossible; but the result is visible and permanent enough, and worthy the admiration of the world.

There are two ways of approaching the Stelvio Pass on the Austrian side, which, by the way, is the better for making the ascent. It is easier to drive a car up a steep road with many corners than to bring it down, and not only are the gradients rather steeper on the Austrian than on the Italian side, but the former is more liberally provided with zigzags. Of the two approaches in question the one leads from Landeck to Finstermünz, and then over the Reschen-Scheideck Pass to Mals and Neu Spondinig, while the other follows a valley route to the last-named village from Bozen and through Meran, the picturesquely centred and ancient capital of the Tyrol, as under:—

Place.	Altitude. (Feet.)	Intermediate Distances. (Kils.)	Progressive Totals, (Kils.)
Bozen - - -	876	—	—
Terlan - - -	—	$9\frac{1}{2}$	$9\frac{1}{2}$
Vilpian - - -	—	4	$13\frac{1}{2}$
Gargazon - -	—	4	$17\frac{1}{2}$
Meran - - -	—	$11\frac{1}{2}$	29
Naturns - - -	—	$13\frac{1}{2}$	$42\frac{1}{2}$
Latsch - - -	—	12	$54\frac{1}{2}$
Schlanders - -	—	$7\frac{1}{2}$	62
Laas - - -	—	7	69
Eyers - - -	—	4	73
Neu Spondinig -	2,883	3	76

ONE OF THE MANY CASTLES IN THE NEIGHBOURHOOD OF MERAN.

The itinerary of the Stelvio itself, assuming that the junction of the two routes referred to has been reached at Neu Spondinig, is as follows:—

Place.	Altitude. (Feet.)	Intermediate Distances. (Kils.)	Progressive Totals. (Kils.)
Neu Spondinig -	2,883	—	—
Prad - - -	2,940	$2\frac{1}{2}$	$2\frac{1}{2}$
Schmelz - - -	3,035	1	$3\frac{1}{2}$
Bridge over the Sulden - - -	3,773	$3\frac{1}{2}$	7
By-road to Stelvio Village - -	—	2	9
Gomagoi - - -	4,101	$\frac{1}{2}$	$9\frac{1}{2}$
1st bridge over the Trafoier-Bach -	—	1	$10\frac{1}{2}$
2nd bridge over the Trafoier-Bach -	—	$\frac{1}{2}$	11
3rd bridge over the Trafoier-Bach -	—	$\frac{1}{2}$	$11\frac{1}{2}$
4th bridge over the Trafoier-Bach -	—	$\frac{1}{2}$	12
Trafoi - - -	5,079	1	13
Weissen Knott -	—	4	17
Roadmenders' Hut -	—	2	19
Franzensböhe -	7,359	$2\frac{1}{2}$	$21\frac{1}{2}$
Roadmenders' Hut -	—	$3\frac{1}{2}$	25
Ferdinandshöhe— Summit (Hotel and Austrian Customs)	9,041	$2\frac{1}{2}$	$27\frac{1}{2}$
S. Maria (Italian Customs and Entrance to Umbrail Pass) - - -	8,153	$3\frac{1}{2}$	31
S. Ranieri - -	7,677	3	34
Refuge - - -	—	$\frac{1}{2}$	$34\frac{1}{2}$
Roadmenders' Casino	7,103	$1\frac{1}{2}$	36
Roadmenders' Hut -	6,529	$2\frac{1}{2}$	$38\frac{1}{2}$
Roadmenders' Hut -	5,584	3	$41\frac{1}{2}$
Iron Bridge - -	4,347	$5\frac{1}{2}$	47
Fork to New Baths -	—	$\frac{1}{2}$	$47\frac{1}{2}$
Bormio - - -	4,019	$2\frac{1}{2}$	50
S. Antonio Morignone	3,592	9	59
Ponte del Diavolo -	—	$3\frac{1}{2}$	$62\frac{1}{2}$
Le Prese Nuovo -	3,117	$2\frac{1}{4}$	$64\frac{3}{4}$

Place.	Altitude. (Feet.)	Intermediate Distances. (Kils.)	Progressive Totals. (Kils.)
Bridge over Adda R.	—	$\frac{1}{4}$	65
Bolladore - -	2,789	$4\frac{1}{2}$	$69\frac{1}{2}$
Tiolo - - -	2,529	$2\frac{1}{2}$	72
Ponte di Grosio -	2,274	$1\frac{1}{2}$	$73\frac{1}{2}$
Grosio - - -	2,169	$1\frac{1}{2}$	75
Grossotto - -	1,968	3	78
Mazzo di Valtellina -	—	2	80
Tovo di S. Agata -	1,742	2	82
Lovero - - -	1,667	2	84
Colle di Sernio -	1,804	$2\frac{1}{2}$	$86\frac{1}{2}$
Tirano - - -	1,441	3	$89\frac{1}{2}$
Madonna di Tirano (Entrance to Bernina Pass) - -	1,437	1	$90\frac{1}{2}$
Tresenda (Entrance to Aprica Pass) -	1,220	8	$98\frac{1}{2}$
Sondrio - - -	1,017	18	$116\frac{1}{2}$

(*Hotels at Neu Spondinig, Prad, Gomagoi, Trafoi, Franzenshöhe, the Summit, Bormio, Tirano, Tresenda, and Sondrio, and sundry inns.*)

A straight and level road has to be followed to Prad, where the ascent òf the Stelvio is begun in earnest. In respect of the height to be attained it offers the most serious undertaking which the motorist has to face in the Alps, for in 25 kilometres from Prad he must needs rise from 2,940 feet to 9,041 feet, and must swing round forty-six " hairpin " corners.

Truly this seems at first sight a formidable task, and it is at one and the same time easier and more difficult than might be supposed. To take the matter of gradients first, it may be stated that the ascent works out at about 400 feet per mile for $15\frac{1}{2}$ miles. Now this, of course, represents nothing more than an average of 1 in 13, which, for any given half mile, might be regarded as relatively trifling.

Also it may be pointed out that there are no abrupt variations of gradient, and that the steepest portion does not exceed 1 in 10; on the other hand, the task of mounting uninterruptedly for five-and-twenty kilometres with a fairly steep gradient is a more serious undertaking than to traverse a short stage with a much steeper rise. The tourist who drives a motor-car over the Stelvio route, therefore, has no need to fear encountering any pitch which should cause him the least concern in the matter of his gear ratio or the limitations of his engine power; but whether the motor will keep cool under the strain of so much "collar-work" is dependent upon the individual car and the "nous" with which it is driven.

If the radiation be good the car should be well equal to the task, and in any case the driver may call a halt the moment he discerns any tendency to overheating. Armed with the consciousness that there is nothing impossibly steep ahead, and that he has merely to keep himself and the engine cool, he need not feel under the least necessity to hurry, but may count to a certainty on reaching the summit in due course.

And here let me interject a hint as to what my personal experience of innumerable passes has shown me to be the best way of ascending a lengthy mountain road. It is the habit of every driver, in ordinary running, to use the top gear as much as possible without actually causing the engine to labour; so long as it is taking its gear smoothly he does not think it either necessary

A VIEW OF TRAFOI, LOOKING TOWARDS THE STELVIO SUMMIT.

or desirable to change down. He is probably using, however, an open throttle, and on English roads few hills are long enough to render this method unpractical.

In the Alps, nevertheless, the driver must approach the problem from a wholly different point of view, and place first and foremost the question of keeping the engine cool. When

THE THREE HOLY SPRINGS.

embarking on a particularly long climb, therefore, he should think of his throttle more than of the joy of breasting a rise on the top gear, and be determined from the outset not to yield to the temptation of giving the cylinders their full quantum of gas. The engine, when running slowly with the throttle open, will heat up much more qui ckly than if turning much faster on half throttle; and the proper way to mount a lofty pass by car is undoubtedly with the throttle lever only half advanced, selecting one's gears accordingly. Of course, it may be necessary to open the throttle momentarily on occasion; but where there is a protracted ascent, of fairly uniform gradient, it must not be taken on a high gear and with a surfeit of gas.

No one need fear the ascent of the Stelvio, however, from either side, so far as engine-power is concerned, provided the car generally is in good running order and has a satisfactory carburetter. So far back as 1899 a voiturette made the ascent, and in 1902 a small car ran out from Milan to the summit and back, a total distance of 279 miles, in one day ; and every summer the road is traversed by cars in plenty. As a matter

THE WEISSEN KNOTT AND PICHLER MONUMENT.

of fact, it is the corners which are the chief item for consideration. Not that they are bad ; the road is mostly 19 feet wide, and there are passes with corners of a much severer kind.

But the fact remains that there are eighty in all to be rounded, including the Italian side, and the whole question resolves itself into one of the ratio of wheelbase to lock. If a car has a short lock the driver will be sick of the Stelvio before he has finished reversing and manœuvring at everyone of the "hairpins"; but, if the lock is a good one, the car can be swung round without reversing at all. The tourist should tackle other passes before the Stelvio, however, and it is for that reason that I have not described this pass immediately after the Arlberg; but, if he has found that he could round the corners of the Pordoi, for example, without reversing at all, and

A ROADSIDE VIEW ABOVE TRAFOI.

turn the sixty corners without fatigue, he can safely adventure the Stelvio and its 25 per cent. more turns.

If intent upon crossing the Stelvio at all costs, however, even if the lock of the car be far from ideal, the driver should take two practical precautions. In the first place, while making sure that his brake-fittings generally are sound, he should adjust the foot-brake as tightly as possible

THE FRANZENSHÖHE HOTEL, WITH THE MAGNIFICENT ORTLER AND
THE MADATSCH GLACIER.

—short of actual binding, of course; for when manœuvring at a corner it is absolutely essential to be able to stop the car dead within a foot. Secondly, he should provide himself with a substantial block of wood, armed with which a fellow passenger, or the chauffeur, must be ready to scotch the car as soon as it has been backed to the limit, and thus enable the driver to let in

his clutch from a standstill, which is a much easier matter than if the car is running backwards at the time, or being held up hard by the brake.

Given equal conditions as to gradients and the radial curves, it is harder to descend a zigzag road than to mount it if there is any reversing to be done.

ON THE LAST STAGE, AUSTRIAN SIDE.

When ascending, the car may be allowed to drop back by gravity at a "hairpin," and there is no need to put in the reverse gear; but, when descending, the case is very different. The driver must needs apply all his skill in apportioning the requisite degree of power when he has to reverse uphill; on the one hand he must not stop his engine, and, on the other, must not accelerate

A "TOURNIQUET" ON THE STELVIO PASS, ITALIAN SIDE.

(As the photograph was taken from below it makes the zigzags appear more formidable than is actually the case, as to gradient and corners alike. It will be noticed that a car is rounding the right-hand corner on the lowest stretch with room to spare.

so much as to overshoot the mark. The wooden scotch referred to comes in even more usefully downhill than up, and must be brought to the aid of the driver; and he should also be assisted in pulling the front wheels round, as is done in town garages where turning space is restricted.

I have said that there is nothing steeper than 10 per cent. on the Austrian side of the Stelvio; and, as a matter of fact, this figure is only attained over one short stretch. From Prad to Gomagoi the rise is from 5 to 6 per cent., and increases to 9 from there to just below Trafoi. After a break of $4\frac{1}{2}$ per cent. the gradient reverts to 9, and then to 10 per cent. at Capanna. From there to the summit is almost uniformly 9 per cent., with one kilometre of 4 per cent., not far from Franzenshöhe.

On the Italian side the percentages are rather lower, the descent beginning with $7\frac{3}{4}$, and increasing to $8\frac{1}{2}$. After five kilometres the fall moderates to $2\frac{3}{4}$ per cent., but soon increases to $7\frac{1}{2}$. Excepting for a short stage of $8\frac{1}{2}$, about nine kilometres from the summit, there is nothing over 7 per cent. on the remainder of the journey. On more modern passes it is rare for the final stages to be cut at a greater angle than 8 per cent.; consequently the Austrian side of the Stelvio, with its 9 per cent., and more particularly its great altitude, may be regarded as specially worthy the car's prowess. I have dwelt the longer on these technical details by reason of the fact that they are essentially the data that are unobtainable from the ordinary guide-book, and are yet so necessary to the automobilist.

And what is there on the Stelvio which makes it so attractive on other grounds than that of a desire for conquest ? The answer may be emphatic ; on no other road can such magnificent views be enjoyed. The windings of this grand highway themselves are worth going thousands of miles to see, but in the splendour of its peaks and glaciers the Stelvio is quite without a rival. This is the more remarkable from the fact that the road winds up a narrow valley, hollowed out by the rushing Trafoi-bach, and does not command actual panoramas until the summit is attained.

It is dominated, nevertheless, by the magnificent Ortler (12,800 feet), the loftiest peak in the Tyrol, while the Madatsch glacier, which almost adjoins the road, is one of the most brilliantly beautiful in the Alps. Nor is this all, for above Trafoi, in addition to the fresh glories which ever unfold themselves ahead as one mounts the pass, the backward view is picturesquely complete to an unusual degree, from the fact that the vista is closed in by the snowy Weisskugel, which is over 12,000 feet in height. As far as the eye can reach everything seems ideally symmetrical and sublime.

In the earlier stages of the pass the chief things of note are that, high up on the right, one sees the village of Stelvio, or Stilfs, from which the pass derives its name, and that at Gomagoi the road runs right through an Austrian fortress. The first splendours of the higher peaks are realised when approaching Trafoi, at a point where the Madatsch glacier bursts into view with sudden and startling effectiveness. As to Trafoi itself, it is one of the most beautifully situated villages in the world, and I cannot recall any spot in the whole of my experiences of road travel where I would more ardently long to linger for an indefinite period. Primarily the place is a mere hamlet; but the manifold attractiveness of its situation has led to the erection of several hotels.

Above Trafoi one enters upon the magnificent series of windings which are cut along the slopes of the valley with such amazing prodigality; as a feat of engineering the road is stupendously impressive. The scenery, however, plays no second part, and particularly entrancing is the view from a spot known as the Weissen Knott, four kilometres from Trafoi. A long halt should be called here, and a walk will not be ill repaid into the depths of the wooded valley in order to view the Chapel of the Three Holy Springs, and the awe-inspiring outlook therefrom (*vide* p. 226). Two memorials in the neighbourhood of the Weissen Knott should also be mentioned, one being an obelisk to the memory of Josef Pichler, who was the first man to ascend the Ortler, and the other a tablet to Madeleine de Tourville, an Englishwoman who was hurled over the roadside and down the precipice by her husband in 1876.

Five kilometres of recurring windings bring one to Franzenshöhe, and just off the road stands an hotel on a small plateau. There is a motor garage attached, and it is probably the highest in the world unless one has been established at the summit since I crossed the Stelvio a second time. The Austrian custom-house also used to be situated here, but is now transferred to the summit. The wavy line of the road which one

THE STELVIO.

SUMMIT OF PASS

Distance 1 - 100,000
Altitude 1 - 10·000

ITALY

AUSTRIA

TRAFOI

BORMIO

CONTOUR OF THE STELVIO, MAGNIFIED TEN TIMES

Distance 1 - 100,000
Altitude 1 - 50,00

ITALY

AUSTRIA

TRAFOI

BORMIO

THE SAME CONTOUR, MAGNIFIED FIVE TIMES.

THE STELVIO AS IT REALLY IS.

Exaggerated contours of hilly roads are only useful when there are numerous undulat
ntervals. With a straightforward ascent, such as characterises most of the Alpine Passes,
uperfluous if actual, and delusive if magnified, as is effectually shown by these diagrams o
oad in Europe.

THE DELUSIVENESS OF CONTOURS.

has left behind stands out with particular pro-
minence as viewed from this point; but, immediately after quitting the hotel, one enters upon a
series of zigzags of a different kind, the strata
being shorter and cut much more vertically up
the face of the mountain side. Though the road
is cleared and thrown open to diligence traffic
in the middle of June, it is flanked even in July
by high walls of snow of inviting coolness.

When the last corner has been rounded a
straight stretch of road leads to the summit,
9,041 feet above the sea. The scene is now one
of much greater bustle than when I first crossed
several years ago, the little restaurant having
given place to the "Ferdinandshöhe Hotel," while
the Austrian customs, as I have said, have been
transferred from Franzenshöhe. It is also, of
course, a halting-place for diligences, and the
Stelvio, it may be remarked, is one of the few
Austrian passes on which the horsed diligence has
not been superseded by the all-conquering motor;
but a change may be expected to take place any
moment even here. The panorama from the summit is far-reaching, and particularly impressive in
July, when one may look down upon vast fields of
snow; but, even in August, there is plenty of snow
about, while the glories of the noble Ortler and
the Madatsch and Eben glaciers are even then un-
dimmed. Nevertheless the difference in the lower
peaks is appreciable, as I found to my regret
when visiting the Stelvio a second time, late in
August, whereas I first crossed it early in July.

On the Italian side of the pass the scenery is
less overwhelmingly beautiful, but singularly wild

ON THE WAY TO THE SUMMIT, ITALIAN SIDE.

(*Though this photograph was taken in August it will be seen that snow is still present on the roadside.*)

and suggestive of complete isolation from the world. Habitations are soon encountered, however, at Santa Maria, where there is a large Italian custom-house, and where also the Umbrail Pass — branches off and leads to another Santa Maria in the Münsterthal.

In sweeping curves the road now winds down the Braulio valley into the Diroccamento defile, and runs through a series of winter galleries, five in all, which must be driven through with care owing to the slippery condition of the surfaces. At length, where the Braulio joins forces with the Adda, the road swings round to the south and opens up a striking view of the Bormio valley, with an environment of high mountains which include the Piz Tresero, nearly 12,000 feet in height. Three kilometres above Bormio an iron bridge is crossed, near which is a tablet commemorating the opening of the road. Shortly afterwards a road is passed on the right which leads to the finely situated New Baths of Bormio, and then, after passing a final pair of "hairpin" bends, one soon reaches Bormio town itself.

Here the steep portion of the descent is ended, and the driver, at all events, may well heave a sigh of relief. The remainder of the journey presents a gentle incline, and no feature of risk whatsoever, save for the possibility of an occasional cow wandering on to the road. The long defile of S. Antonio Morignone is reached in nine kilometres, and at the Devil's Bridge (Ponte del Diavolo) lower down, the river Sulden is crossed, and one enters the Valtellina, and before long, amid verdure and vegetation of characteristic

Italian opulence, the grim wildness of the upper slopes of the descent is for the time forgotten.

Onward we speed through Le Prese Nuovo (not to be confounded with Le Prese on the Bernina Pass), Bolladore, Grosio, and other villages in quick succession, until Tirano is reached. A little further on, at Madonna di Tirano, the Bernina Pass branches off to the right, while at Tresenda, eight kilometres further, we join the route from Bozen, already described, by way of the Mendel, Tonale and Aprica passes.

CHAPTER XX.

MORE ABOUT THE TYROL.

ALTHOUGH the main attractions of the Tyrol have already been dealt with in preceding chapters, the resources of this motorists' paradise have by no means been exhausted, and I may say in a word that the

THE HOCH-FINSTERMÜNZ DEFILE.

district is worth exploring in almost every corner. Besides pass-climbing there is much easy driving to be enjoyed, especially in the neighbourhood of Trient, a fine city which is well worth visiting. The blue lake of Garda is only 40 kilometres away, and the road to Arco and Riva is interesting

NAUDERS, ON THE RESCHEN-SCHEIDECK PASS.

and picturesque alike.   There is no difficulty, by
the way, in buying petrol even in the mountain
districts of the Tyrol, and of hotels there are
plenty; at the same time it must be remembered
that some of them occupy much-sought-after
positions, and when possible it is better to secure
accommodation in advance.

But we have not even done with the passes
as yet.   There are still the Reschen-Scheideck,

MALS, ON THE RESCHEN-SCHEIDECK PASS.

the Fern, the Griesen, the Scharnitz, the Campiglio, the Fugazza, and others to be considered,
though several of these are not wholly Tyrolese,
but are partially in Bavaria or Italy.   While in
the Dolomites region, moreover, the tourist may
have time to run up to the Karer summit and
back for the sake of seeing the charming lake,
and he might do worse than stroll down the
forbidden side in order to explore the ravines of
the Eggenthal.

The Reschen-Scheideck.

The road over the Reschen-Scheideck, if not quite worth a chapter to itself, is none the less very beautiful, and should be taken without hesitation whenever opportunity allows. Indeed it is essential to anyone proposing to " do " the Stelvio before exploring the Dolomites, in which case he would proceed southwards from Landeck and through Hoch-Finstermünz to the foot of the famous pass at Neu Spondinig, by the following itinerary :—

Place.	Altitude. (Feet.)	Intermediate Distances. (Kils.)	Progressive Totals. (Kils.)
Landeck - - -	2,677	—	—
Prutz - - -	—	12½	12½
Ried - - -	--	3	15½
Pfunds - - -	—	14	29½
Hoch-Finstermünz -	—	7½	37
Nauders - - -	4,468	5	42
Summit - - -	*4,901*	7	49
Reschen - - -	4,888	½	49½
Graun - - -	—	2½	52
St. Valentin - -	4,698	6	58
Mals - - -	3,428	9½	67½
Schluderns - -	3,011	5	72½
Neu Spondinig - -	2,883	6	78½

(Hotels or Inns at all points.)

More often than not this pass is known as the Finstermünz, but its correct name is as given above. It is a grand road almost throughout, and offers the easiest of travelling so far as gradients are concerned. At Hoch Finstermünz there is a very picturesque defile, and then follows a winding rise to Nauders, centred in a spacious valley, the most impressive view of which, however, is gained when crossing from

the Engadine at Martinsbruck. To the summit
at Reschen-Scheideck is a gentle ascent of seven
kilometres from Nauders. There is a pretty lake
here and the environment is very pleasing; but in
pasing through Reschen village, a short distance
below the summit, a really marvellous view is
unfolded of the Ortler chain. As a matter of
fact this is the best way of approaching the
Stelvio route, but it may not always be easy to
bring within the scope of a 'general tour.

Thenceforward the route is level for 13 kilometres, and, after a steep fall into Mals, there
is more level running to Neu Spondinig, at the
foot of the Stelvio. The surface throughout is
excellent.

The Toblach.

Strictly speaking, the continuation of the
Pusterthal route, which we have already traced
from Mühlbach to Toblach village, is a "pass,"
and connects the Brenner route with the Drave
Valley. The itinerary is as follows:—

Place.	Altitude. (Feet.)	Intermediate Distances. (Kils.)	Progressive Totals. (Kils.)
Toblach - - -	3,965	—	—
Innichen - - -	3,855	5	5
Sillian - . - -	3,600	11	16
Abfaltersbach - -	3,220	8	24
Mittewald - -	2,890	$6\frac{1}{2}$	$30\frac{1}{2}$
Thal - - -	2,660	$6\frac{1}{2}$	37
Lienz - - -	2,215	9	46

(*Hotels at Toblach, Sillian, Mittewald and Lienz.*)

Toblach village itself is practically the summit
of the pass, and a glance at the altitudes will
show that the road involves nothing in the way

of climbing, but simply affords a pleasant and virtually level run along the Puster Valley.

The Fern.

The Fern Pass is not of sufficient note to be worth a special journey in that direction; but, on the other hand, it lies on the route of anyone entering or leaving the Tyrol by way of Munich.

A MOTOR DILIGENCE ON THE FERN ROUTE.

The pass breaks off from the Landeck-Innsbruck route at Imst, and crosses to Reutte by the following itinerary:—

Place.	Altitude. (Feet.)	Intermediate Distances. (Kils.)	Progressive Totals. (Kils.)
Landeck - - -	2,677	—	—
Imst - - -	2,716	19	19
Nassereith - -	2,742	13½	32½
Summit - -	*3,969*	9	41½
Bieberwier - -	—	8	49½
Lermoos - - -	·3,244	2	51½
Biehlbach - -	—	9½	61
Reutte - - -	2,800	12½	73½

(Hotels all along the route.)

The road is good throughout, and the scenery is essentially romantic, the attractions of the landscape including not only fine mountain prospects, but well-wooded slopes, a series of lakes, and several picturesque old castles. I may add that this is the best and most popular route to the famous village of Ober Ammergau.

The Griesen and Scharnitz.

These two passes are in close contiguity with the Fern Pass, and are chiefly interesting as forming alternative routes to Ober Ammergau. The Griesen Pass breaks off from the Fern Pass at Lermoos, and leads to Garmisch by the following itinerary :—

Place.	Altitude. (Feet.)	Intermediate Distances. (Kils.)	Progressive Totals. (Kils.)
Lermoos -	3,265	--	—
Frontier -	—	12	12
Griesen -	2,690	1	13
Garmisch -	2,295	13	26

(*Hotels at Lermoos and Garmisch.*)

The Scharnitz road strikes north from Zirl, on the Landeck-Innsbruck road, and veers round to Partenkirchen, which is close to Garmisch, the itinerary being as follows :—

Place.	Altitude. (Feet.)	Intermediate Distances. (Kils.)	Progressive Totals. (Kils.)
Innsbruck -	1,885	—	—
Zirl -	2,040	12	12
Seefeld (*summit*) -	3,870	12	24
Scharnitz -	3,160	10	34
Frontier -	—	2	36
Mittenwald -	3,020	$5\frac{1}{2}$	$41\frac{1}{2}$
Partenkirchen -	2,350	$18\frac{1}{2}$	60

(*Hotels all along the route.*)

Though this road figured in the itinerary of one of the Herkomer Trophy contests, it is not altogether desirable, being exceptionally steep. By covered or otherwise heavily loaded cars it should certainly be avoided—as regards engine—power on the ascent and brake-power on the descent.

The Madonna Di Campiglio.

On the whole this pass is hardly to be recommended to the tourist. Though not on the list, it is true, of passes which are barred to motor-cars on the score of danger by the Tyrolese authorities, it is none the less a difficult road on the Italian side; nor is it in any way inevitable as regards the line of route. It breaks off from the foot of the Tonale Pass at Dimaro, and runs down to Brescia; but of other ways of reaching that city there are enough and to spare. The itinerary, however, is as follows:—

Place.	Altitude. (Feet.)	Intermediate Distances. (Kils.)	Progressive Totals. (Kils.)
Dimaro - - -	2,559	—	—
Distillery - - -	—	12½	12½
Campo di Carlomagno (*summit*) - -	5,413	3	15½
Madonna di Campiglio	4,970	3	18½
S. Antonio - -	—	8½	27
Pinzolo - . - -	2,525	6½	33½
Strembo - - -	2,230	5	38½
Spiazzo - - -	—	2½	41
Pelugo - - -	2,165	2	43
Tione - - -	1,853	7½	50½
Storo - - -	1,296	26	76½
Preseglie - - -	1,266	34	110½
Brescia - - -	488	29½	140

(*Hotels at Dimaro, Campo di Carlomagno, Madonna di Campiglio, Pinzolo, Tione, and Brescia.*)

The road is fairly good to the summit, but part way down the Italian side becomes very steep and narrow, with bad corners, between S. Antonio and Pinzolo. Thenceforward to Tione, however, it improves considerably, and is good to Brescia.

The Buco Di Vela.

This is a small pass which may be mentioned as a connecting link between the large town of Trient and Tione, on the Madonna di Campiglio Pass, the route being as follows:—

Place.			Altitude. (Feet.)	Intermediate Distances. (Kils.)	Progressive Totals. (Kils.)
Trient	-	-	625	—	—
Summit	-	-	*1,640*	4½	4½
Cadine	-	-	1,520	1	5½
Vezzano	-	-	1,238	8	13½
Padergnone	-	-	1,088	2½	16
Alle Sarche	-	-	830	8	24
Comano	- . -	-	1,198	5½	29½
Ponte delle Arche	-	-	1,286	2	31½
Tione	- -	-	1,853	13	44½

(*Hotels at Trient and Comano ; Inns at Comano and Tione.*)

The road is hardly to be described as first-class, but it is at all events practicable, and is served by a motor diligence in summer.

The Fugazza.

Like the preceding route, this is partly Tyrolese and partly Italian. Though affording fine views it is very little known, being transverse to the usual main lines of travel; the road, in fact, is a connecting link between Rovereto, not far from the Lake of Garda, and Schio, whence there is a direct connection with Vicenza, Padua, and Venice. The itinerary is as follows :—

Place.	Altitude. (Feet.)	Intermediate Distances. (Kils.)	Progressive Totals. (Kils.)
Rovereto - - -	673	—	—
Spino - - -	1,280	4	4
Acheni - - -	1,788	4	8
Valmorbia - -	2,100	3	11·
Zocchio - - -	2,224	1	12
Anghebeni - -	2,067	$2\frac{1}{2}$	$14\frac{1}{2}$
Fochesi - - -	2,165	$1\frac{1}{2}$	16
Raossi - - -	2,398	2	18
Parocchia - - -	2,667	1	19
AustrianCustom-house	2,881	1	20
Ponte di Pietra - -	2,986	3	23
Inn - - - -	3,707	2	25
Summit - - -	*3,819*	1	26
Frontier - - -	3,786	$\frac{1}{2}$	$26\frac{1}{2}$
Hotel Dolomiti -	3,510	1	$27\frac{1}{2}$
Teza del Biasi - -	2,638	3	$30\frac{1}{2}$
Teza del Frane -	2,543	1	$31\frac{1}{2}$
La Tagliata - -	1,959	$1\frac{1}{2}$	33
S. Antonio - -	1,844	1	34
Italian Custom-house	1,342	$1\frac{1}{2}$	$35\frac{1}{2}$
Valli dei Signori -	1,158	2	$37\frac{1}{2}$
Torrebelvicino - -	869	$4\frac{1}{2}$	42
Schio - - -	630	4	46
Vicenza - - -	361	18	64

(*Hotels at Rovereto, Schio and Vicenza; inn at the 25th kilometre.*)

The road does not in any sense offer an uninterrupted rise, but is unusually undulating throughout, with an average gradient which is very slight; but, as is natural to expect in the circumstances, there are occasional short pitches which are steep, though in no sense formidable. In the way of a uniform rise, however, nothing is encountered until at a point three kilometres beyond the Austrian custom-house—namely, at the Ponte di Pietra; and from there to the inn the gradient is $10\frac{1}{2}$ per cent., followed by a slight rise to the summit. The descent, however, is steeper than on the average Tyrolean or Italian Alpine carriage-road, and from the summit to Valli dei Signori the gradients range from $7\frac{1}{2}$ to as much as 13 per cent., after which there is level running. The road, it may be added, is of about the same age as the Stelvio, having been completed in 1822, and it is interesting to note that it is traversed by motor diligences.

The Della Mauria.

Though this pass is really in Italy, it is on the extreme northern fringe of that country, and is in close contiguity to well-known Tyrolese resorts. As a matter of fact, it is a continuation of the road to Lake Misurina, and the itinerary throughout from Schluderbach, over the pass, and down to Udine is as follows:—

Place.	Altitude. (Feet.)	Intermediate Distances. (Kils.)	Progressive Totals. (Kils.)
Schluderbach (Austrian Customs) -	4,730	—	—
Frontier - - -	5,627	$4\frac{1}{2}$	$4\frac{1}{2}$
Misurina Hotel- -	5,761	$1\frac{1}{2}$	6
Al Palus (Italian Customs) - - -	3,648	$9\frac{1}{2}$	$15\frac{1}{2}$
Auronzo - - -	2,851	15	$30\frac{1}{2}$
Lozzo - - -	2,444	5	$35\frac{1}{2}$
Pelos - - -	2,581	1	$36\frac{1}{2}$
Summit - - -	4,262	$12\frac{1}{2}$	49
Vico - - -	2,976	9	58
Tredolo - - -	2,543	$9\frac{1}{2}$	$67\frac{1}{2}$
Ampezzo di Carnia -	1,837	12	$79\frac{1}{2}$
Socchieve - -	1,312	6	$85\frac{1}{2}$
Esemon - - -	1,286	$5\frac{1}{2}$	91
Villa Santina - -	862	2	93
Tolmezzo - - -	1,059	8	101
Amaro - - -	942	8	109
Stazione per la Carnia	853	4	113
Udine - - -	374	$38\frac{1}{2}$	$151\frac{1}{2}$

(*Hotels at Schluderbach, Misurina, Vico, Ampezzo and Udine.*)

It should be mentioned at the outset, however, that the road to the beautiful Lake of Misurina is narrow and difficult, and that, though there is no actual embargo against motor-cars, it is not an altogether desirable route. The best way, indeed, to reach the Della Mauria Pass is to start from Pieve di Cadore (*vide* Chapter XIV.), whence it is only 18 kilometres to Lozzo.

The road undulates from Pieve to Pelos, and then descends for a short distance before entering on the final ascent of 10 kilometres to the Della Mauria summit. It then descends by an easy gradient to Vico and undulates to Socchieve, whence there is a level run to Esemon. After a steep fall to Villa Santina there is again a level run to Stazione per la Carnia and Udine. The pass is pleasantly picturesque, but in effect, unless one is bound for Trieste, it merely provides an alternative route from the Tyrol to Venice in lieu of the Via Ampezzo itself, and is only likely to be used by those who have time to make a long stay in the Tyrol and explore its manifold attractions from end to end.

The Broccon and Gobera.

The road over these two new passes, which was only opened in the summer of 1910, affords a convenient means of making a round trip in south Tyrol without crossing the Italian frontier. We may assume, for example, that the tourist has crossed the San Lugano and Rolle passes,

and neither wishes to return on his tracks nor
to descend into Italy.   In this case he may leave
the Rolle road below Imer, and turn to the right
for the ascent of the Gobera Pass from Fiera di
Primiero, the itinerary being as follows : —

Place.		Altitude. (Feet.)	Intermediate Distances. (Kils.)	Progressive Totals. (Kils.)
Fiera di Primiero	-	2,346	—	—
Imer	-	2,133	5	5
Gobera Summit	-	*3,339*	3	8
Canal S. Bovo	-	2,490	$3\frac{1}{2}$	$11\frac{1}{2}$
Broccon Summit	-	*5,305*	21	$32\frac{1}{2}$
Castel Tesino -	-	2,887	13	$45\frac{1}{2}$
Bieno	-	2,856	$8\frac{1}{2}$	54
Strigno -	-	1,114	6	60
Alla Barricata Inn	-	980	2	62
Castelnuovo	-	1,010	$1\frac{1}{2}$	$63\frac{1}{2}$
Borgo	-	1,254	$4\frac{1}{2}$	68
Roncegno	-	2,000	5	73
Levico	-	1,542	14	87
Pergine	-	1,550	9	96
Trient	-	623	$11\frac{1}{2}$	$107\frac{1}{2}$

(*Hotels at Primiero, Roncegno, Levico, Pergine, and
Trient; Inns at Castel Tesino, Strigno, and Borgo.*)

As with all the new Tyrolean roads, the
maximum gradients do not exceed 8 per cent., and
the average is 4·8 per cent.   For the most part
the surface is excellent, while the road is fairly
wide, with liberal curves.   Strictly speaking, it is
not absolutely necessary to pass through Roncegno
on the way from Borgo to Levico.   Roncegno,
however, is the best place on the whole route for
a halt.   Tourists will find, moreover, in Dr. Alfonso
Waiz, who is the proprietor of the Grand and
Palace Hotels, one who is himself a keen automobilist and a mine of information on the subject

of motoring in the Tyrol. His was the first çar, I may add, to ascend the Broccon Pass after it was opened. It may also be mentioned here that those who wish to proceed to Venice will find the road from Roncegno to Padua an 'excellent, if not preferable, alternative to the more easterly route from Feltre referred to' elsewhere.

The Jaufen.

As with the case of the Dolomitenstrasse, the new road over the Jaufen Pass is a striking illustration of Tyrolese enterprise, and alike an object lesson to the whole civilised world. For it is yet another example of what road-building ought to be—namely, the making of a through route between more or less distant terminal points without regard to what may lie between. Here is no parochial method of linking two neighbouring villages by a road, and then waiting until another village has grown up before extending the highway; it is the needs of the through traveller which have primarily been considered.

A single glance at the map of the Tyrol, facing p. 129, will reveal at once the importance of the Jaufen Pass. It connects Sterzing, on the Brenner, with St. Leonhard, near Meran. The road between the two last-named towns has been in existence for some time, but is narrow and closed to motor traffic; in due course, however, it will be improved, following on the construction of the Jaufen road. When this route in its entirety is complete, travellers will have the option of passing from the Brenner to the Stelvio, or vice-versa, without the necessity of going round by Bozen. Every visitor, of course, to Tyrolese territory will need to go to Bozen for the sake of traversing the Brenner, Mendel, Dolomitenstrasse, Rolle, and other important passes already described; but no one can tour extensively among the Tyrolese passes without wishing to avoid, as far as possible, the unnecessary retracing of his tracks, and this boon is what the building of the Jaufen will confer, even if it were not worth visiting for its own sake. The date announced for its completion is July of the present year, 1911, while the widening of the Meran–St. Leonhard road will probably occupy another year. While road-making operations such as these are in progress, however, it is necessary for the tourist to make enquiries in the vicinity; when, for example, I crossed the Falzarego Pass it had only been opened a couple of days, and no one knew that it was actually ready until I arrived at Bozen itself.

That the Jaufen is worth crossing for its own sake, however, there can be no doubt. Its height alone commands attention, for it has an altitude of 6,869 feet, and is thus exceeded only by the Stelvio, Pordoi, and Falzarego among the passes of the Tyrol. It represents the last word in the art of road-building, for, great as is the height to be attained, the gradient never exceeds 6 per cent., while wherever zigzags occur they have easy, sweeping bends; the road, moreover, is of 17 feet width throughout, and of first-class surface. All this has been done in direct recognition of the importance of automobile traffic ; and no more striking example could be adduced of the difference between the Swiss and Austrian points of view.

As yet, of course, the itinerary lacks detail, as the villages have yet to come; suffice it to say that, for the present, the following are the only places to be mentioned :—

Place.	Altitude. (*Feet.*)	*Intermediate* Distances. (*Kils.*)	*Total* Distances. (*Kils.*)
Sterzing - - -	3,115	—	—
Gasteig - - -	4,281	4	4
Summit - - -	*6,869*	11	15
Walten - - -	4,141	12	27
St. Leonhard - -	2,230	9	36
Meran - - -	1,050	22	58

(*Hotels at Sterzing, St. Leonhard, and Meran.*)

The kilometric figures of the route between Gasteig and the summit, and thence to St. Leonhard, are only to be regarded as approximate, as official details are not yet forthcoming.

Forbidden Routes.

It has already been mentioned that motor-car traffic, save for Government purposes, is forbidden on the Eggenthal side of the Karer Pass. There are two other roads, however, on which automobile locomotion is not allowed within the Dolomite district. One is the Tre Croci Pass, between Schluderbach and the road down from Lake Misurina, and the other is the Campolungo Pass, which connects Arabba on the Pordoi route with Bruneck in the Pusterthal. It is permissible to drive over the summit (6,125 feet) to Corvara (5,110 feet), but the rest of the route is barred. Certain other roads in the Tyrol are also barred, but they are mostly much further east, and are — of relatively minor importance.

CHAPTER XXI.

THE MINOR FRENCH PASSES.

IT is a truism to say that France possesses the finest highways in the world, but though this fact is so well known it is often made the medium of erroneous deductions. Not by any means is it in quality of surface alone that French roads are supreme. Other countries have well-surfaced roads, if in less degree as to mileage; and there are parts even in England where, if quality were the only desideratum, the heart of the tourist would have nothing of which to complain.

The distinctive glory, however, of the French highway system is that it is national, not local, and that it provides a means of free locomotion in every direction from Paris to the uttermost confines of the country. The genius of the great Napoleon has left an imprint that will endure for all time. So all-embracing is the system of *routes nationales* which he established that, if every line of railway were to be uprooted in France to-morrow, the business of the nation would only be impeded to the extent of there not being enough motor-cars to go round; but the existing owners of large cars could proceed from any part of France to any other, however remote, in less time than any train could carry them, simply because of the construction of the roads from the point of view of through locomotion.

R

In England, on the contrary, no matter how powerful a car a man might possess, he could not hope to rival the train on an express route, such as from London to Glasgow, for the simple reason that British high-roads are too narrow and too tortuous to permit of speedy travelling. If the whole route were guarded by military, and not a single vehicle or person were allowed on the roadway, a man would still be unable to drive a car in England, or any other country save France, as comfortably and expeditiously as can be done on French roads even under ordinary conditions of traffic on any day of the week. Perfection of surface is only one factor in the making of a good road; its width, its straightness along the plains, and its scientific grading over rising ground, are even more important.

Strangely enough, however, Napoleon's prescience in this respect was marvellous and colossal, and almost it might be imagined that he had foreseen the advent of something very much speedier in the way of locomotion than the horsed vehicle; and, as his object in building his *grandes routes* was not merely to facilitate internal locomotion, but also to provide means for rapid transit to other countries, it naturally follows that the Alpine regions of France were not excluded from his wonder-working scheme. Despite the rise of the railway system, moreover, the good seed sown in Napoleon's time has been fructified by later generations, and we find as a result that the French Alps are as easy of access in almost every part, by means of magnificently constructed highways, as even the lowlands themselves, and that, on through routes to Switzerland and Italy, the Alps offer no obstruction whatever other than that of height.

To those unfamiliar with the distribution of the Alpine ranges it will presumably come as a revelation to learn that there are as many roads of high altitude in France (excluding those already dealt with) as the following list will show :—

	Altitude (Feet.)
Col du Parpaillon	8,694
Col du Galibier	8,399
Col d'Izouard	7,903
Col de la Cayolle	7,716
Col d'Allos	7,382
Col de Vars	6,939
Col des Champs	6,791
Col de Larche	6,545
Col du Glaudon	6,400
Col de la Viste	5,266
Colle St. Michel	4,938
Col des Aravis	4,915
Col des Montets	4,741
Col de Morgins	4,530
Col de Porte	4,429
Col de Maure	4,429
Col de la Faucille	4,331
Col d'Ornon	4,331
Col St. Jean (Dauphiné)	4,331
Col di Tenda	4,331
Col du Rousset	4,298
Col Bayard	4,117
Col du Labouret	4,042
Col du Cucheron	3,871
Col de Plainpalais	3,871
Col de la Croix-Haute	3,858
Col des Gets	3,845
Col du Frène (Grande Chartreuse)	3,818
Col St. Pierre	3,773
Col de Mégève	3,674
Col de Vergons	3,380
Col de Moriez	3,297
Col de Braus	3,281
Col de la Savine	3,248

	Altitude. (Feet.)
Col de la Faye - - - - -	3,232
Col du Frène (Bauges) - - - -	3,133
Col du Fau - - - - - -	2,986
Col de Leschaux - - - - -	2,966
Col de Brouis - - - - -	2,887
Col de Mont Sion - - - - -	2,592
Col du Pilon - - - - - -	2,575
Col de Vence - - - - -	2,461
Col de Castillon - - - - -	2,461
Col de Chatillon - - - - -	2,428
Col de Pérus - - - - -	2,165
Col de St. Jean (Nice) - - - -	2,116
Col du Chat - - - - -	2,100
Col de Nice - - - - - -	1,247

It should be noted that French territory extends into the Jura Mountains, and that two of the passes above named, the Col de la Savine and the Col de la Faucille, are not strictly Alpine. The Col di Tenda, moreover, in the Maritime Alps, is not in France but in Italy; it nevertheless forms a portion of *route nationale* No. 204 to Nice.

It will be seen at once that the list of minor French passes is very heavy, and from considerations of space it is impossible to deal with them individually at great length. I propose, therefore, to give the itineraries of each, but to reduce the descriptive portions of the text to minimum dimensions. It may be postulated in the first place, however, that the majority of the roads are of good surface, and well graded; where the case is otherwise the fact will be mentioned accordingly. So far as the routes are concerned, some of the passes must be taken willy-nilly if it is desired to reach this or that town; others are off a main line of route, but

are worth traversing for their own sakes; others combine great picturesqueness with necessity as regards direction; while the crossing of others may be regarded as a purely sporting experience.

One word of caution may be enjoined at the outset. The French standard of roads is so high, and the country has so many broad plains, across which *routes nationales* run in perfectly straight lines for miles at a time, that local opinion has often to be taken with a grain of salt. In any town or village which marks the beginning of a pass route, the tourist is likely to be told that the road is both difficult and bad, simply because the inhabitants base their standard upon that of the *routes nationales*. If he has the good sense not to be affrighted by what he is told on the spot, he will probably find that the gradients are easy, that the surface is mostly good, and that the corners are not particularly acute; and, after crossing that particular pass, he will have so greatly enjoyed both the scenery and the driving experience alike as to congratulate himself very heartily on not having been dissuaded from his purpose.

The Cols de la Savine and de la Faucille.

The French Alps, as has already been explained in an earlier chapter, extend from the confines of Geneva to the Riviera, but high ground is to be found even further north, though not in the Alps but in the Juras. The majority of tourists bound for a cruise among the Alpine passes will probably make for Geneva in the first instance, and therefore the mountain ridges which would be the first to be crossed would be the Jura passes of the Col de la Savine and the Col de la Faucille. For the sake of convenience, therefore, we will ignore the technical distinction between the Juras and the Alps, and regard the two passes named as Alpine routes.

They offer an excellent breaking in to motor mountaineering. It is enough to mention that the roads were built by Napoleon to imply that they are superexcellent in quality, as to surface, width, and gradient alike. Following the grand high road from Dijon to Geneva, we enjoy a splendid run as far as Poligny, where the ascent of the Col de la Savine may be said to begin, and the itinerary from here to Geneva is as follows:—

Place.	Altitude. (Feet.)	Intermediate Distances. (Kils.)	Progressive Totals. (Kils.)
Poligny - - -	—	—	—
Champagnole - -	—	22	22
St. Laurent - -	3,001	22	44
Col de la Savine -	*3,248*	$4\frac{1}{2}$	$48\frac{1}{2}$
Valet - - -	—	$1\frac{1}{2}$	50
Morbier - - -	—	$2\frac{1}{2}$	$52\frac{1}{2}$
Morez - - -	2,247	$2\frac{1}{2}$	55
Gouland - - -	—	6	61
Les Rousses (French Customs) - -	3,740	$3\frac{1}{2}$	$64\frac{1}{2}$
La Cure (Fork to Col de St. Cergues) -	—	$2\frac{1}{2}$	67
Col de la Faucille -	*4,331*	16	83
La Maladière - -	—	$7\frac{1}{2}$	$90\frac{1}{2}$
Gex - - -	1,985	$3\frac{1}{2}$	94
Cessy - - -	—	$2\frac{1}{2}$	$96\frac{1}{2}$
Segney - - -	1,542	$2\frac{1}{2}$	99
Ornex - - -	1,578	3	102
Ferney - - -	1,444	$1\frac{1}{2}$	$103\frac{1}{2}$
Frontier - - -	1,362	$2\frac{1}{2}$	106
Grand Saconnex (Swiss Customs) -	1,525	1	107
Geneva - - -	1,247	4	111

(Hotels at Poligny, Champagnole, St. Laurent, Morez, Les Rousses, Gex and Geneva.)

A MOTOR DILIGENCE ASCENDING TO THE COL DE LA FAUCILLE.
(*Note the excellence of the road.*)

The road winds through woods to St. Laurent, whence there is a drop of nearly two kilometres, followed by a rise of three kilometres to the summit, the steepest gradient being only 7 per cent. The Jura mountains have meanwhile begun to open out, with fine vistas. An enjoyable descent follows to Morez, where the ascent of the Col de la Faucille is begun. It represents a rise of eight kilometres to Les Rousses, with a gradient in parts of 8 per cent., though the average is much less. At Les Rousses one must be careful not to miss the French custom-house, which is on the right in the middle of the town. At La Cure, two kilometres beyond Les Rousses, we take the right-hand turn at the fork, the road to the left leading into Switzerland over the Col de St. Cergues. There is a slight rise of three kilometres, followed by almost level running to the summit of the Col de la Faucille.

Then comes a grand drop to Geneva, the first portion of which has short sections of 9 per cent. The road is carved in beautiful windings on the hill-side, and soon brings into view a truly glorious prospect of the spacious lake of Geneva, with a chain of Alps, and, on a clear day, the famed Dent du Midi at the far end of the lake. As a foretaste of what delights may be derived from cruising by motor-car over still loftier roads, this journey is perhaps the very best that could be taken.

Of its type it is impossible to speak too highly of the view from the Col de la Faucille; and, having crossed it in both directions, I cannot say which is the more enchanting, the view as first

THE WINDINGS OF THE FAUCILLE ROAD, WITH THE LAKE OF GENEVA BEYOND.

seen when coming from the west, or when taken retrogressively as a farewell glimpse on the return journey. One way or the other, however, the Col de la Faucille should certainly be crossed.

On the way down from the summit a motor diligence will probably be met—one of the many which ply on the French Alpine roads, and which at once dismiss any idea of the impracticability of motor mountaineering. If a heavily laden diligence can ascend Alpine gradients, it should be but short work for a relatively light touring car, probably with a far more powerful engine, and with four or five passengers at most, to tackle anything which the great Alpine carriage-roads present in the way of gradients or corners.

At Gex, 11 kilometres below the summit, care must be taken to find the continuation of the road to Geneva, as there are two divergent routes. The remainder of the descent is slight, with sundry undulations to Grand Saconnex, where the Swiss custom-house has to be dealt with. Bear in mind that mid-European time has now come into play, and that the custom-house is supposed to close at six o'clock. If you have made the journey in the afternoon, however, you may not only be a little late, but also an hour out of your reckoning. I do not know how late it is possible to get through, but in my own case I passed at about 7.15 p.m. by mid-European time, and got my triptyque stamped on payment of a fine of 1 franc 50 c.

A run of four kilometres from the custom-house brings one into Geneva. To those who have occasion to take this journey in the opposite direction, I may proffer the advice not to fill up their tanks with petrol at Geneva.   Just beyond the custom-house at Grand Saconnex, and inside French territory, petrol can be obtained at a very much lower price than is possible in Geneva itself.

The Col Du Mont Sion.

We have now to consider a number of high roads among the Alps of Savoy and Dauphiny, and· will first deal with those lying between Geneva and Grenoble.   Here is the itinerary of the road over the Col du Mont Sion :—

Place.	Altitude. (Feet.)	Intermediate Distances. (Kils.)	Progressive Totals. (Kils.)
Geneva - - -	1,243	—	—
Frontier (Swiss Customs) - - -	—	8	8
St. Julien - -	—	1	9
La Chable - -	—	6	15
Summit - · -	2,592	3	18
Jussy - - -	—	2	20
Cruseilles · -	2,576	5	25
Pont de la Caille -	2,428	3	28
Allonzier (French Customs) - -	—	$2\frac{1}{2}$	$30\frac{1}{2}$
Pringy - - -	—	$7\frac{1}{2}$	38
Annecy - - -	1,476	6	44

(*Hotels at Geneva, St. Julien, and Annecy.*)

As will be seen, it does not boast any great height, but is on an essentially interesting route. The city of Geneva should be left by the bridge over the Rhone, and at the first fork the left-hand road should be taken for St. Julien.   At the next fork the Annecy road on the left should be followed.   It is fine and broad, and rises with a gradient nowhere exceeding. 6 per cent. to

the summit of the Col du Mont Sion, which
affords pleasant views, if not on a grandiose scale.
A slight descent follows to Jussy, where the
road swings to the left and rises slightly to
Cruseilles, at which point it is •only 16 feet lower
than the Col du Mont Sion.

A moderately steep descent of three kilometres
follows to the Pont de la Caille, a particularly fine
suspension bridge spanning a deep ravine. At
the opposite end is situated the custom-house,
where the *douaniers* are for some reason more
pertinacious in examining baggage than elsewhere.
A nearly level stretch of four kilometres follows;
after which there is a run down of five kilometres, and then a level run into Annecy.
Meanwhile, at a point 10 kilometres from the
first custom-house, another will be encountered,
at which it is necessary to show one's papers a
second time, though only for a momentary inspection.

Annecy is a fine old town, and the chief in
Savoy. It is surrounded by mountains, and is
situated at the north end of the placid Lac
d'Annecy, which is nine miles in length. A road
winds along the whole of its western bank, and
leads to Ugines and Albertville; but for the
continuation of our present route we turn to the
right in Annecy, and then to the left at the fork,
proceeding over an undulating road to Alby.
There is a steep rise out of this town, followed by
undulations to Albens, Aix-les-Bains and Chambéry. Aix-le-Bains, of course, is always worth
visiting in the season, being a place of much
gaiety, and pleasantly situated near the Lac du

Bourget. Throughout this entire route the road-surfaces are excellent.

The Cols du Frène (Grande Chartreuse), Du Cucheron, De Porte, and De Vence.

This quartette of passes, quite apart from any others, would serve to show the folly of travelling along the plains when alternative mountain routes are available. From Chambéry to Grenoble there

THE DENT DU GRANIER, AS SEEN FROM THE
COL DU FRÈNE.

are two *routes nationales*, pleasant enough in their way, but not to be compared for picturesqueness with the route over the intervening ranges of hills midway between the two. Yet such is French human nature that everyone in Chambéry will do his best to dissuade the tourist from crossing this very modest series of passes, albeit the road is good almost throughout, while neither

gradients nor corners are difficult. The following
is the itinerary :—

Place.	Altitude. (Feet.)	Intermediate Distances. (Kils.)	Progressive Totals. (Kils.)
Chambéry - - -	886	—	—
Savons - - -	—	6	6
Pont du Var - -	—	1	7
Tunnel - - -	2,838	2	9
Inn - - - -	—	1	10
Col du Frène -	*3,818*	5	15
Entremont-le-Vieux -	2,756	4	19
St. Pierre d'Entremont	2,100	5	24
Chenevez - - -	2,526	2	26
Les Vialles - -	3,117	4	30
Col du Cucheron -	*3,871*	2	32
St. Pierre de Chartreuse	2,887	3½	35½
La Chartreuse road fork - - -	2,559	1½	37
La Martinière - -	2,920	2	39
Col de Porte - -	*4,429*	6	45
Le Sappet - -	3,150	5	50
Col de Vence - -	*2,461*	4	54
Corene - - -	—	3	57
La Tronche - -	—	3	60
Grenoble - - -	689	2	62

(*Hotels at Chambéry, St. Pierre de Chartreuse, Col de Vence
and Grenoble.*)

Particular care should be taken at Chambéry
to ask for the road over the Col du Frène, and
not simply for Grenoble, or people will just
point out one or the other of the valley roads.
The right exit having been found, however, and
the ascent having been begun, care must again
be taken to turn to the right a short way up.
The road thenceforward is not difficult to follow.
It ascends fairly steeply—averaging from 6 to
8 per cent. for the most part, but with one brief
stretch of 13 per cent.—for nine kilometres,
where a short tunnel is passed through at the
Pas de la Fosse.

Not only are there fine views from this point, but very soon afterwards a complete change of scene is unfolded, and a range of snow-capped peaks appears to the south-east, while to the south towers the huge square-topped mountain known as the Dent du Granier. The gradient moderates for a couple of kilometres, and then in less than four more, averaging 8 per cent., the summit is attained, this final stage being

THE ERSTWHILE MONASTERY OF LA GRANDE CHARTREUSE.

mostly through a wood. From the summit an extensive panorama may be enjoyed. A run down of 10 kilometres follows, through Entremont-le-Vieux to St. Pierre d'Entremont, over a surface that is better than on the Chambéry side.

At St. Pierre d'Entremont avoid the road to the right, and, after continuing straight on for a short distance, swing round to the left, and so enter upon the Col du Cucheron, which is one of eight kilometres, with a gradient in parts of 10 per cent. The surface is better than that over the Col du Frène. Like the ascent, the descent to St. Pierre de Chartreuse is wooded all the way, and at two points is as steep as 11 per cent. It is from St. Pierre de Chartreuse that a road ascends on the right in four kilometres to the famous Chartreuse monastery, which is no longer, however, occupied by the monks of liqueur-making fame.

It is not difficult to trace the road over the Col de Porte, as indications are provided which are unmistakable, whereas at St. Pierre d'Entremont, without the directions given above, the road to the Col du Cucheron would be by no means easy to locate. The ascent of the Col de Porte is one of eight kilometres, and is practically identical in steepness with its immediate predecessor. The road winds up a wooded valley, with several changes of view, all of which are interesting and well reward the climb.

Then follows a descent of 17 kilometres, which gradually grows more and more picturesque, until at the Col de Vence the great valley of Grenoble is unfolded, with its magnificent environment of peaks. Even if every yard from Chambéry to here had been uninviting, the journey would have been worth taking for the sake of this final stage, which is of a character which would be entirely lost to a traveller along the plains.

The Col de Leschaux and the Col de Plainpalais.

The only inducement to follow the route from Annecy to Chambéry is that of seeing Aix-les-

Bains, but there is an alternative which leads over the mountains and affords finer prospects accordingly. The itinerary is as follows :—

Place.	Altitude. (Feet.)	Intermediate Distances. (Kils.)	Progressive Totals. (Kils.)
Annecy - - -	1,476	—	—
Letraz - - -	—	4	4
Sévrier - - -	1,526	1	5
Machevaz - -	—	4	9
Col de Leschaux -	*2,966*	8	17
Glapigny - -	—	3½	20½
Route de Bellecombe	—	2	22½
Route d'Aix - -	—	1	23½
Route du Chatelard -	1,936	1½	25
Lescheraines · - -	2,165	1	26
Le Mont - - -	2,707	3½	29½
Le Noyer - -	—	2	31½
Col du Plainpalais -	*3,871*	5	36½
Plainpalais - -	—	1	37½
Pont de la Jacco -	—	1	38½
Les Deserts - -	2,969	2	40½
St. Jean d'Arvey -	1,903	5½	46
Tunnel - - -	1,608	2½	48½
Villaret - - -	1,033	1½	50
Chambéry - -	886	3½	53½

(*Hotels at Annecy, Lescheraines and Chambéry.*)

The west bank of the lake of Annecy is followed for five kilometres, and there, instead of taking the left at the fork for Albertville, we keep to the right, and ascend to the Col de Leschaux by an easy gradient in 12 kilometres. The road rises high above the Gorge of Aiguedon, and commands fine retrospective views of the Annecy lake. A quick run down of seven kilometres follows, shortly after which the ascent of the Col du Plainpalais is begun.

For three or four kilometres it averages from 6 to 8 per cent., undulates for two more kilometres, and then rises steeply, with one slight break, to the summit, the gradient being in places as much as 10 per cent. Though the summit itself is not striking, the ascent is picturesque. The descent to Chambéry, in 17 kilometers, is mostly steep, and at one point is as stiff as 12 per cent., or 1 in 8½. The road throughout is less good and wide, of course, than the *route nationale*, but is adequate, and the owner of a good car need not hesitate as to which he should follow where picturesqueness is the chief objective.

The Col du Chat.

A favourite excursion from Chambéry or Aix-les-Bains is that over the Col du Chat, which may either be used as a morning's excursion, out and home, or as a cross route to Yenne by the following itinerary :—

Place.	Altitude. (Feet.)	Intermediate Distances. (Kils.)	Progressive Totals. (Kils.)
Chambéry - - -	886	—	—
Le Bourget - -	787	10	10
Hotel de la Dent du Chat - - -	—	7	17
Col du Chat - -	*2,100*	1	18
St. Jean de Chevelu	1,017	4	22
Yenne - - -	787	5½	27½

(*Hotels at Chambéry, Le Bourget, and below the Col.*)

The road is level to Le Bourget, and then rises in zigzags to the summit, with gradients ranging from 4 to 9 per cent. The Col du Chat takes its name from the neighbouring mountain, the Dent du Chat, which towers above it on the left. Though the Col is only 2,100 feet high, it affords fine views of the Lac de Bourget and the neighbouring mountains. If the journey be continued to Yenne the gradients on the descent to St. Jean de Chevelu will be found similar to those on the Le Bourget side, followed by an easy run to Yenne. From Yenne one may either proceed. to Geneva, or to Ruffieux and follow the east bank of the Lac de Bourget to Aix-les-Bains.

The Col du Frène (Bauges).

In addition to the Col du Frène already mentioned above, there is another Savoyan mountain road of the same name in the district of Bauges. It is not on any main line of route, however, and merely provides an opportunity for an excursion from Aix-les-Bains or Annecy. From the latter town the first portion of the journey would cross the Col de Leschaux (q.v., p. 268); but instead of continuing over the Col du Plainpalais the left-hand road would have to be taken at the bridge of Bange. From Aix-les-Bains, however, the itinerary is as follows:—

Place.	Altitude. (Feet.)	Intermediate Distances. (Kils.)	Progressive Totals. (Kils.)
Aix-les-Bains -	850	—	—
Grésy-sur-Aix -	—	5	5
Cusy -	—	9½	14½
Pont de Bange -	—	6	20½
Pont de la Charniat -	—	3	23½
Le Rocher -	—	3½	27
Le Chatelard -	2,477	3	30
Pont d'Ecorchevel -	2,198	1	31
École -	—	3½	34½
Summit -	*3,133*	8½	43
La Plantar -	—	4	47
St. Pierre d'Albigny -	1,345	2½	49½
Junction with Petit St. Bernard Road -	—	3	52½

(*Hotels at Aix-les-Bains, Le Chatelard, and St. Pierre d'Albigny.*)

Leaving Aix-les-Bains in a northerly direction, we proceed for about three kilometres and take the right-hand road at the fork, and then proceed through Grésy-sur-Aix on gradually rising ground. At four kilometres from Grésy the road grows steeper, and continues to rise until, at $2\frac{1}{2}$ kilometres short of Cusy, there is a level stretch. A gentle rise of over two kilometres beyond Cusy is followed by a descent of $3\frac{1}{2}$ kilometres to the Pont de Bange, after which the road rises and falls to the Pont de la Charniat.

A rise of six kilometres follows to Le Chatelard, a small town which is growing in popularity as a centre for excursions. Then follows a moderately steep drop to the bridge of Ecorchevel, from which there is a rise of 12 kilometres to the summit, mostly of inappreciable gradient, but as steep as 8 per cent. in the penultimate kilometre. The view from the summit is decidedly attractive, as it commands a wide prospect over the broad plains in which the Arc and the Isère join forces on the Petit St. Bernard road.

From the summit the road winds, with about a dozen zigzags, through St. Pierre d'Albigny, with a gradient of 7 to 11 per cent., and continues to fall rather less steeply to the junction of the Petit St. Bernard road, five kilometres west of Pont Royal, where the Petit St. Bernard and Mt. Cenis routes diverge. The road throughout from Aix-les-Bains is of good width, and the scenery quite picturesque enough to justify the excursion.

The Col de Morgins.

Known sometimes by the name given above, and at others as the Col d'Abondance, this road

PASSES OF HAUTE SAVOIE AND SAVOIE, WITH THE
ST. BERNARD.

leads from Thonon, on the south side of Lac Léman, to Monthey, in the Rhone Valley, not far from Martigny; but the latter portion is, unfortunately, in Swiss territory, and is barred to motor vehicles. As in many other cases, however, we have an illustration of Swiss stupidity in preventing a through route being utilised by an automobilist without any rhyme or reason. So far as concerns the French portion of the route, it terminates a kilometre below the summit, and the pass itself may be reached either from Evian or Thonon, while the journey from the latter town is worth taking because the road leads through the picturesque gorges of La Dranse. The itinerary is as follows:—

Place.	Altitude. (Feet.)	Intermediate Distances. (Kils.)	Progressive Totals. (Kils.)
Thonon - - -	1,411	—	—
Fork (road to Evian)	2,592	18	18
Abondance - -	—	$11\frac{1}{2}$	$29\frac{1}{2}$
La Chapelle - -	3,315	$6\frac{1}{2}$	36
Chatel - - -	—	$5\frac{1}{2}$	$41\frac{1}{2}$
Vonne - - -	—	1	$42\frac{1}{2}$
Frontier - - -	—	2	$44\frac{1}{2}$
Summit - - -	4,530	1	$45\frac{1}{2}$
Morgins (Swiss Customs) - - -	—	1	$46\frac{1}{2}$
Trois-Torrents - -	2,494	10	$56\frac{1}{2}$
Monthey - - -	1,362	5	$61\frac{1}{2}$

(*Hotels at Thonon, Abondance, Morgins, and Monthey.*)

There is no gradient exceeding 6 per cent. between Thonon and the fork where the Evian road joins in, and from there the ascent is almost imperceptible to Abondance, a pleasantly situated town with about 1,500 inhabitants, and continues easy to La Chapelle, beyond which, however, it is rather steeper, amounting in places to 9 per cent.

A kilometre below the summit, amid pine woods, is a small lake, and the frontier line is crossed here, but the road rises another 50 feet or so before reaching its highest point, which is in Swiss territory. The village of Morgins, a kilometre lower down, is a summer station, and the seat of the Swiss customs. From there a winding descent of 17 kilometres leads to Monthey, with a gradient of 10 per cent. in parts. The road surfaces throughout are mostly good, and, as in other cases of the kind, it is regrettable that the senseless embargo should prevail on the Swiss side.

The Cols des Gets and de Chatillon.

In the ordinary way the tourist bound for Chamonix by road will proceed either from Geneva or from Chambéry and Albertville; but anyone staying on the south side of Lac Léman may make Thonon his starting point instead of Geneva, and proceed over the two Cols named above, by the following itinerary :—

Place.	Altitude. (Feet.)	Intermediate Distances. (Kils.)	Progressive Totals. (Kils.)
Thonon - - -	1,411	—	—
Le Jotty - - -	2,297	15	15
Pont de Gys - -	2,133	2½	17½
St. Jean d'Aulph -	2,526	7½	25
Les Gets (*Col des Gets*)	*3,845*	12	37
Pont des Gets - -	3,199	4½	41½
Taninges - - -	2,100	6½	48
Bridge over River Giffre	2,018	1½	49½
Col de Chatillon -	*2,428*	2½	52
Cluses - - -	1,591	6½	58½
Sallanches - -	1,837	15½	74
Le Fayet - - -	1,936	7	81
Tunnel - - -	2,641	6½	87½
Les Montées - -	2,838	3	90½
Chamonix - -	3,412	10½	101

(*Hotels at Thonon, Les Gets, Taninges, Cluses, Sallanches, Le Fayet and Chamonix.*)

This itinerary is chiefly interesting as forming the initial stage of the projected " Grande Route des Alpes," about which further details will be found in Chapter XXVI. The road to Les Gets is a *route nationale*, and is both wide and of excellent surface. The gradients are easy to inappreciable all the way to the village of Les Gets, which constitutes the summit, and was founded in the fourteenth century by Jews expelled from Tuscany. The village is very pleasantly situated amid woods and grassy slopes.

There is nothing steeper than 7 per cent. on the descent to Taninges, where the direct route from Geneva, 39 kilometres away by St. Jeoire, is joined. The rise to the Col de Chatillon averages 2 to 6 per cent., and, though low in altitude, affords a fine outlook. A winding descent follows to Cluses, where an alternative road from Geneva (40½ kilometres), comes in on the right. The gradients average from 3 to 7 per cent., after which the road is level to Sallanches. From there to Le Fayet is also level, followed by a moderate rise to the tunnel, with easy running over the remainder of the journey to Chamonix.

The Col des Aravis.

This pass occurs in the course of the cross-country journey from Annecy to Chamonix. It has more than ordinary claims to picturesqueness, and should certainly be taken if one's programme will permit. The pass itself lies between St. Jean de Sixt and Flumet. So far as the connecting link is concerned, however, from Annecy to St. Jean de Sixt, the itinerary is as follows :—

Place.			Altitude. (Feet.)	Intermediate Distances. (Kils.)	Progressive Totals. (Kils.)
Annecy	-	-	1,476	—	—
Veyrier	-	-	1,558	5	5
Bluffy	-	-	2,100	5	10
Thônes	-	-	1,051	11	21
Pont des Villards	-	2,165	2	23
Les Villards	-	2,444	1½	24½
St. Jean de Sixt	-	3,149	4½	29

(*Hotels at Annecy, Thônes and St. Jean de Sixt.*)

Up to the Villards bridge there is no gradient of any particular moment, but the rise to St. Jean de Sixt ranges from 4 to 8 per cent.

The road over the Col des Aravis is by the following itinerary :—

Place.			Altitude. (Feet.)	Intermediate Distances. (Kils.)	Progressive Totals. (Kils.)
St. Jean de Sixt	-	3,149	—	—
Brunier	-	-	—	1	1
La Clusaz	-	-	3,412	2	3
Inn	-	-	—	7	10
Summit	-	-	*4,915*	1	11
Tunnel	-	-	—	1	12
La Giettaz	-	-	3,642	4½	16½
Tunnel	-	-	3,330	4½	21
Flumet	-	-	3,008	2	23

(*Hotels at St. Jean de Sixt, La Clusaz, La Giettaz and Flumet.*)

For the most part the gradients are from 6 to 8 per cent., with seven bends between La Clusaz and the summit. Though the road is not particularly wide, however, the curves are not abrupt, and, as a matter of fact, a motor diligence plies over this route. The views from the summit, and on the downward run to Flumet, are particularly fine, commanding as they do the entire

Mont Blanc range, which is tantamount to saying that the scenery is amongst the most magnificent in the Alps.

The Col de Mégève.

This is another of the various routes which lead to Chamonix, the connection in this case being at Albertville on the Petit St. Bernard Pass. The itinerary is as follows:—

Place.	Altitude. (Feet.)	Intermediate Distances. (Kils.)	Progressive Totals. (Kils.)
Albertville	1,115	—	—
Fork to Annecy	1,345	8	8
Flumet	3,008	14	22
Mégève (*Col de Mé-gève*)	3,674	$9\frac{1}{2}$	$31\frac{1}{2}$
Combloux	3,314	5	$36\frac{1}{2}$
St. Gervais	2,707	9	$45\frac{1}{2}$
Le Fayet	1,936	$3\frac{1}{2}$	49

(*Hotels at Albertville, Flumet, Mégève, St. Gervais, and Le Fayet.*)

The road is normally good, though needing repair. After 10 kilometres of level running it rises easily to near Flumet, with a slight dip before the town is reached. After three kilometres of ascent the road is nearly level to Mégève. Mégève itself is charmingly situated, and an excellent centre for excursions. Magnificent views of Mont Blanc and the Valley of the Arve are forthcoming on the descent to Combloux and St. Gervais, while the gradients are very easy. At Le Fayet one joins the road to Chamonix from the Col de Chatillon.

The Col du Rousset.

Whether or not one's itinerary may render it desirable to proceed over the Col du Rousset and down to Die, the first portion, or north side, of

the pass constitutes a favourite excursion from
Pont-en-Royans, inasmuch as the town is within
close touch of the famous gorges of the Petits
and Grands Goulets. Pont-en-Royans itself is situated 56 kilometres to the south-west of Grenoble,
by way of Sassenage and Villard-de-Lans, and
on this route also are some fine gorges—namely,
those of Engins and de la Bourne. From Pont-en-
Royans, an ancient and exceedingly picturesque
town, the itinerary is as follows:—

Place.	Altitude. (Feet.)	Intermediate Distances. (Kils.)	Progressive Totals. (Kils.)
Pont-en-Royans -	738	—	—
Ste. Eulalie - -	—	$3\frac{1}{2}$	$3\frac{1}{2}$
Les Baraques - -	2,198	$10\frac{1}{2}$	14
La Chapelle-en-Vercors	2,986	6	20
St. Agnau - -	2,575	4	24
Les Chaberts - -	2,739	$4\frac{1}{2}$	$28\frac{1}{2}$
Rousset - - -	3,035	3	$31\frac{1}{2}$
Exit of Tunnel - -	4,298	7	$38\frac{1}{2}$
Chamaloc - - -	1,706	$14\frac{1}{2}$	53
Die - - - -	1,212	$5\frac{1}{2}$	$58\frac{1}{2}$

(*Hotels at Pont-en-Royans, Les Baraques, and Die.*)

The gorge of the Petits Goulets is situated
just beyond Ste. Eulalie, the road running above
the ravine through a series of tunnels 500 feet
above the river Vernaison, which winds through
the gorge. An ascent follows, averaging 3 to 7
per cent., to Les Baraques, and passing through
the higher gorge known as the Grands Goulets.
    The road is carved on the hillside, with
frequent tunnels hewn out of the solid rock,
high above the river, and in its general characteristics strongly resembles the first stage of the
Petit St. Bernard route, in the neighbourhood
of the Sieix tunnels. From Les Baraques the

gradient continues about the same to La Chapelle, after which there is a fall to St. Agnan, followed by a gentle rise to the hamlet of Rousset, from which there is a rise of a little over six kilometres, round four hairpin corners, with a gradient of 7 per cent. to the entrance of the tunnel which passes beneath the summit. This tunnel is no less that 612 metres in length, and

ONE OF THE TUNNELS IN THE GORGE OF LES GRANDS GOULETS.

has been built owing to the exposed nature of the actual summit.

A picturesque descent follows, with a dozen zigzags, to Chamaloc; the gradients, however, do not exceed 6 per cent. After a slight rise from the village there is a fall of three kilometres, followed by a short level run into Die—a thermal station, and the centre of many excursions.

The Col des Montets.

This is merely a short excursion from Chamonix, and constitutes the first stage of the

Col de la Forclaz route to Martigny. The itinerary is as follows:—

Place.			Altitude. (Feet.)	Intermediate Distances. (Kils.)	Progressive Totals. (Kils.)
Chamonix	-	-	3,412	—	—
Le Praz	-	-	—	2	2
Les Tines	-	-	3,756	2	4
Les Iles	-	-	—	2	6
Argentière	-	-	4,052	2	8
Trélechant	-	-	—	$2\frac{1}{2}$	$10\frac{1}{2}$
Summit	-	-	4,741	$\frac{1}{2}$	11
Le Nant	-	-	4,265	3	14
Vallorcine	-	-	—	2	16
Le Chatelard	-	-	3,691	2	18

(*Hotels at Chamonix, Le-Praz, Les Tines, and Argentière.*)

On the picturesqueness of Chamonix it is needless to expatiate here; suffice it to say that it is one of the most beautifully situated villages in the world. The road to the Col des Montets runs parallel with the Mont Blanc range, passing all the famous Aiguilles in turn, and rising gently to Argentière, where the gradient grows steeper, and at one point reaches 9 per cent. It is hardly worth while to go beyond the summit, but it may be mentioned that there is a run down of seven kilometres to Le Chatelard, of from 3 to 8 per cent. The continuation of the route over the Col de la Forclaz and down to Martigny, being in Swiss territory, is barred to motor-cars. Further reference to that pass, however, will be found in the chapter on the Swiss routes.

The Col du Galibier.

Especial interest attaches to this road by reason that it is the highest carriage road of fair quality in France, and only exceeded in the whole

of Europe by the Stelvio itself.   It is true that
the Col du Parpaillon, which is also in France,
is 141 feet higher than the Galibier, but though
it is not impracticable, and has occasionally been
crossed, it can hardly be recommended for purposes
of ordinary touring as a normal carriage road.

Few tourists, however, will find it convenient
to drive over the Galibier Pass from end to end,

THE GALIBIER TUNNEL, LAUTARET SIDE.

unless they return on their tracks and make the
journey twice over.   It is merely a cross route
between the two main high roads of the Col du
Lautaret and the Mont Cenis.   If the former be
quitted, therefore, in order to cross the Galibier,
the eastern side of the Lautaret and the pass
over Mont Genèvre would have to be missed
entirely ; while, if one ascended the Galibier
from the north, it would be impossible to cross
the Mont Cenis Pass, and one of the most

enjoyable drives available for the motorist would thus be missed.

The Galibier road may be traversed in its entirety, however, by any one making excursions with Grenoble as a centre, in which case the Lautaret road should be ascende l to the summit, and descended for a couple of kilometres on the other side. A narrow road will then be perceived on the left, and this is the entrance to the Galibier route, of which the itinerary is as follows:—

Place.	Altitude. (Feet.)	Intermediate Distances. (Kils.)	Progressive Totals. (Kils.)
Junction with Lautaret road	6,480	—	—
La Mandette	7,415	2	2
Tunnel	8,530	3½	5½
Châlets du Galibier	7,546	3½	9
Plan Lacha	6,381	5	14
Barricade des Pestiférés	5,381	3½	17
Le Verney	5,118	2½	20
Serroz	—	1	21
Valloire	4,593	1½	22½
Les Granges	—	1½	24
Le Clos	5,036	1	25
Telegraph Tunnel	5,102	2	27
La Léchère	4,347	4	31
Pont Lancélot	3,543	3	34
St. Martin d'Arc	—	4	38
St. Michel de Maurienne	2,329	1	39

(*Hotels at Valloire and St. Michel.*)

The ascent is one of six kilometres only, but the gradients are steeper than on the main routes, inasmuch as they average from 11 to 14 per cent. over the first three kilometres, and 9 to 11 per cent. over the remainder. There are about a dozen "hairpin" corners which are somewhat acute, but cars with really good locks can round them without reversing. The road generally is somewhat narrow, and often none too good in quality, while at times its nearness to the precipice's edge makes some amount of demand upon the nerves of the driver. Naturally, however, at such an altitude the views available are extremely picturesque, and even tourists proceeding directly into Italy by the Lautaret and Mont Genèvre should make a point of at least ascending the southern side and returning to the main road.

THE GALIBIER TUNNEL, ST. MICHEL SIDE.

The road traveller does not actually cross the Col, as a tunnel is bored through the mountain at a point 190 feet below the summit. It is worth one's while, however, to leave the car and go up to the Col for the sake of enjoying the ample panorama. The drive through the tunnel requires care, as the surface is invariably greasy.

On the descending side there is a gradient of 9 to 10 per cent. for six kilometres, followed by a brief drop of 13 per cent., and then comes nine kilometres of varying gradient to Valloire, the steepest portions being 10 per cent. From Valloire the road rises for four kilometres to the telegraph tunnel, from which there is a descent of 12 kilometres to the foot of the pass at St. Michel de Maurienne, with gradients of from 6 to 9 per cent. It is regrettable that the journey does not come conveniently within the scope of a comprehensive tour, as it not only affords magnificent mountain views, but passes through smiling prairies and ravines of much attractiveness.

The Col Bayard.

This route leads through the heart of the Dauphiné, and is one that may be taken as a sporting experience by tourists on the way to the Riviera when the spring season is far advanced. Later, of course, the Côte d'Azur will be unbearably hot, while in the winter all the mountain roads will be snow-bound. The Col Bayard lies on the road from Grenoble to Gap, and the itinerary is as under:—

Place.	Altitude. (Feet.)	Intermediate Distances. (Kils.)	Progressive Totals. (Kils.)
Grenoble - - -	689	—	—
Vizille - - -	919	17	17
Laffrey - - -	3,051	7½	24½
St. Théoffrey - -	—	7½	32
La Mure - - -	2,904	6	38
Pont Haut - -	2,001	4½	42½
Les Egats - -	2,805	4½	47
La Salle - - -	2,526	3	50
Quet - - -	2,986	4½	54½
Corps - - -	3,068	8½	63
Le Motty - -	2,575	5½	68½
La Trinité - -	2,543	2	70½
Chauffayer - , -	3,018	3½	74

GRENOBLE, WITH THE ALPS BEYOND.

Place.	Altitude. (Feet.)	Intermediate Distances. (Kils.)	Progressive Totals. (Kils.)
Les Baraques - -	—	11	85
Brutinel - - -	3,248	2	87
Les ·Roberts - -	—	2	89
Laye' - ↳ -	3,937	1	90
Summit - - -	*4,117*	2	92
Chauvel - · - -	—	2	94
Route d'Orcières -	3,314	1	95
·Gap· - · - -	2,382	4	99

(*Hotels at Grenoble, Vizille, Laffrey, La Mure, Corps, and Gap.*)

Up to Vizille the Col du Lautaret route (*q.v.* Chapter VI) may be followed, or either of the alternatives through Pont de Claix or Eybens. At Vizille one leaves the Lautaret road on the left and crosses the Romanche river, after which a steep ascent is entered upon of seven kilometres to Laffrey, the gradients averaging from 6 to 12 per cent.

A picturesque and undulating run follows, past the three lakes of Laffrey, Petit Chat, and Pierre Chatel, to La Mure, from which a rather steep descent leads by several zigzags to the Pont Haut. At the fork beyond the bridge the Valbonnais road is passed on the left, and a steep rise follows to Les Egats, with a short descent to La Salle, and then an undulating road to Corps.

In the next nine kilometres are several steep rises and falls, with sharp corners, followed by a nearly level stage to Chauffayer. After a drop to a bridge, $2\frac{1}{2}$ kilometres from the town, there is a gradual rise of 11 kilometres to Les Baraques, but the remaining five kilometres to the summit are much steeper, but afford fine views. The descent to Gap is also steep, with numerous windings. Though the highest point of the journey is only 4,117 feet, the route throughout is more difficult than many of the really lofty passes.

The Col d'Ornon.

In the preceding route we have seen how a road to Valbonnais branched off near the Pont Haut. It leads, in fact, to the Col d'Ornon and down to Bourg d'Oisans, on the Lautaret Pass, by the following itinerary :—

Place.	Altitude. (Feet.)	Intermediate Distances. (Kils.)	Progressive Totals. (Kils.)
Pont Haut - -	2,001	—	—
Malbuisson - -	2,297	3	3
Pont du Prétre -	2,247	$2\frac{1}{2}$	$5\frac{1}{2}$
Valbonnais - -	2,625	$3\frac{1}{2}$	9
Pont Lafayette -	2,461	2	11
Entraigues - -	2,674	2	13
Le Perrier - -	2,904	5	18
Les Dorens - -	—	$2\frac{1}{2}$	$20\frac{1}{2}$
La Chalp - -	—	$1\frac{1}{2}$	22
Chantelouve - -	3,504	2	24
Villelonge - -	—	$1\frac{1}{2}$	$25\frac{1}{2}$
Les Siands - -	—	1	$26\frac{1}{2}$
Summit - - -	4,331	1	$27\frac{1}{2}$
Le Rivier - -	—	3	$30\frac{1}{2}$
La Potuire - -	—	2	$32\frac{1}{2}$
Pont des Oulles (near Ornon) - -	3,150	$\frac{1}{2}$	33
La Pallud - -	2,953	$1\frac{1}{2}$	$34\frac{1}{2}$
La Paute - -	2,359	$4\frac{1}{2}$	39
Bourg d'Oisans (Lautaret) - - -	—	$2\frac{1}{2}$	$41\frac{1}{2}$

(*Hotels at Valbonnais and Bourg d'Oisans, and inn at Entraigues.*)

As this is merely a branch route it will pro-bably be missed by the average tourist. Almost the only circumstances in which it is likely to be followed are those of a car-owner who wishes to cover the maximum possible amount of high ground, and, instead of proceeding by the direct road. to the Col du Lautaret, elects to make a wide detour embracing the ascent of the lakes of Laffrey and afterwards the rise to the Col d'Ornon.

The road thrice crosses the River Bonne, on each side of Valbonnais and just before Entraigues. It then follows the course of the Malsanne, some-times on the right bank, sometimes on the left. The surface is moderate only, and there are occasional gullies. The gradients, however, are mostly easy all the way to the top, with half-a-dozen zigzags in the last five kilometres. The Pic du Col d'Ornon flanks the summit, together with the Cime des Mayes.

On the descending side there are four more windings, and gradients ranging from three to nine per cent. The road takes its name from the village of Ornon, which lies away on the left about half-way down; some Roman tombs were excavated here in 1866. At La Paute the Lautaret road is joined, on the straight and poplar-lined run from Sables to Bourg d'Oisans.

The Cols du Fau and de la Croix Haute.

The resources of Grenoble in the way of mountain carriage-roads are not to be exhausted in a moment, and we have still another route to consider of which this beautifully centred city is the starting point. The Col du Fau and the Col de la Croix Haute are passed successively on the main road from Grenoble to Sisteron.

From the point of view of the pass-climber, however, who revels in the possession of a car

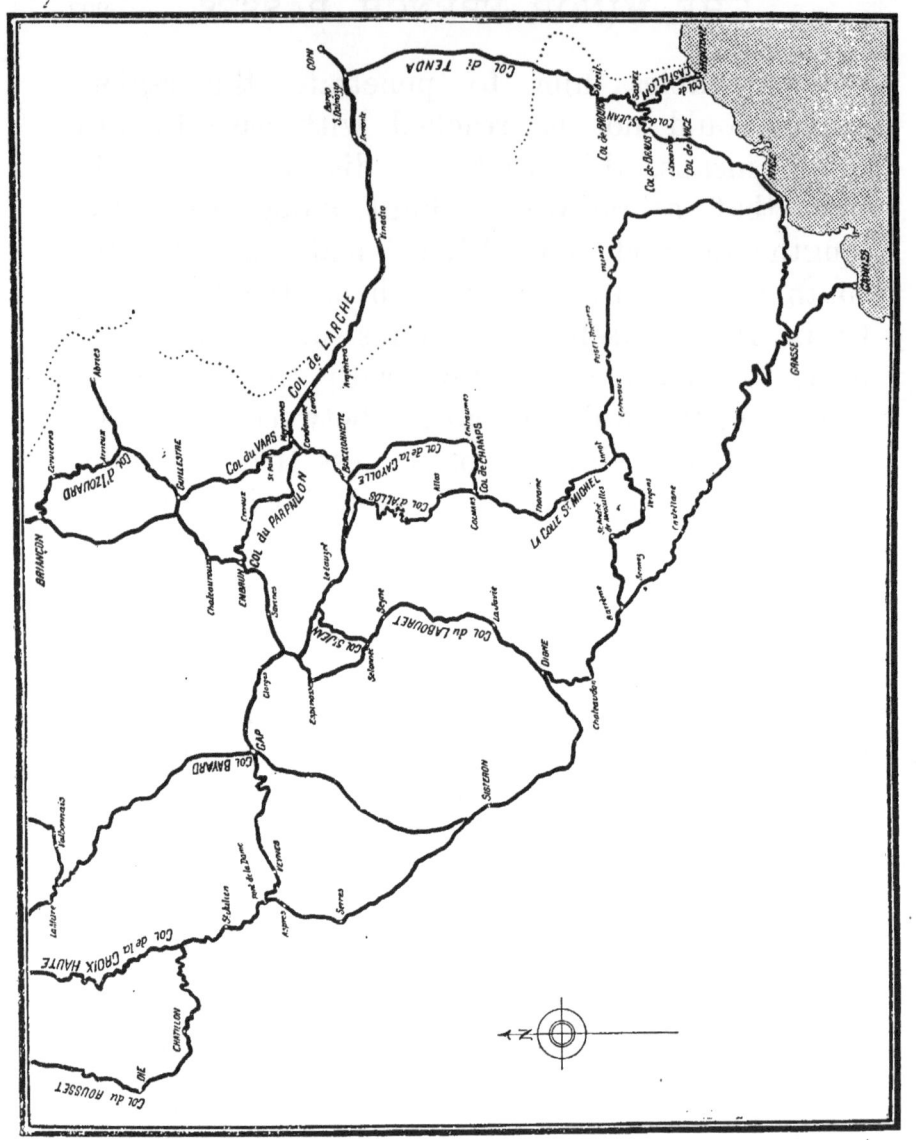

THE PASSES BETWEEN GRENOBLE AND THE RIVIERA.

which enables him to penetrate the regions
which could not be reached with ease by any
other means, this route is discounted by the
fact that a railway is built along its entire
length; in fact, the P.L.M. main line to the
south of France rises as high as the Col de la
Croix Haute itself. At Aspres-sur-Buech, moreover, it effects a junction with the line from
Briançon, the railway journey between that town
and Grenoble being one of no less than 218 kilometres, whereas the road traveller who proceeds
over the Col du Lautaret may bridge the distance in 115 kilometres—a striking testimony to
the superiority of motor-car locomotion, especially
when it is considered that the ability to attain
higher ground than the railway itself can compass at the same time confers the advantages of
enjoying much grander scenery.

The itinerary of the route in question is as
follows :—

Place.	Altitude. (Feet.)	Intermediate Distances. (Kils.)	Progressive Totals. (Kils.)
Grenoble - -	689	—	—
Pont de Claix - -	801	8	8
Varces - - -	—	$4\frac{1}{2}$	$12\frac{1}{2}$
Vif - - -	1,050	4	$16\frac{1}{2}$
Crozet - - -	—	2	$18\frac{1}{2}$
Le Poyet - -	1,542	$1\frac{1}{2}$	20
Station of St. Martin de la Cluze - -	2,041	5	25
Monestier-de-Clermont	2,776	$8\frac{1}{2}$	$33\frac{1}{2}$
Col du Fau - -	2,986	$1\frac{3}{4}$	$35\frac{1}{4}$
St. Michel Station -	—	$4\frac{3}{4}$	40
Pont de St. Michel -	2,247	$2\frac{3}{4}$	$42\frac{3}{4}$
Les Riperts - -	2,592	$4\frac{1}{4}$	47
Pont de l'Orbanne -	—	1	48
Les Chaffaud - -	2,723	$\frac{3}{4}$	$48\frac{3}{4}$
La Commanderie Station - -	2,838	$13\frac{1}{4}$	62

U

Place.	Altitude. (Feet.)	Intermediate Distances. (Kils.)	Progressive Totals. (Kils.)
Col de la Croix Haute	3,858	$8\frac{3}{4}$	$70\frac{3}{4}$
Luz la Croix Haute -	3,323	$2\frac{1}{2}$	$73\frac{1}{4}$
La Caire- - -	—	$5\frac{1}{4}$	$78\frac{1}{2}$
St. Julien-en-Beau-chène - - -	3,021	$4\frac{3}{4}$	$83\frac{1}{4}$
La Rochette - -	—	4	$87\frac{1}{4}$
La Faurie - -	2,756	3	$90\frac{1}{4}$
La Valette - -	—	$1\frac{1}{2}$	$91\frac{3}{4}$
Pont de la Dame -	2,5£9	$2\frac{1}{2}$	$94\frac{1}{4}$
Aspres - - -	2,497	4	$98\frac{1}{4}$
Aspremont - -	2,346	4	$102\frac{1}{4}$
Cross roads and Pont la Barque - -	2,215	$5\frac{1}{2}$	$107\frac{3}{4}$
Serres - - -	2,205	3	$110\frac{3}{4}$
Laragne - - -	—	17	$127\frac{3}{4}$
Sisteron - - -	1,585	14	$141\frac{3}{4}$

(*Hotels at Grenoble, Vif, Monestier-de-Clermont, Luz la Croix Haute, St. Julien-en-Beauchène, Aspres, and Sisteron.*)

From Grenoble, which is left by the Avenue de Vizille, the road is almost level to Vif, and then rises gradually to Monestier-de-Clermont, after which the gradient is rather steeper to the Col du Fau. It is sufficient to mention that this is a *route nationale* to indicate that the road is good and wide throughout. There is a gentle descent from the summit to the bridge of St. Michel, followed by a slight ascent to Les Chaffaud, after which the road is level for six kilometres. It then undulates to the railway station at La Commanderie, a kilometre beyond which the ascent to the Col de la Croix Haute is begun, and represents a rise of 1,020 feet in six kilometres, the steepest gradient being one of 6 per cent. The country is fertile, and the views are attractive without being on a grand scale. After a moderately steep descent to the village of La Croix

Haute the gradient is all but imperceptible for the remainder of the journey, the fall being one of 1,119 feet in 37½ kilometres.

The Col d'Izouard.

The direct road from Briançon follows the River Durance to Guillestre, a distance of 32½ kilometres, by a *route nationale*. An interesting diversion may be made, however, over the Col d'Izouard, at the foot of which the road is joined which follows the course of the River Guil to Guillestre, a total distance of 53 kilometres.

Whether this direct route be taken in preference to the *route nationale* is simply a question of time and preference for a sporting trip among the mountains, the chief attraction of the Col d'Izouard route being its secluded character, the pleasing pastoral scenery, and the opportunity afforded of studying the costumes and customs alike of the Valley of Arvieux. The road itself, however, is mostly steep and narrow, with numerous zigzags and gullies, but at the same time the surface itself is good. The itinerary is as follows:—

Place.			Altitude. (Feet.)	Intermediate Distances. (Kils.)	Progressive Totals. (Kils.)
Briançon	-	-	4,396	—	—
St. Catherine	-	-	3,986	1	1
Cervières -	-	-	5,266	10	11
Le Laus	-	-	5,725	1½	12½
Summit	-	-	*7,903*	7½	20
Brunissard	-	-	5,758	8	28
La Chalp -	-	-	—	1	29
Arvieux	-	-	5,118	2	31
Les Moulins	-	-	—	2	33
Fork	-	-	4,429	2	35
Guillestre -	-	-	3,248	17	52

(*Hotels at Briançon and Guillestre.*)

After descending the steep hill from the Lautaret side of Briançon, the road to Cervières should be followed. It rises steeply for four kilometres, and then undulates for the next six. From Cervières to the summit is a winding ascent of nine kilometres, with gradients ranging from 3 to as much as 14 per cent. On the Briançon side the pass is well wooded, and, when the summit has been passed, the descent runs steeply for several kilometres through a deserted amphitheatre devoid of verdure.

The gradients range from 8 to 12 per cent., and naturally there are numerous zigzags. At the village of Brunissard the scenery grows less wild, and at Arvieux, three kilometres lower, becomes pleasantly pastoral. In four kilometres the foot of the pass is reached, two kilometres short of Château Queyras on the left. We turn to the right, however, and descend by a broad road to Guillestre.

The Cols de la Viste and de Vars.

This is another somewhat difficult route, but one which must be taken of necessity by anyone proceeding from Briançon to Coni, in Italy, unless that country is entered by way of Mont Genèvre. The gradients are stiff, however, and the corners acute, and some of them cannot be negotiated without resort to the reverse. The following is the itinerary :—

Place.	Altitude. (Feet.)	Intermediate Distance. (Kils.)	Progressive Totals. (Kils.)
Guillestre	3,248	—	—
Haute Peyre	4,377	3	3
Col de la Viste	5,266	$3\frac{1}{4}$	$6\frac{1}{4}$
Vars	5,466	$3\frac{1}{2}$	$9\frac{3}{4}$
Sainte Marie	5,426	$1\frac{3}{4}$	$11\frac{1}{2}$

Place.	Altitude. (Feet.)	Intermediate Distances. (Kils.)	Progressive Totals. (Kils.)
Refuge - - -	6,562	$5\frac{1}{2}$	17
Col de Vars - -	6,939	$2\frac{1}{4}$	$19\frac{1}{4}$
Intra - - -	—	$4\frac{1}{4}$	$23\frac{1}{2}$
Le Mélézin - -	5,463	1	$24\frac{1}{2}$
St. Paul - - -	4,823	$3\frac{1}{2}$	28
Pas de la Reyssole -	—	2	30
Gleizolles - -	4,429	$3\frac{3}{4}$	$33\frac{3}{4}$
Fork - - -	4,331	$\frac{1}{4}$	34
Condamine - -	4,291	$1\frac{1}{2}$	$35\frac{1}{2}$

(Hotels at Guillestre and Condamine.)

From Guillestre to the Col de la Viste is a steep rise ranging from 6 to 14 per cent., with zigzags all the way, but is rewarded by fine views from the summit. The road then undulates for several kilometres, passing through the village of Vars to that of Sainte Marie, from which begins the steep ascent to the Col de Vars, with gradients ranging from 3 to 12 per cent.

The route is a classic one in the sense that it has been crossed by several armies from the 17th century onwards. It affords fine views, save at the summit, which is shut in on every side; it marks, by the way, the boundary between the Hautes and Basses Alpes. According to an obelisk to be found here, the road in its present form was built in 1891. A steep descent, ranging from 10 to 14 per cent., follows to Mélézin, thence there is a level kilometre, and the road again descends steeply to St. Paul, and then more gradually to a cross road. To the right one may proceed to Barcelonnette, passing on the way the town of Condamine-Chatelard, from which the ascent of the Col du Parpaillon is to be made, while the road to the left leads over the Col de Larche to Coni.

The Col du Parpaillon.

This pass is interesting from one point of view alone. It is the highest road in France. At the same time, although it *is* a road, and can be traversed by a car, it is not such as to offer the prospect of an easy or even picturesque journey, and therefore makes no appeal to the tourist on pleasure bent. As a matter of fact, it was constructed by the military in 1900 purely for strategical purposes, and is a mere cross route between two points, without leading to or from anywhere in particular, or, at all events, any towns which cannot be reached from other directions.

The pass lies between Condamine and Embrun, in the territory immediately south of Briançon, and connects the road over the Col de Vars with the main road from Briançon to Embrun and Gap. The itinerary is as follows:—

Place.	Altitude. (Feet).	Intermediate Distances. (Kils.)	Progressive Totals. (Kils.)
Condamine	4,298	—	—
Les Pras	5,676	4¾	4¾
Ste. Anne	5,722	¾	5½
Pont de Bérard	6,053	1¾	7¼
Parpaillon River	6,496	2¾	10
Cabane du Grand Parpaillon	—	¾	10¾
Refuge	—	6	16¾
Tunnel	8,671	¾	17½
Barracks	8,300	1¼	18¾
Refuge	7,841	1½	20¼
Refuge	6,824	3¼	23½
Canal de St. Sauveur	—	2¼	25¾
Canal Chenevier	6,020	1	26¾
Crévoux	5,151	3	29¾
Praveyral	4,888	1½	31¼
Champrond	—	3¼	34½
Le Villard	—	1¾	36¼

Place.	Altitude. (Feet.)	Intermediate Distances. (Kils.)	Progressive Totals. (Kils.)
Le Serre - - -	3,642	1¼	37½
Bridge of St. Privat -	2,657	5	42¼
Embrun - - -	2,854	2	44½

The gradients are very steep. From Condamine to Les Pras the rise averages from 9 to 15 per cent.; to the Parpaillon river it fluctuates between 3 and 10 per cent.; and then follows a virtually uniform climb of 9 to 11 per cent., over 7½ kilometres, to the summit. On the descending side the gradient is the same for a like distance, and, save for a brief section of 3 per cent., ranges from 7 to 10 per cent. to Crévoux. After 1½ kilometres of 10 per cent. there is a kilometre rise of 4 per cent. followed by a steep drop of 10 to 15 per cent. to Champrond. There is nearly level running to Le Serre, and the road then falls again, between 4 and 10 per cent., to the bridge of St. Privat, whence a rise of 1 to 8 per cent. leads to Embrun.

In the way of surface the road leaves much to be desired, judged by the normal French standard, but at the same time is neither so bad nor so steep as English roads such as those round Exmoor. The actual *col* is 640 feet higher than one needs to rise, as underneath the summit there is a tunnel, no less than 1,535 feet long, with an iron gate at either end.

I may add that considerable doubt has hitherto existed as to the relative heights of the Cols du Galibier and Col du Parpaillon respectively; but I am able to give the official figures, as above, thanks to the kindness of M. Lethier, the Inspecteur-Général of the French Ponts et Chaussées.

The Col de Larche.

Though only one side of this pass is in France it may for convenience be included in the present chapter. The road is a continuation of the Col de Vars route from Guillestre, or the Col du Parpaillon from Embrun, and connects Condamine with Borgo S. Dalmazzo and the Col di Tenda route to Nice. It is variously known as the Col de Larche, the Col de l'Argentière and the Col de la Madeleine, the first and second names being derived from villages *en route*, and the third from a lake situate between the two. The itinerary is as follows :—

Place.	Altitude. (Feet.)	Intermediate Distances. (Kils.)	Progressive Totals. (Kils.)
Condamine - -	4,298	—	—
Meyronnes - -	5,036	8	8
Certamussat - -	5,398	3	11
Larche (French Customs) - - -	5,545	2	13
Summit - - -	6,545	6½	19½
Italian Customs -	—	1	20½
Madeleine Lake -	6,476	2½	23
Les Granges - -	5,905	1	24
Argentera (2nd douane)	5,495	2	26
Bersezio - - -	5,380	3½	29½
Ponte Bernardo -	—	6½	36
Pietraporzio - -	4,462	2	38
Pianche - - -	3,215	8½	46½
Vinadio - - -	2,986	5	51½
Aisone - - -	2,723	4	55½
Lavoira - - -	2,707	3	58½
Demonte - - -	2,559	4	62½
Mojola - - -	2,198	7½	70
Gajola - - -	2,244	2½	72½
La Stura River -	—	1	73½
Borgo S. Dalmazzo -	2,083	6	79½
Coni (Cuneo) - -	1,542	8	87½

(*Hotels at Condamine, Meyronnes, Larche, Argentera, Borgo S. Dalmazzo, and Coni.*)

The road is good and well maintained, while the gradients are easy throughout. Between Meyronnes and Larche are two forts, the second of which, the Batterie de Viraysse, stands at 9,121 feet, and is probably the highest dwelling in Europe which is inhabited all the year round. At the village of Larche the French customs have to be dealt with, but the actual frontier is at the summit. The flora of the wide meadows adjoining the *col* are particularly rich and varied.

An Italian custom-house stands about 200 yards below, and there is a second at Argentera; between the pair the road describes six sweeping curves, with gradients of from 6 to 8 per cent. The road becomes characteristically Italian the lower one descends until it enters wine-growing territory at Vinadio, a picturesque and strongly fortified town. Thenceforward the road is virtually flat, and runs through the plain of Piedmont to Borgo S. Dalmazzo. Here one may strike to the north-east for Coni, or continue southwards for the Col di Tenda.

The Cols of St. Pierre, de la Faye, and du Pilon.

This is the most direct route to the Riviera for anyone travelling from the direction of Grenoble. We may assume that by one or other of the many routes the tourist has come as far south as Digne, and from there to Cannes the itinerary is as follows :—

Place.	Altitude. (*Feet*.)	Intermediate Distances. (*Kils*.)	Progressive Totals. (*Kils*.)
Digne - - -	1,952	—	—
Chateauredon - -	1,936	12	12
Norante - - -	2,264	12	24
Barrême - - -	2,362	6	30

Place.	Altitude. (Feet.)	Intermediate Distances. (Kils.)	Progressive Totals. (Kils.)
Tunnel - - -	3,412	12	42
Taulanne - -	3,461	1½	43½
Col St. Pierre -	*3,773*	1½	45
Castellane - -	2,362		54
La Garde - -	3,035	9	60
La Batie - -	3,084	6	66
Le Mousteiret -	3,625	5	71
Road to Mons - -	3,839	12	83
Escragnolles - -	3,314	6	89
Bridge - - -	2,838	9	98
Col de la Faye -	*3,232*	3	101
St. Vallier - -	2,346	5½	106½
Col du Pilon - -	*2,575*	3	109½
Grasse - - -	1,148	8½	118
Mouans-Sartoux -	361	7½	125½
Les Baraques -	525	3	128½
Cannes - - -	—	7½	136

(*Hotels at Digne, Barrême, Castellane, Grasse, and Cannes.*)

The road is a *route nationale* throughout, and
mostly good and wide. It undulates from Digne
to Chateauredon, and is then practically level to
Barrême, eight kilometres beyond which, however,
there is a fairly steep rise of nearly two kilometres to the Col St. Pierre. A descent follows
to Castellane, with nothing steeper than 8 per
cent., and after a couple of level kilometres
there is another rise to four kilometres beyond
La Garde, where the road attains an altitude of
3,461 feet before descending. in two kilometres
to La Batie. Anothere rise of three kilometres
follows, after which the road undulates to a
point where there is a branch road to Mons.
From the fork the general tendency of the road
is downwards save for a kilometre rise out of
Escragnolles, until a bridge is reached nine kilometres further on.

Then follows a rise of 4 to 6 per cent. in

three kilometres to the Pas de la Faye, with a subsequent run down of 5½ kilometres to St. Vallier. A gentle rise leads to the Col du Pilon, from which there is mostly a moderate descent to Grasse, with nothing steeper than 7 per cent. The road continues to fall for five kilometres, and after a level stage of four kilometres undulates gently to Cannes.

The Cols du Labouret and de Maure.

This is an alternative route between Gap and Digne, in preference to the valley road which follows the River Durance to Sisteron and Volonne, and thenceforward the Bléone river to Digne. Travellers to the Riviera in winter would naturally take the latter, but the higher route would prove the more picturesque for the return journey in spring, as soon as the road was cleared of snow. The following is the itinerary:—

Place.	Altitude. (Feet.)	Intermediate Distances. (Kils.)	Progressive Totals. (Kils.)
Digne - - -	1,952	—	—
Le Brusquet - -	2,592	11	11
La Javie - - -	2,657	4	15
Beaujeu - - -	2,887	4	19
Col du Labouret -	*4,042*	7	26
Pont de Verdaches -	3,757	2	28
Le Vernet - -	3,937	3	31
Colloubroux - -	—	3½	34½
Col de Maure - -	*4,429*	1½	36
Pont de la Blanche -	4,003	3	39
Seyne - - -	3,970	3	42
Selonnet - - -	3,445	4½	46½
Ermite - - -	3,018	5	52
Tunnels - - -	2,543	7	59
Espinasses - -	2,165	2	61
Remollon - -	2,231	6	67
La Madeleine - -	1,968	7	74
Gap - - -	2,379	12	86

(*Hotels at Digne and Gap; inn at Seyne.*)

There is nothing difficult between Digne and Beaujeu, where the ascent, however, becomes somewhat more marked, and between the village and the Col du Labouret the gradients range from 4 to 13 per cent. A descent follows to the Verdaches bridge, with a moderate fall to the Pont de la Blanche, and then level running to Seyne. After a gradual descent to Selonnet the road undulates to Ermite, with one or two steep bits, and then falls gradually to Espinasses, with a level run into Gap. From Digne to Selonnet the road is wide, though not without gullies, but between Selonnet and Espinasses it is narrow and of inferior surface.

The Col St. Jean.

From Selonnet, on the foregoing route, a short cross road goes over the Col St. Jean by the following itinerary to Le Lauzet and Barcelonnette :—

Place.	Altitude. (Feet.)	Intermediate Distances. (Kils.)	Progressive Totals. (Kils.)
Selonnet - - -	3,445	—	—
Summit - - -	*4,331*	8	8
Fork - - -	2,986	10	18
Le Lauzet - .	2,936	2	20
Le Martinet - -	3,166	6	26
Thuiles - - -	3,642	$7\frac{1}{2}$	$33\frac{1}{2}$
Barcelonnette - -	3,740	7	$40\frac{1}{2}$

(*Hotels at Le Lauzet and Barcelonnette.*)

The gradients are easy, and do not exceed 5 per cent. on the Selonnet side, nor 6 per cent. on the descent to Le Lauzet. The road is narrow and of poor surface to the *col*, but is very attractive. From Le Lauzet to Barcelonnette the road is excellent.

The Cols de Moriez and de Vergons.

The tourist bound for Nice could follow the foregoing route and proceed along the coast through Antibes and Cannes. He has great variety of choice, however, in other directions, and we may consider in the first instance a route which breaks off from the road to the Col St. Pierre at Barrême, and proceeds as follows:—

Place.	Altitude. (Feet.)	Intermediate Distances. (Kils.)	Progressive Totals. (Kils.)
Barrême - - -	2,362	—	—
Moriez - - -	2,986	10	10
Col de Moriez - -	3,297	2	12
St. André-de-Méouilles	2,936	2	14
Pont de St. Julien -	2,821	4	18
St. Julien - - -	2,992	3	21
Vergons - - -	3,380	4	25
Col de Vergons - -	3,691	2½	27½
Rouaine - -	2,936	6	33½
Scaffarels - - -	2,149	5	38½
Pont de Gueydan -	1,755	6½	45
Entrevaux - -	1,591	5½	50½
Puget-Theniers - -	1,329	7	57½
Touët-de-Beuil - -	1,083	9½	67
La Mescla - -	623	18	85
Levens-Vesubie - -	459	7	92
Colomars - - -	180	12	104
Var - - - -	—	12	116
Nice - - - -	33	5	121

(*Hotels at Barrême, St. André-de-Méouilles, Entrevaux, Puget-Theniers, and Nice.*)

The ascent is slight to within one kilometre of Moriez, from which there is a rise to the Col du Moriez of three kilometres, ranging from 4 to 6 per cent., with a shade steeper fall to St. André-de-Méouilles; this also, by the way, is a *route nationale* of good width. After several kilometres of practically level running the road rises moderately from St. Julien to the Col de Vergons, which is also known as the Col de Toutes-Aures and the Col de Chamatte.

In the descent which follows to Scaffarels there is nothing steeper than 8 per cent., while the general average is considerably lower. From Scaffarels to the Rivieran coast at Nice the descent of some 2,000 feet is extended over so great a distance as to constitute, to the eye at all events, a flat road.

The Col d'Allos and the Colle St. Michel.

Though the route is marked as impracticable in the Taride map it is nothing of the kind. The gradients are easy, and though the road varies in width it is nowhere very narrow. It starts at Barcelonnete and runs southward by the following itinerary :—

Place.	Altitude. (Feet.)	Intermediate Distances. (Kils.)	Progressive Totals. (Kils.)
Barcelonnette - -	3,740	—	—
Pont du Faut - -	4,396	6	6
Mourjuan · - -	—	8	14
Col d'Allos - -	7,382	6	20
La Foux - - -	5,577	$8\frac{1}{2}$	$28\frac{1}{2}$
La Baumelle - -	5,184	$2\frac{1}{2}$	31
Allos - - -	4,724	$4\frac{1}{2}$	$35\frac{1}{2}$
Colmars - - -	4,085	8	$43\frac{1}{2}$
Villars - - -	4,003	$2\frac{1}{2}$	46
Beauvezer - -	3,806	3	49
Bridge over River Verdon - - -	3,478	6	55
La Colle St. Michel -	4,938	9	64
Fugeret - - -	2,821	$11\frac{1}{2}$	$75\frac{1}{2}$
Annot - - -	2,329	$5\frac{1}{2}$	81
Scaffarels - - -	2,149	2	83
Nice (*see* Col de Vergons route) -	33	$82\frac{1}{2}$	$165\frac{1}{2}$

(*Hotels at Barcelonnette, Allos, Colmars, and Nice.*)

Three kilometres from Barcelonnette begins an almost uninterrupted ascent of 17 kilometres to the Col d'Allos, otherwise known as the Valgelaye. The gradients nowhere exceed 8 per cent. There is a hospice at the summit, which offers magnificent views. A picturesque descent, winding at first, and following the course of the River Verdon, leads through Allos and Colmars to a bridge near the village of Thorame-Haute, in 35 kilometres. Here the road again rises with a . moderate gradient to the Colle St. Michel. The descent to Fugeret ranges from 2 to 7 per cent., and continues gently to Annot and Scaffarels, where the Col de Vergons route to Nice is joined (*q.v.*, p. 301).

The Col de la Cayolle.

I have included this *col* because it is an important link in the projected "Grande Route des Alps." The road has been in course of construction by the military for several years past, and so far as the engineering is concerned was completed last year; but I was informed by the late M. Lethier, Inspecteur-Général des Ponts et Chaussées, that there was a section of 11 kilometres between the *col* and Entraunes which had still to be *empierré*, or surfaced. This, however, was to be accomplished before the end of the year. The following itinerary shows the line of route, but the distances are only approximate, as the exact figures are not yet available:—

Place.	Altitude. (Feet.)	Intermediate Distances. (Kils.)	Progressive Totals. (Kils)
Barcelonnette - -	3,740	—	—
Uvernet - - -	3,970	4	4
Le Villiard d'Abas	4,888	8	12

Place.	Altitude. (Feet.)	Intermediate Distances. (Kils.)	Progressive Totals. (Kils.)
Fours St. Laurent -	5,479	4	16
Bayasse - - -	5,905	4	20
Summit - - -	7,716	7	27
Entraunes- - -	4,167	20	47

(Hotels at Barcelonnette and Entraunes.)

Though the gradients on the old mule-path
were very steep, M. Lethier informed me that
those on the new road would not exceed 8 per
cent. The making of this highway reduces the
distance between Barcelonnette and Nice. An
interesting feature of the route is the colouring
of the rocks of the adjoining mountains, masses
of deep reddish-brown being interspersed with
thin lines of brilliant green.

The Col des Champs.

This is a cross route, built purely for military
purposes, and connects the Col d'Allos route
with the new road over the Col de la Cayolle.
The itinerary is as follows :—

Place.	Altitude. (Feet.)	Intermediate Distances. (Kils.)	Progressive Totals. (Kils.)
Colmars - - -	4,134	—	—
Summit - - -	6,791	12	12
Chastelonnette - -	5,315	7	19
St. Martin d'Entraunes	3,461	10	29
Villeneuve d'Entraunes	3,084	4	33
Guillaumes - -	2,543	8	41
First of five tunnels -	2,956	4	45
Fifth tunnel - -	—	4	49
Pont de Gueydan -	1,755	11	60
Nice (*see* Col de Vergons route) -	33	77	137

(Hotels at Colmars, Guillaumes, and Nice.)

The rise to the summit, which divides the
Basses Alpes from the Alpes Maritimes, is steep,
being mostly between 8 and 10 per cent., with
several zigzags. Though the road is narrow it

affords fine views. The descent is equally steep, with two short breaks of level going. At the foot of the pass (St. Martin d'Entraunes) the road from the Col de Cayolle is joined, and runs southwards until it meets, in its turn, the road to Puget-Theniers and Nice, as already mentioned.

The Cols di Tenda, de Brouis, de Pérus, de St. Jean, de Braus, and de Nice.

Yet another way of journeying to Nice is by linking up the Col de Larche route with that over the Col di Tenda and the other *cols* mentioned in the headlines; and, though part of the route is in Italian territory, it is one of Napoleon's making, and to all intents and purposes is French. There is now a regular motor diligence service, moreover, between Nice and Viévola, whence there is a railway line to Coni and Turin, though there is, of course, a high-road also.

The Col de Larche route (*q.v.*, p. 296) brought us as far as Borgo S. Dalmazzo, and from there we may proceed southwards as follows:—

Place.	Altitude. (*Feet.*)	Intermediate Distances. (*Kils.*)	Progressive Totals. (*Kils.*)
Borgo S. Dalmazzo -	2,083	—	—
Roccavione - -	2,116	2	2
Vernante - -	2,543	10	12
Limone - - -	3,297	$6\frac{1}{2}$	$18\frac{1}{2}$
Entrance to *Col di Tenda* tunnel -	4,331	6	$24\frac{1}{2}$
Exit from tunnel -	4,199	$3\frac{1}{2}$	28
Viévola (railway tunnel)	3,133	4	32
Tenda - - -	2,608	5	37
St. Dalmas (Italian Customs) - -	2,428	4	41
Frontier - - -	1,739	4	45
Fontan (French Customs) - - -	1,476	4	49
La Giandola - -	951	$7\frac{1}{2}$	$56\frac{1}{2}$

X

Place.	Altitude. (Feet.)	Intermediate Distances. (Kils.)	Progressive Totals. (Kils.)
Col de Brouis - -	2,887	9	65½
Custom House -	2,362	3½	69
Col de Pérus - -	2,165	1	70
Sospel - - -	1,132	7	77
Col de St. Jean -	2,116	6	83
Fort du Barbonnet -	2,657	2½	85½
Col de Braus - -	3,281	3½	89
Touët de l'Escarène -	1,329	9	98
L'Escarène - -	1,050	1	99
Col de Nice - -	1,247	1½	100½
Drap - - -	361	9½	110
La Trinité - -	197	2½	112½
Nice - - -	33	6½	119

(*Hotels at Borgo S. Dalmazzo, Tenda, La Giandola, Sospel, L'Escarène, and Nice.*)

The rise from Borgo S. Dalmazzo is very gradual to Limone, where a railway tunnel is cut through the mountain and emerges at Viévola. From Limone the rise is rather steeper up to the road tunnel which is cut beneath the Tenda summit. The tunnel is over three kilometres in length, and often very damp; and, though professedly illuminated by electricity, is dim enough to make the lighting of the car lamps desirable.

The descent from the other end to Viévola has a gradient of from 7 to 9 per cent., with innumerable sweeping zigzags, but moderates for the remainder of the fall to La Giandola, passing meanwhile the Italian custom-house at S. Dalmas and the French custom-house at Fontan. At La Giandola, where the direct road to Ventimiglia is quitted, the ascent is begun of the Col de Brouis, which is one of 1,936 feet in nine kilometres, with the short piece of 13 per cent. Then follows a descent to Sospel, passing midway over the Col de Pérus, with a gradient nowhere exceeding 8 per cent.

THE WINDINGS OF THE COL DI TENDA ROAD.

The valleys through which this undulating route passes are mostly somewhat bare, but there are extensive views from the summits themselves. Care is required in descending the Col de Braus to L'Escarène, as the zigzags are of the gridiron type; that is to say, they follow very quickly one upon another, with sharp turns. Still, as I have said, there is a public service over this route, and what a motor diligence with many passengers can tackle is scarcely beyond the powers of the ordinary touring car. The gradients are rather steeper than on the Sospel side, and range from 5 to 11 per cent. From L'Escarène there is a short rise to the Col de Nice, followed by a run down of several kilometres, and a level run to Nice along the valley of the Paillon.

The Col de Castillon.

From Sospel, on the Col de Braus route, a diversion may be made to Menton over the Col de Castillon. As this is only 2,461 feet in height I should not have mentioned it but for the fact that there is now a motor diligence service plying between Sospel and the coast. The following is the itinerary :—

Place.	Altitude. (Feet.)	Intermediate Distances. (Kils.)	Progressive Totals. (Kils.)
Sospel - - -	1,148	—	—
La Cinièra - -	—	$3\frac{1}{2}$	$3\frac{1}{2}$
Tunnel under Col -	2,461	$3\frac{1}{2}$	7
Baraque - - -	1,739	4	11
Bridge over the Carei	—	2	13
Monti - - -	656	4	17
Menton - - -	—	$5\frac{1}{2}$	$22\frac{1}{2}$

(*Hotels at Sospel and Menton.*)

The Col du Glandon.

Purely as a side excursion this route may be mentioned, especially as it bridges a large tract of mountainous territory not otherwise provided with any highway. Like the Col du Galibier, in fact, it is a connecting link between the two important main routes of the Col du Lautaret and the Mt. Cenis respectively. The itinerary is as follows:—

Place.	Altitude. (Feet.)	Intermediate Distances. (Kils.)	Progressive Totals. (Kils.)
Les Grandes Sables (see p. 54).	2,330	—	—
Allemont - - -	—	3	3
Le Verney - -	2,607	$4\frac{1}{2}$	$7\frac{1}{2}$
Le Rivier - - -	4,101	$4\frac{1}{2}$	12
Summit - - -	6,400	$14\frac{1}{2}$	$26\frac{1}{2}$
St. Columban - -	3,510	$11\frac{1}{2}$	38
La Chambre (see p. 78).	1,509	9	47

(Hotels at St. Columban and La Chambre; Inns at Allemont and the Summit.)

The road is of varying width and surface quality, with gradients amounting at times to 11 per cent. Above Le Rivier there is a water-splash, of a depth which varies according to the season. On the St. Columban side the zig-zags are acute, but not impracticable. For the most part the route is essentially picturesque, and provides an excursion of a sporting kind for those who have time to make it.

MISCELLANEOUS.

Exclusive of the main routes dealt with in separate chapters we have now reviewed no fewer than 48 *cols* in France. There are yet others which might be mentioned, but I have adopted the principle of dealing with no road under 3,000 feet in height unless it offers a through connection, or has some special claim to notice. Other *cols* there are, moreover, which have not been included because the roads are only of inferior quality.

CHAPTER XXII

THE SWISS PASSES.

ON the subject of the Swiss Passes it is difficult to think, speak, or write with patience, so entirely ridiculous and indefensible is the wholesale embargo which the authorities have placed upon automobiles. We have already seen how several Alpine high-roads outside Switzerland are even higher than those within the Republic, and there is not one solitary reason that can be adduced in favour of banning motor-cars on the Swiss carriage-roads as compared with the mountain highways of other countries.

The climax of absurdity is reached, moreover, when on one and the same road, part of which may be in Switzerland and part in another country, motor traffic is allowed on one side and not on the other; or when three passes converge to a point of great altitude, as in the case of the Stelvio, and cars are allowed to ascend or descend on one or two of the sides but not on the third.

Swiss opposition to motor vehicles, in short, is without rhyme or reason. It has nothing whatever to do with the nature of the roads themselves, the conditions of road traffic being identical over all the ranges of the Alps. The real cause of the boycott is simply and solely the power of the Swiss peasant. Switzerland is not only an ultra-democratic country, but delegates its internal management to local authorities to an extent which is without parallel elsewhere.

Each particular canton does practically what it likes within its own borders, and it has become only too clear that the inhabitants thereof are unconscious of anything that is done beyond. If one asked a Swiss peasant why a motor-car should be allowed on one side of a main pass and not on the other, albeit the road was of similar width and character throughout, he would shrug his shoulders and offer no reply. The forces of prejudice, stupidity, and pusillanimity alike combine to make the natives of the cantons place obstacles in the way of motor-car loco-motion; and the Swiss Government cannot say them nay.

Nevertheless it must be remembered that it is the system which is mainly at fault. Let us suppose that in England, instead of there being a statute law providing for the use of automobiles everywhere, each individual district had the power of saying yea or nay. It may be taken for granted that in certain territories motor-cars would not be allowed; even as it is, every effort is made to strain to the utmost the application of special speed limits of ten miles an hour through the Local Government Board.

The Swiss Government, however, has realised the undesirability of this wholesale prohibition of motor-car locomotion in the mountainous cantons, but under the Constitution its hands are power-less. Feeling is growing, however, in favour of passing a Federal law for the legalisation of

motor-cars to the same degree as in other countries; and, in the belief that before long some
such enactment will have taken practical shape,
I summarise below the chief features of the
Swiss and Swiss-Italian Alpine roads. Incidentally I may explain, of course, that my knowledge of these highways was of necessity gained
in the main by other means than that of the
automobile; as a matter of fact I started cycling
in Alpine territory as far back as 1895, and had
made the acquaintance of most of the Swiss
passes before the motor-car was a practical
vehicle.

It should first be mentioned, however, that
there are three passes on which motor-cars are
allowed under certain restrictions—namely, the
Simplon, the St. Gotthard, and the Brunig. The
first has already been dealt with in a separate
chapter. There is one piece of road, moreover,
which is sometimes called a pass, namely, the
Bötzberg, on which no special restrictions against
motor-cars exist; and the same remark applies
to the Swiss side of the Col de St. Cergues,
which breaks off from the Col de la Faucille
route to Geneva and strikes the lake further
east at Nyon, and to the Col de Pillon, the
Saanen Möser Pass and the Les Mosses Pass,
which lead from Aigle to Saanen and Lake
Thun.

The Bötzberg.

The Bötzberg only rises to 1,945 feet, but is
worth mentioning as an illustration of the way
in which the road traveller scores over the train-
borne passenger, inasmuch as the latter is carried

through a tunnel. The road route, on the other hand, low as it is, offers a surprise view of the most striking and agreeable kind. It occurs on the main road from Basel to Zurich, in the course of the following itinerary:—

Place.	Altitude. (Feet.)	Intermediate Distances. (Kils.)	Progressive Totals. (Kils.)
Basel - - - - -	830	—	—
Rheinfelden - - -	863	$17\frac{1}{2}$	$17\frac{1}{2}$
Mohlin - - - -	—	5	$22\frac{1}{2}$
Mumpf - - - -	1,025	$5\frac{1}{2}$	28
Stein - - - -	1,025	2	30
Eiken - - - -	—	3	33
Frick - - - -	1,190	4	37
Hornussen - - -	1,364	$3\frac{1}{2}$	$40\frac{1}{2}$
Boezen - - - -	—	$1\frac{1}{2}$	42
Effingen (ry. tunnel) -	1,522	2	44
Bötzberg summit - -	*1,945*	3	47
Brugg - - - -	1,160	$5\frac{1}{2}$	$52\frac{1}{2}$
Gebenstorff - - -	—	$1\frac{1}{2}$	54
Baden - - - -	1,260	$8\frac{1}{2}$	$62\frac{1}{2}$
Dietikon - - -	1,280	$10\frac{1}{2}$	73
Zurich - - - -	1,342	11	84

(*Hotels all along the route.*)

The railway enters a tunnel at Effingen, but a good road leads one several hundred feet higher and suddenly unfolds one of the most expansive prospects which could be found at so low an altitude, extending right away to Zurich and its lake. The quality of the view which they have missed is quite unsuspected by the railway passengers when they emerge at the Brugg end of the tunnel.

From Zurich the lake side may be followed, on the right bank, until a junction is effected with the route from Lucerne already referred to in the chapter on the Arlberg Pass.

The Col de St. Cergues.

The road over the Col de St. Cergues only rises a couple of kilometres from the fork at La Cure, where France is left behind, and then falls in six kilometres to St. Cergues, and continues to drop all the way to Nyon, on the north side of Lac Léman. The gradients are pretty much the same as on the Col de la Faucille, but there are a few more "hairpins." In the nature of things the descent affords fine views of Lac Léman and the Alps beyond. The itinerary is as follows:—

Place.	Altitude. (Feet.)	Intermediate Distances. (Kils.)	Progressive Totals. (Kils.)
La Cure (Swiss Customs)	—	—	—
Summit - - -	4,051	2	2
St. Cergues - - -	—	6	8
Trélex - - - -	—	9½	17½
Nyon - - - -	1,345	5½	23

This route is seldom likely to be used by the touring automobilist, inasmuch as he will certainly wish to see Geneva if approaching Lac Léman from Dijon, and will therefore choose the Col de la Faucille route. It may not suit his purpose, moreover, to come near the lake on his return. If it should so happen, however, that he has occasion to pass the lake twice, or if he already knows the Col de la Faucille or Geneva city, there is no reason why he should not utilise the St. Cergues road for the sake of variety. It is also somewhat shorter if the traveller is proceeding directly to or from the Rhone valley.

The Col de Pillon and the Saanen-Möser Pass.

Taken in conjunction with the Saanen-Möser Pass, the Col de Pillon enables one to cross from Aigle, between Martigny and the eastern end of

Lac Léman, to the Lake of Thun; or, instead of the Col de Pillon, the Pass of Les Mosses may be taken to Saanen, the remainder of the journey

THE NEW AND THE OLD: A MOTOR-CAR AND A HORSED DILIGENCE AT LES DIABLERETS.

being common to both. The itinerary, by way of the Col de Pillon, etc., is as follows :—

Place.	Altitude. (Feet.)	Intermediate Distances. (Kils.)	Progressive Totals. (Kils.)
Aigle - - -	1,335	—	—
Le Sépey - - -	.3,212	10	10
Vers l'Eglise - -	3,707	7	17
Les Diablerets - -	3,871	3	20
Col de Pillon - -	*5,085*	4	24
Gsteig - - -	3,911	7½	31½
Feutersoey - -	—	3	34½
Gstaad - - -	3,455	7	41½
Saanen - - -	3,327	2½	44
Saanen-Möser Summit	*4,193*	6	50
Zweisimmen - -	3,100	7½	57½
Boltigen - - -	2,726	10	67½
Erlenbach - -	2,244	14	81½
Wimmis - - -	2,231	6½	88
Thun - - -	1,844	9½	97½

(Hotels at nearly every stage.)

The road is fairly good throughout, and the gradients range from 4 to 10 per cent. The chief attraction of the route is that it leads through Les Diablerets, which is a favourite tourists' resort, with a finely-situated hotel. It may be noted in passing that the horsed diligence is still in use on this road, and takes four hours to do the 21 kilometres from Aigle to

LES DIABLERETS.

Les Diablerets. Needless to say, a motor diligence would accomplish the journey in less than half the time.

Between Les Diablerets and the summit the road passes the fine Cascades of the Dard, and also a curious isolated rock which is known as "Lot's Wife." There is a moderate descent to Gsteig, and then practically level running to Saanen. Another moderate rise leads to the summit of the Saänen-Möser Pass, whence there is a run down of equal length to Zweisimmen, followed by more or less level running to the Lake of Thun. At Wimmis there is the option of either turning to the left for Gwatt and the town of Thun, or keeping to the right and descending to Spiez, whence a run of 18½ kilometres brings one by the lakeside to Interlaken.

The Les Mosses Pass.

This alternative route to the Col de Pillon has also its well-known place of attraction in Château d'Oex, which of recent years has become a favourite winter as well as summer resort. The itinerary is as follows:—

Place.	Altitude (Feet.)	Intermediate Distances. (Kils.)	Progressive Totals. (Kils.)
Le Sépey -	3,212	—	—
La Comballaz -	4,432	6	6
Summit -	4,751	2½	8½
La Lechetteraz -	4,534	3	11½
Contour de l'Etivaz -	3,865	3	14½
Les Moulins -	—	8	22½
Château d'Oex -	3,182	3½	26
Rougemont -	3,264	6½	32½
Saanen -	3,327	4	36½

(*Hotels at Le Sépey, La Comballaz Contour de l'Etivaz, Château d'Oex, Rougemont and Saanen.*)

The ascent from Le Sépey to the summit is less irregular than that of the Col de Pillon route, and does not exceed 8 per cent. On reaching the *col* a surprise view is obtained of the famed Dent du Midi. There is an easy run down, with one short portion of 10 per cent., to Les Moulins, followed by a very slight rise to Château d'Oex, after which the road undulates to Saanen, and connects with the Saanen-Möser Pass above mentioned.

The Brunig.

Only the motorist who has never been to Switzerland before, and therefore wishes to ·visit Interlaken, should drive over the Brunig Pass; otherwise it is best avoided. It is neither lofty nor particularly picturesque; it can just as well be done at any time by rail as by road; and, if for no other reason, it should be boycotted because of the wholly senseless restrictions which are imposed upon automobilists alone, although horse drivers and cyclists are free to go as fast as they please.

Notwithstanding the fact that the road is wide, free from sharp zigzags, and, in fact, entirely devoid of dangerous conditions, cars are only allowed to drive at ten kilometres (six miles) an hour between the summit and Alpnachstad. They are only permitted on the road, moreover, between the hours of seven in the morning and four in the afternoon, and not at all on holidays. Permits have to be obtained at the station buffets at Giswil or Brunig, and are gratis; but the prospect of compulsorily taking three hours to cover 18 kilometres of easy road is so uninviting that the fewer applications that are made by motorists the better. *Timeo Danaos et dona ferentes* should be their motto. For the benefit of those, however, whom necessity compels to cross the pass, I append the itinerary as follows:—

Place.			Altitude. (Feet.)	Intermediate Distances. (Kils.)	Progressive Totals. (Kils.)
Interlaken	-	-	1,863	—	—
Ringgenberg	-	-	—	5	5
Oberried	-	-	—	$6\frac{1}{2}$	$11\frac{1}{2}$
Brienz	-	-	1,857	$6\frac{1}{2}$	18

Place.			Altitude. (*Feet.*)	*Intermediate* *Distances.* (*Kils.*)	*Progressive* *Totals.* (*Kils.*)
Brienzwiler	-	-	1,890	6	24
Summit	-	-	*3,396*	6	30
Lungern	-	-	2,477	6	36
Giswil	-	-	1,601	8	44
Sachseln	-	-	1,568	6	50
Sarnen	-	-	1,558	3	53
Alpnach	-	-	1,493	6	59
Alpnachstad	-	-	1,444	2	61
Hergiswil	-	-	—	$7\frac{1}{2}$	$68\frac{1}{2}$
Horw	-	-	—	4	$72\frac{1}{2}$
Lucerne	-	-	1,437	$4\frac{1}{2}$	77

(*Hotels all along the route.*)

It may be remarked in passing that there are plenty of ways of reaching Lucerne other than by Brunig, and even if coming from the west one may go straight across from Berne to Lucerne through Langau. Those who really wish to see Interlaken, however, might do worse than drive thither from Berne over a mere 50 kilometres of level road, and then return to Berne round the other side of the lake.

The St. Gotthard.

From the strictly motoring point of view it is possible to rate the St. Gotthard Pass too highly. As a railway route it is quite without a rival, neither the Mt. Cenis (so-called) nor the Simplon line being at all comparable with it in interest or picturesqueness. A good deal of glamour, moreover, attaches to the St. Gotthard line because of the magnificence of its approach before the pass is reached, for the journey from Brunnen to Fluelen, on the south-eastern arm of the Lake of the Four Cantons, is one of the most attractive in Europe.

On the other hand, "everybody knows" the St. Gotthard railway, and probably nine-tenths of those who may consider the desirability of including the pass in a motoring tour will already have seen much of it by rail. The same thing cannot be said of the Mt. Cenis, because, as we have seen in Chapter VII, the railway has practically nothing to do with the pass, and the tunnel is bored through another mountain altogether; while the Simplon rail route, besides being of recent origin, is incapable of conferring on the train passenger even the faintest idea of the nature of the road journey.

But the St. Gotthard line does undoubtedly afford characteristic views up to a fairly high point, and this is material when puzzling out the programme of a tour among the Alps. If one had nothing else to consider but a single journey from Lucerne to Milan, and asked one's self whether the road or rail were preferable, the answer, of course, for the motorist would be obvious and emphatic; the road traveller would score at every point, and rise another 3,000 feet while the train was buried in the great tunnel. But I am weighing not the St. Gotthard railway against the St. Gotthard Pass, but the pass against the other passes which are so numerous, so attractive, and so difficult to embrace within a single tour; and in the circumstances it seems to me that this particular pass should not be included until one has exhausted the list of those which must be crossed by road or not at all.

Then, again, there is the question of restrictions. One may waive these in the case of the

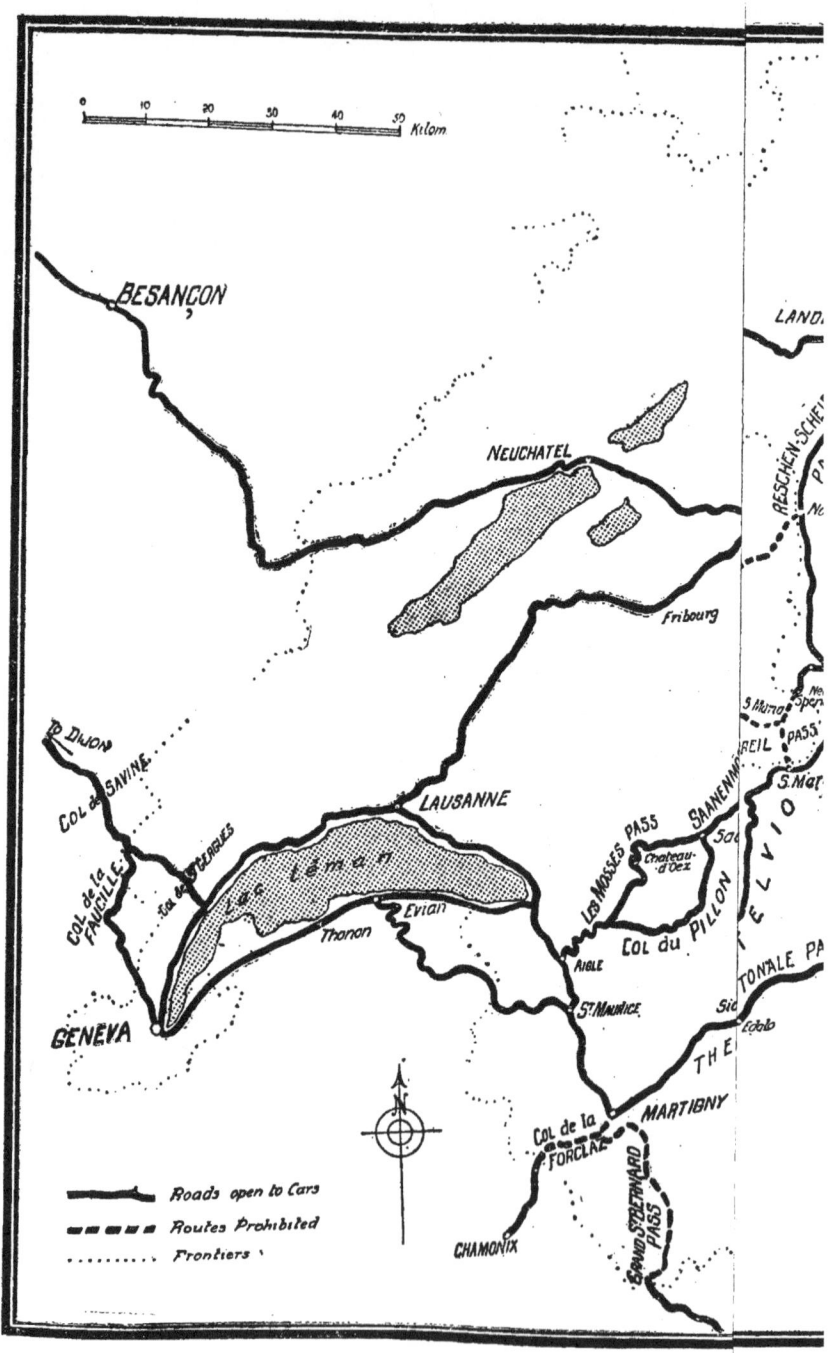

THE C

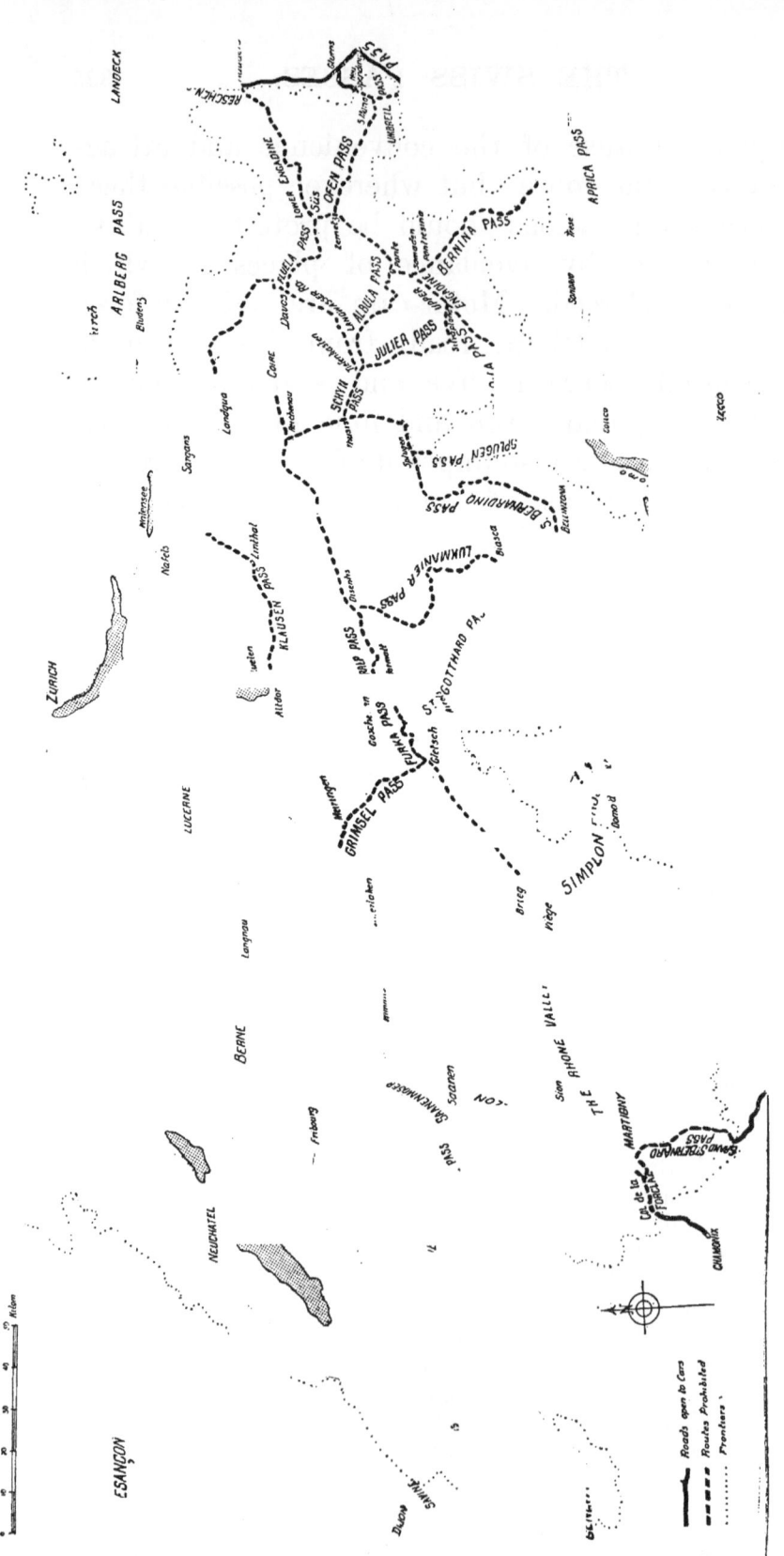

THE CENTRAL ALPINE ROUTES, FROM GENEVA TO THE STELVIO.

Simplon, because of the convenience and attractiveness of the route; but wherever possible these vexatious regulations should be protested against, if in silence, by avoidance of places in which they are enforced. Motor-cars are only suffered on the St. Gotthard road, from Göschenen to Hospenthal, between five and eight o'clock in the morning and seven and nine in the evening. A speed limit is also imposed of 12 kilometres an hour. This means, of course, either a very early start or a late finish.

Assuming, however, that the tourist is visiting Switzerland for the first time, and naturally wishes to see Lucerne and its many neighbouring attractions, the St. Gotthard route must needs be taken if he proposes to go on to Italy direct, instead of by way of the Tyrol, and the itinerary is as follows:—

Place.				Altitude. (Feet.)	Intermediate Distances. (Kils.)	Progressive Totals. (Kils.)
Fluelen	-	-	-	1,637	—	—
Altdorf (entrance to Klausen Pass)			-	1,512	3	3
Erstfeld	-	-	-	1,558	6½	9½
Silenen	-	-	-	1,739	4	13½
Amsteg	-	-	-	1,713	3	16½
Wiler	-	-	-	2,500	7	23½
Wassen	-	-	-	3,018	3½	27
Göschenen		-	-	3,704	5	32
Devil's Bridge	-		-	4,596	3½	35½
Andermatt (entrance to Oberalp Pass)			-	4,760	1½	37
Hospenthal (entrance to Furka Pass)			-	5,010	2½	39½
Summit	-	-	-	*6,926*	10	49½
Hospice	-	-	-	6,870	1	50½
Airolo	-	-	-	3,865	16	66½
Piotta	-	-	-	3,320	5½	72
Ambri Sotto	-		-	3,212	2½	74½
Fiesso	-	-	-	3,182	3	77½

Place.	Altitude. (Feet.)	Intermediate Distances. (Kils.)	Progressive Totals. (Kils.)
Faido - - -	2,365	6	83½
Chiggiogna - -	2,198	2	85½
Lavorgo - - -	1,713	3½	89
Giornico - - -	1,247	6	95
Bodio - - -	1,037	4	99
Pollegio - - -	968	2½	101½
Biasca (entrance to Lukmanier Pass) -	1,001	2	103½
Osogna - - -	965	5½	109
Cresciano - - -	919	3½	112½
Fork to S. Bernardino Pass - - -	781	7½	120
Bridge over Moesa River - - -	797	½	120½
Bellinzona - -	761	3½	124

(*Hotels at Fluelen, Altdorf, Göschenen, Andermatt, Hospenthal, summit, Airolo, Faido, Biasca, and Bellinzona.*)

Altdorf, the first village on the route after leaving Lucerne, is, of course, associated with the name William Tell, a memorial to whom is a prominent object on the roadside, while a play is annually performed here in commemoration of the exploits of the "national hero." The celebration is maintained despite the fact that all the Tell episodes are now regarded as myths, and even his very name has been officially struck out from the school-books in the Canton Glaris.

The road is nearly level to within a kilometre of Wasen, and is in close touch throughout with both the railway and the River Reuss. A short steep rise to Wasen is followed by a nearly level run, and then a moderate rise to Göschenen, where the railway enters the great tunnel. The motorist crossing the St. Gotthard from north to south, will, of course, find it convenient to finish his day's journey at Göschenen, obtain his permit from the gendarmerie (price two francs) over night, and be ready to make an early start next morning.

From the scenic point of view the next five kilometres are the most interesting on the route, the road entering and winding through the Schöllenen defile, through which the Reuss rushes madly between rocks which tower to a great height. In the nature of things the road is exposed to avalanches, and it is not surprising to find a long gallery about midway in the gorge. Further on, the famous Devil's Bridge is encountered, where the Reuss drops 100 feet. The present bridge, though eighty years old, is called the "new," but old travellers will remember that there were two bridges superimposed up to 1888, when the older and lower one was swept away by a flood.

It was the old bridge which was the scene of the memorable struggles at the close of the eighteenth century between the French and Suworoff's army of Austrians and Russians, and a lofty granite cross of comparatively recent erection to the memory of the Russian commander may now be seen above the bridge on the left. Beyond the new bridge the road rises to a rocky tunnel, with fortifications in the neighbourhood, and Andermatt is quickly reached by way of the green Urseren valley.

For the next two and a half kilometres there is a level stretch of road, from Andermatt to Hospenthal, which is practically common to the St. Gotthard, Oberalp, and Furka routes. Once through Hospenthal the motorist need no longer worry about time-limits, the remainder of the road being available between 5 a.m. and 9 p.m., only night-driving being forbidden. The gradients to the summit range from 4 to 10 per cent., with zigzags at intervals. Between the summit and the hospice, opposite which there is an hotel, the road is level, and is adjoined by several small lakes. Speaking generally, however, the scenery is bleak rather than picturesque.

It is the descent from the summit to Airolo which offers the chief attraction from the driving point of view, as the road is a fine example of the ribbon type, and in some respects resembles the Stelvio. The surface is not first-class, but is fairly good, and the corners, though not of the modern type, are nevertheless practicable. The Val Tremola, through which the road descends, is grim rather than grand. Airolo is reached after a rapid fall of 16 kilometres, and the region of the railway is once more entered upon. Following a moderate descent of four kilometres, there is a level run for six more to Fiesso. Then comes a fall of 1 in 14 for three kilometres, followed by a short level run to Faido, the River Ticino being crossed meanwhile several times.

Save for one short pitch when nearing Giornico the road is now almost level all the way to Biasca and Bellinzona, through scenery which, like that of all the southern sides of the Swiss Passes, is thoroughly Italian in character.

The Klausen.

With less reason than any other should this pass be closed to motor-cars. The road is good throughout and well graded, with better corners than on any other in Switzerland, and the element of extraordinary risk does not enter into the situation to the slightest degree. From two causes, moreover, it is a distinct deprivation to the automobilist on tour that he should be denied the opportunity of crossing the pass, for in the first place it is a very attractive one, while, in the second place, it offers a very convenient route for anyone wishing to proceed from Lucerne to Ragatz or the Arlberg Pass.

The Klausen Pass links the railway terminus at Linthal, south of Glarus and the Lake of Wallenstadt, with the village of Altdorf on the St. Gotthard Pass, by the following itinerary:—

Place.	Altitude. (Feet.)	Intermediate Distances. (Kils.)	Progressive Totals. (Kils.)
Linthal - - -	2,164	—	—
Fruttberg - -	3,386	6	6
Urnerboden - -	4,557	$7\frac{1}{2}$	$13\frac{1}{2}$
Summit - - -	6,404	9	$22\frac{1}{2}$
Balm - - -	6,034	1	$23\frac{1}{2}$
Urigen - - -	4,068	$7\frac{1}{2}$	31
Unterschächen -	3,261	$3\frac{1}{2}$	$34\frac{1}{2}$
Spiringen - -	3,038	4	$38\frac{1}{2}$
Burglen - - -	1,811	$6\frac{1}{2}$	45
Altdorf - - -	1,512	$2\frac{1}{2}$	$47\frac{1}{2}$

(Hotels at Linthal, Urnerboden, Balm, Urigen, Unterschächen, Spiringen, and Altdorf.)

There is a steep rise of about nine kilometres from Linthal, followed by a level run to Urnerboden, while from there to the summit represents a rise of 1,847 feet in nine kilometres. The backward views over the Linthal valley when rising to Urnerboden are very satisfying, while the rise to the summit brings nearer and nearer to view not only fine peaks but glistening glaciers and numerous waterfalls.

The descent on the other side, however, is even finer, and it is simply impossible to hurry, though the road itself is excellent. There are several hotels on the way down which are so agreeably situated that one or other of them should be chosen either for a luncheon halt or staying the night, if, and when, it comes to pass that motorists are allowed to travel by this route.

The Furka.

A mere glance at a map of Switzerland will reveal at once the practical inconvenience of barring the Furka Pass to motor-cars, as it not only offers a direct route across the heart of Switzerland from the south-west, but is linked up with several other passes, the Grimsel, St. Gotthard, and Oberalp all actually being inter-connected with it, while the Lukmanier, S. Bernardino, Splügen, and Maloja are within measurable distance. The Furka, in fact, is just as necessary for the crossing of the Swiss Alps from west to east, roundly speaking, as the St. Gotthard is from north to south; but under present conditions it is impossible to proceed by car from the Rhone valley to Coire, although it is a diligence route of long standing.

None the less, even if the embargo were removed forthwith, I should not be keen on counselling the motorist to take the Furka route until, at all events, the cantonal authorities evinced some desire to put it into decent condition. Primarily a good road, it has been allowed to deteriorate considerably in quality. Five-horsed diligences, descending with the skid-pan fixed the whole way, are hardly conducive to the maintenance of a smooth surface, and by the end of every season the heavy traffic has made mincemeat of the road generally, particularly at the corners, which are decidedly sharp. They manage things better in the Tyrol; tourists have been diverted thither in thousands as a consequence; and the fact that this is being realised by the Swiss renders by no means remote the prospect of a change.

A run of fifty kilometres along the Rhone valley from Brigue leads to Gletsch, where the Grimsel Pass and the Furka Pass diverge. The Furka connects with the St. Gotthard and Oberalp Passes by the following itinerary:—

Place.	Altitude. (Feet.)	Intermediate Distances. (Kils.)	Progressive Totals. (Kils.)
Gletsch - - -	5,777	—	—
Hotel Belvedere -	7,454	$7\frac{1}{2}$	$7\frac{1}{2}$
Summit - - -	7,976	$2\frac{1}{2}$	10
Tiefenbach - -	6,863	5	15
Galenstock - -	6,594	2	17
Realp - - -	5,075	$5\frac{1}{2}$	$22\frac{1}{2}$
Hospenthal - -	5,010	6	$28\frac{1}{2}$
Andermatt - -	4,737	$2\frac{1}{2}$	31

(*Hotels at Gletsch, the Belvedere, the summit, Galenstock, Hospenthal, and Andermatt; inns at Tiefenbach and Realp.*)

As Gletsch itself has an altitude of 5,777 feet, the ascent to the Furka summit, high as it is, is one of 2,199 feet only, and averages 220 feet per kilometre. The road winds above the bed of the Rhone and then crosses to the shoulder adjoining the Rhone Glacier, one of the largest in the Alps. By a series of seven zigzags the road rises to the top of the glacier and all but touches it; indeed, the mule-path to Montanvert, above Chamonix, brings one less closely to the Mer de Glace than the Furka Pass to the Rhone Glacier.

At the corner stands the Hotel Belvedere, beyond which the road leaves the ice-fall and turns eastward towards the summit, which boasts two hotels, as well as barracks and fortifications. All the way up the retrospective views have been remarkably impressive, in that they embrace some of the best-known peaks of the Bernese Oberland, towering above a hillside on which the lines of the Grimsel Pass, on the Gletsch side, may distinctly be traced.

The descent of the Furka is fairly steep to Realp, averaging as it does 231 feet per kilometre. The scenery is less striking than on the Grimsel side, but when about half-way down one may trace the zigzags of the Oberalp in the distance, just as those of the Grimsel which have been left behind. The road now runs through the grassy Urseren valley, and is all but level to Hospenthal, where the St. Gotthard Pass is crossed, and thence to Andermatt.

The Grimsel.

Historically and otherwise the Grimsel route is full of interest. It was the scene of a great battle at the end of the eighteenth century between the French and the Austrians, in which the latter were defeated. It has also been a favourite vantage ground for the investigations of many naturalists and explorers, including such famous men of science as Agassiz and Tyndall. From end to end, moreover, the pass provides one long continuity of picturesque and interesting scenery. The itinerary is as follows:—

Place.	Altitude. (Feet.)	Intermediate Distances. (Kils.)	Progressive Totals. (Kils.)
Gletsch - - -	5,777	—	—
Summit - - -	*7,126*	6	6
Hospice - - -	6,152	4	10
Handegg - -	4,528	7	17
Tschingel Bridge -	3,740	2	19
Guttannen - -	3,442	3	22
Im Hof - - -	2,054	9	31
Kirchet - - -	2,313	2	33
Meiringen - -	1,952	4	37

(*Hotels at Gletsch, Guttannen, Im Hof, Kirchet and Meiringen.*)

From Gletsch, at the foot of the Rhone Glacier, the Grimsel road rises, with a gradient of 8 per cent., by a series of zigzags from which the glacier and the Furka road are in view throughout. A steep fall through a rocky valley leads to the Hospice and Todten See, or the "Lake of the Dead," so called because its surface is nearly always frozen. The environment is unique in its barren wildness, but before long one descends into the zone of trees, passing meanwhile through three tunnels, four rock galleries, and over five bridges formed out of huge blocks of granite.

At length the famous Handegg Fall is reached, and it justifies its reputation, being the most striking of its type to be found in the Alps. It is seen to great advantage from the roadway, and its unbroken drop of over 100 feet, the thunderous roar of the waters, and the brilliant iridescence of the tossing spray go to make an ineffaceable impression on the mind of the spectator.

From the fall to Guttannen the road runs through wildly picturesque scenery, with the river Aar rushing tempestuously alongside, until it is crossed by the Schwarzbrunnen Bridge, while two kilometres further it is again crossed by the Tschingel Bridge, the valley then opening out to the village of Guttannen, a centre of the crystal-seeking industry. Gorges and green valleys now alternate on the descent to Meiringen, but, after making the winding ascent to Kirchet, the tourist should leave his vehicle and visit the famous Gorge of the Aar, which may be walked through from end to end, and should on no account be missed, the driver having meanwhile kept to the main road and waited at the Meiringen end of the gorge.

The wonders of the pass, however, are not yet exhausted, for between the gorge and Meiringen a striking waterfall adjoins the road, and, though of a different type from the Handegg, is particularly impressive. Meiringen, of course, is too well known a tourist centre to need description. When the Swiss Passes come to be opened to motor-cars the Grimsel is one of the first that should be visited; though it may be found convenient to return on one's tracks from the Hospice rather than descend to Gletsch and go over the Furka.

The Oberalp.

The Oberalp is the least picturesque of the Swiss Passes; at the same time it is a continuation of the Furka route, and if cars were not banned would certainly have to be taken by those who wish to proceed eastwards to Disentis or to Coire. The following is the itinerary :—

Place.	Altitude. (Feet.)	Intermediate Distances. (Kils.)	Progressive Totals. (Kils.)
Andermatt - -	4,737	—	—
Lake - - -	6,653	8½	18½
Summit - - -	*6,719*	2	10½
Tschamut - -	5,407	5½	16
Rueras - - -	4,596	4½	20½
Sedrun - - -	4,596	2½	23
Disentis . - - -	3,793	9	32

(*Hotels at Andermatt and Disentis.*)

From Andermatt the road rises with nine zig-zags to the summit, and, as in the case of the Furka, the surface generally is very stony and much cut about with diligence traffic. The total rise represents an average of nearly 200 feet per kilometre, and in parts it is as steep as 9 per cent. The sole object of interest is the lake, two kilometres from the summit, the trout from which are said to be the finest in the world. From the lake to the summit is virtually level. Then follows a descent, round ten zigzags, to Tschamut, with a kindred gradient to that of the Andermatt side. The valley is comparatively featureless, and a constant prey to avalanches. To Rueras the descent is rather less steep, and thenceforward the road is practically level for several kilometres, with a gentle fall to Disentis.

Here the Lukmanier Pass turns off to the right, while the forward road leads to Ilanz and Coire. It is thick with dust in dry weather, and almost impassable from mud in wet, from which it will be seen that to tempt automobilists along this east to west route the Swiss must not only remove their embargo, but also improve what is an important, and should also be a first-class, highway from west to east.

The Lukmanier.

Unique in its way is the Lukmanier, for though it is off the beaten track, and probably traversed less by the ordinary tourist than any other, save perhaps the S. Bernardino, it is exceedingly well populated, and its normal aspect is not wild but charmingly pastoral. Village succeeds village, particularly on the southern side, and the slopes are literally gay in the sunshine with innumerable white cottages between Biasca and Olivone. For the most part the road is good, if not of the broadest, while it has few steep gradients or sharp corners. The itinerary is as follows:—

Place.	Altitude. (Feet.)	Intermediate Distances. (Kils.)	Progressive Totals. (Kils.)
Biasca - - -	1,001	—	—
Loderio - - -	—	$2\frac{1}{2}$	$2\frac{1}{2}$
Chiesa di Malvaglia -	1,230	$2\frac{1}{2}$	5
Malvaglia - -	1,388	2	7
Motto - - -	—	2	9
Dongio - - -	—	2	11
Pozzo - - -	—	1	12
Acquarossa - -	1,814	1	13
Lottinga - - -	—	3	16
Torre - - -	—	2	18
Dangio - - -	2,644	1	19
Aquila - - -	—	$\frac{1}{2}$	$19\frac{1}{2}$
Olivone - - -	2,930	$3\frac{1}{2}$	23
Camperio - -	4,029	$5\frac{1}{2}$	$28\frac{1}{2}$
Campra - - -	4,675	3	$31\frac{1}{2}$
Pontelegno - -	5,476	3	$34\frac{1}{2}$
Acquacalda - -	5,866	2	$36\frac{1}{2}$
Casaccia - - -	—	$2\frac{1}{2}$	39

Place.	Altitude. (Feet.)	Intermediate Distances. (Kils.)	Progressive Totals. (Kils.)
Summit - - -	6,289	1	40
Santa Maria - -	6,043	2½	42½
Perdatsch - -	5,092	8½	51
Platta - - -	4,528	3½	54½
Curaglia - -	4,370	1½	56
Disentis - - -	3,793	6	62

(*Hotels at Biasca, Olivone, and Disentis.*)

The northern side of the pass is chiefly remarkable for the fine views it affords of the approach to Disentis, which is reached by way of several tunnels bored through the rocks. Given a sunny day, the Lukmanier would provide a thoroughly enjoyable run, and one which, if the ban upon motor-cars were removed, the motorist could take with every prospect of satisfaction.

The S. Bernardino.

Though this pass is entirely in Switzerland, its characteristics throughout are Italian, as indeed are those of the Lukmanier in the main. The S. Bernardino is an ancient road, and is therefore more irregular and less skilfully engineered than a modern pass, but for the most part offers good going; but on the lower portions the surface is loose or muddy according to the weather. The itinerary is as follows:—

Place.	Altitude. (Feet.)	Intermediate Distances. (Kils.)	Progressive Totals. (Kils.)
Bellinzona - - -	761	—	—
Bridge - - -	797	3½	3½
Fork to St. Gotthard -	781	½	4
Lumino - - -	840	1½	5½
S. Vittore - - -	935	3½	9
Roveredo - - -	978	2	11
Grono - - -	1,132	1½	12½
Leggia - - -	1,050	2½	15

Place.	Altitude. (Feet.)	Intermediate Distances. (Kils.)	Progressive Totals. (Kils.)
Cama - - -	1,119	1	16
Lostallo - - -	1,394	6	22
Cabbiolo - - -	1,476	2	24
Soazza - - -	1,968	6	30
Mesocco - - -	2,549	3	33
S. Bernardino - -	5,272	13	46
Cantoniera - -	6,266	$4\frac{1}{2}$	$50\frac{1}{2}$
Hospice (Summit) -	6,768	4	$54\frac{1}{2}$
Hinterrhein - - -	5,328	8	$62\frac{1}{2}$
Nufenen - - -	5,144	$3\frac{1}{2}$	66
Splügen (Swiss Customs) - - -	4,757	7	73

(*Hotels at Bellinzona, S. Bernardino, and Splügen.*)

Though the journey over the S. Bernardino is less pleasant, perhaps, than that over its neighbour, the Lukmanier, the former has the advantage in respect of the view from the summit. The village of S. Bernardino itself is nicely situated, and is a favourite summer station, with a mineral spring and quite a number of hotels. Everything, by the way, about the village is so entirely Italian that it is difficult to realise that the frontier line is so many miles away. The pass comes to an end on entering the Rhine valley, but a turn to the right leads to Splügen village, from which one may either proceed to Thusis or ascend the Splügen Pass.

The Fluela.

When the Engadine is thrown open to the motor-car the Fluela Pass will be one of the numerous ways of reaching it. The choice of route, of course, depends upon the point from which one starts; the Fluela, however, would

suit the convenience of anyone who was visiting
Davos Platz, a place, by the way, which is particularly attractive in summer, although best
known perhaps to winter visitors. The itinerary
is as follows:—

Place.			Altitude. (Feet.)	Intermediate Distances. (Kils.)	Progressive Totals. (Kils.)
Davos Platz	-	-	5,118	—	—
Davos Dorf	-	-	5,174	$2\frac{1}{2}$	$2\frac{1}{2}$
Tschuggen	-	-	6,368	$7\frac{1}{2}$	10
Summit -	-	-	7,835	6	16
Süs	-	-	4,659	13	29
Zernetz -	-	-	4,911	$6\frac{1}{2}$	$35\frac{1}{2}$

(*Hotels at Davos Platz, Davos Dorf, Süs, and Zernetz; inn
at Tschuggen.*)

I have twice crossed the Fluela, which is one
of the highest passes in Switzerland, and may
say that its chief points of attraction are the
wealth of *alpenrosen*, the beauty of the cattle
one meets, and the wildness of the scenery on
the upper stages, while one of the two lakes at
the summit is of a delicate silvery blue. The
pass as a whole, however, is not one of the most
picturesque, while the surface on the Engadine
side had much deteriorated the last time I passed
that way.

Since the building of the Engadine railway,
however, the amount of traffic has probably been
reduced, and the road should be less cut up in
consequence. There is a short steep stage about
half-way down, and the last two kilometres into
Süs also require care. By turning to the right
at Süs, and following the Engadine valley for a
few kilometres, one may reach the foot of the
Ofen Pass at Zernetz.

The Albula.

When the Albula railway to St. Moritz was completed, there was some talk of throwing the pass open to motorists on the ground that the bulk of the traffic had been removed from the road. No special exemption, however, has been made, and, like other roads in the Canton Grisons, it is still barred to cars. Truth to tell, it is not by any means one of the best routes from the automobilist's point of view, as it is an ancient highway, and mostly narrow in consequence. While the surface is fairly good over some portions of the route, in others it is distinctly bad. The itinerary is as follows:—

Place.	Altitude. (Feet.)	Intermediate Distances. (Kils.)	Progressive Totals. (Kils.)
Ponte - - -	5,548	—	—
Summit - - -	7,595	9	9
Weissenstein - -	6,660	4	13
Preda - - -	5,880	2	15
Bergün - - -	4,511	5	20
Alvaneu Bad - -	3,100	12	32
Tiefenkastel - -	2,910	4	36

(*Hotels at Ponte, Bergün, Alvaneu, and Tiefenkastel.*)

As one winds up the steep ascent to the summit the views of the peaks adjoining the Engadine valley become more and more prominent; but the views are less picturesque than those from the Julier, inasmuch as one is out of range of the wonderful line of lakes for which the Engadine valley is specially distinguished. The descent to Tiefenkastel passes through the savage hollow known as the Teufelsthal, surmounted by rugged crags, and pleasant pastures, the village of Bergün being particularly attractive, nestling as it does in a broad basin of vivid green. The road through the Bergünerstein, running hundreds of feet above the rushing river, is very badly surfaced, and requires to be taken

THE VILLAGE OF BERGÜN, ON THE ALBULA PASS.

with care, as it is very narrow, and in wet weather is liable to be greasy. Lower down, however, the road improves, and the descent to the village of Tiefenkastel, always a scene of animation owing to the converging of several diligence routes, is of a much more pleasing character.

The Julier.

The journey over the Julier Pass, which leads from Tiefenkastel to Silvaplana in the Upper Engadine, is worth taking, if only for the sake of the surprise view it unfolds of the Engadine

z

on the Silvaplana side. The itinerary is as follows :—

Place.	Altitude. (Feet.)	Intermediate Distances. (Kils.)	Progressive Totals. (Kils.)
Tiefenkastel	2,910	—	—
Conters	3,901	7½	7½
Savognin (Schweiningen)	3,970	1½	9
Tinzen	4,068	2	11
Roffna	4,659	3½	14½
Molins (Muhlen)	4,793	4	18½
Marmorera	5,361	4	22½
Bivio (Stalla)	5,827	3½	26
Hospice	7,349	7½	33½
Summit	*7,503*	½	34
Silvaplana	5,958	8½	42½

(Hotels all along the route.)

This pass is less susceptible to avalanches than either the Fluela or the Albula, and is also one of the earliest routes to be cleared of snow. The ascent is less uniform than is usually the case, having many level, or nearly level, stages in between the more or less steep rises. From Tiefenkastel, for example, there is an ascent of about four kilometres, with a gradient of 1 in 13, followed by eight kilometres of nearly level road. The road then rises steeply to Roffna, with another level stage to Molins. Then comes another short rise with easy gradients to Stalla, but thence to the summit is a matter of zigzags.

The most picturesque portion on the route is between Molins and Stalla, but the remainder of the ascent is through stony wastes. The road at the summit is flanked by two pillars of bluish stone, known as the columns of Julius, but whether they are of Roman or mediæval origin has never been satisfactorily determined.

Two or three kilometres beyond the summit a sublimely beautiful view is suddenly unfolded of the green lakes of the Engadine, with the snowy peaks of the Bernina group beyond, and it is one which, once seen, can never be forgotten. The last five kilometres into Silvaplana are steep, and require care, but the road surface is good.

THE JULIER HOSPICE.

The Schyn.

This pass is virtually a continuation of the Albula and Julier routes. It offers a most effective illustration of the superiority of road to rail travelling. Since I first crossed the Albula and Schyn I have made the same journey by the new line, and can state most emphatically that there is not the slightest comparison between the two methods in point of picturesqueness. The line winds about, with a suggestion of aimlessness, in enormous spirals, but the road gets down to the heart of things. The itinerary is as follows :—

Place.	Altitude. (Feet.)	Intermediate Distances. (Kils.)	Progressive Totals. (Kils.)
Tiefenkastel - -	2,910	—	—
Summit - - -	*3,333*	3	3
Solis Bridge - -	2,782	2	5
Thusis - - -	2,349	9	14

(*Hotels at Tiefenkastel and Thusis.*)

The pass of the Schyn is one of the most impressive things in Switzerland, owing to the exceptional picturesqueness of the ravine itself. The road is cut along the solid rock, and four times right through it, as well as passing under several avalanche galleries of masonry ; and while massive crags mount perpendicularly above, the road itself is nevertheless high above the Albula river, which swirls swiftly between sheer precipices that almost touch each other.

The road frequently crosses and recrosses the ravine, and there are more than a dozen bridges in all, one of which, the Solis, has a single span of 80 feet, and stands 250 feet above the stream. Other elements of the romantic, moreover, there are on this route in the shape of numerous ruined castles; and this short run from Tiefenkastel to Thusis is perhaps more replete with dramatic beauty than any similar stretch of road.

The Ofen.

This is another pass on which the exclusion of motorists can in no sense be justified. There is very little traffic on the road, which is well engineered, and for the most part the surface is excellent. The scenery through which the pass

THE UPPER ENGADINE VALLEY, INTO WHICH THE BERNINA, JULIER, ALBULA, OFEN AND MALOJA PASSES ALL LEAD.

leads is everywhere attractive, and exceptionally secluded. The itinerary is as follows :—

Place.	Altitude. (Feet.)	Intermediate Distances. (Kils.)	Progressive Totals. (Kils.)
Zernetz - - -	4,911	—	—
Roadmenders' Hut. -	5,997	7	7
Ofenberg - - -	5,919	8	15
Summit - - -	7,070	7	22
Cierfs - - - -	5,577	6	28
Fuldera - - -	5,384	3½	31½
Valcava - - -	4,708	2½	34
Santa Maria (Münsterthal)	4,547	2	36

(*Hotels at Zernetz and Santa Maria, and inn at Ofenberg.*)

Unlike the majority of the passes, the road does not present a practically unbroken ascent to the summit, with a corresponding fall, but is undulating in character. After a moderately steep rise of seven kilometres with one intervening stretch of level road, there is a winding fall of five kilometres down the wild ravine of Ova del Fuorn. The road then rises gently to the inn at Ofenberg, and undulates thenceforward to the summit, with nothing really steep, save on the last kilometre. A sublime panorama is unfolded from the top, commanding as it does both views of the Ortler range on the one hand, and the peaks of the Engadine on the other.

A steep descent from the summit, with numerous zigzags, leads through pine woods to Cierfs, and from there the road undulates to Santa Maria. From here the Umbrail Pass may be ascended, or the descent may be continued through the Münsterthal, until the Reschen-Scheideck route is joined at Schluderns.

The Umbrail.

The Umbrail is the newest Swiss carriage-road, having been opened as recently as 1901. It is merely a connecting link, however, between the Münsterthal and the Italian side of the Stelvio, and was built by the Swiss in order to avoid the need of making a detour in the Tyrol. The itinerary is as follows :—

Place.	Altitude. (Feet.)	Intermediate Distances. (Kils.)	Progressive Totals. (Kils.)
Santa Maria (Münsterthal)	4,547	—	—
Planteal - - -	6,427	$5\frac{1}{2}$	$5\frac{1}{2}$
Alpmuranza - - -	7,146	4	$9\frac{1}{2}$
Summit - - -	*8,241*	$2\frac{1}{2}$	12
Santa Maria - -	8,156	$1\frac{1}{2}$	$13\frac{1}{2}$

(*Hotels at the terminal points.*)

I crossed this pass as soon as it was opened, and found the surface extremely loose, but since then it has settled down. The road is well engineered throughout, but steep, with an average gradient amounting to over 300 feet per kilometre. In the way of scenery the pass is comparatively unattractive, and its chief claim to distinction is the fact that it is the highest carriage-road in Switzerland.

The Col de la Forclaz and the Tête Noire.

The road over the Col de la Forclaz does not in any way constitute a desirable journey, as the road is very narrow, while the gradients are steep and the corners very acute. I am speaking, of course, from the tourist's point of view, and not that of the seeker after adventure. The fact that the automobile is equal to the occasion has been shown by my friend Captain Deasy, who caught the custom-house officials napping, and duly crossed the pass on a car in the early morning. It is not a diligence route, however, and is only used by light carriages, while now even they are seldom resorted to, inasmuch as a new electric railway has been built from Chamonix to Martigny. In case anybody does care to make a sporting trip by this route when the Swiss embargo is removed, I append the itinerary as follows :—

Place.				Altitude. (Feet.)	Intermediate Distances. (Kils.)	Progressive Totals. (Kils.)
Martigny	-	-	-	1,539	—	—
Col de la Forclaz		-		4,997	12½	12½
Trient	-	-	-	4,249	2	14½
Tête Noire (Hotel)		-		3,918	2½	17
Le Chatelard Trient (Swiss Customs)			-	3,921	3	20
Vallorcine	-	-	-	4,137	3	23
Argentière	-	-	-	4,114	5	28
Chamonix	-	-	-	3,396	8	36

(*Hotels all along the route.*)

It is a matter of opinion, of course, but to my thinking the scenery on this route is greatly overrated, and the tourist will not miss much who, finding himself on hospitable French territory at Chamonix, contents himself with driving from there to Argentière and back.

CHAPTER XXIII.

SWISS-ITALIAN AND ITALIAN PASSES.

THE way in which the Swiss embargo militates against free locomotion is not confined to Switzerland itself, but interferes in several cases with the highways leading into Italy. The principle applies whether much or little is on

THE BERNINA LAKE AND HOSPICE.

Swiss soil; so long as a mountain route is common to two countries, and cars are barred on a single kilometre, it is impossible to make a through journey.

The Bernina.

The first case in point is the Bernina Pass, from which the element of danger is entirely absent. Apart from the fact that the pass is exceptionally beautiful, and therefore one to be visited, it would offer a convenient way, if free to motorists, of returning to Switzerland after descending the Italian side of the Stelvio Pass. The following is the itinerary:—

Place.	Altitude. (Feet.)	Intermediate Distances. (Kils.)	Progressive Totals. (Kils.)
Tirano - - -	1,437	—	—
Madonna di Tirano -	—	1	1
Piattamala (Italian Customs) - -	1,706	$1\frac{1}{2}$	$2\frac{1}{2}$
Swiss Custom House	—	1	$3\frac{1}{2}$
Brusio - - -	2,707	3	$6\frac{1}{2}$
Meschino - -	3,160	3	$9\frac{1}{2}$
Le Prese - - -	3,166	3	$12\frac{1}{2}$
Poschiavo - -	3,317	$4\frac{1}{2}$	17
Aino - - -	3,592	2	19
La Rosa - - -	6,161	10	29
Summit - - -	7,644	6	35
Hospice - - -	—	$\frac{1}{2}$	$35\frac{1}{2}$
Bernina Houses -	6,722	$6\frac{1}{2}$	42
Pontresina - -	5,915	$8\frac{1}{2}$	$50\frac{1}{2}$
Samaden - - -	5,669	$5\frac{1}{2}$	56

(*Hotels at Tirano, Brusio, Le Prese, Poschiavo, La Rosa, Pontresina and Samaden.*)

From the frontier to Meschino the gradients range from 5 to 8 per cent., after which there is a level run alongside the lake of Poschiavo, which occupies a pleasing position. The road continues practically level to Poschiavo, from which, however, there is a continuous rise to the summit, averaging $7\frac{1}{2}$ per cent. The road winds up the Poschiavo valley, and as far as La Rosa would offer somewhat dull travelling by any other form of progression than that of the auto-mobile; but a good car will make short work of the ascent, and as a long winter gallery is approached, and the summit is neared, suggestions

THE WINTER GALLERY ON THE BERNINA PASS.

of a glorious panorama to come are unfolded and
are quickly realised.

The Bernina peaks are among the most picturesque that can be found, and are always
covered with snow and glaciers, while the summit
also commands a magnificent prospect of the
unrivalled valley of the Upper Engadine.   The
descent to Pontresina is charming, and, being
easy of gradient, is a favourite run out and home
from Pontresina; consequently there is plenty of

THE MORTERATSCH GLACIER, FROM THE BERNINA ROAD.

carriage traffic to be encountered. Four kilometres below the Bernina houses the road passes
in close proximity to the Morteratsch glacier,
while Pontresina itself, of course, affords a splendid
prospect of the Roseg glacier.   So well known is
this side of the pass to tourists generally that there
is no necessity to expatiate upon its attractions.
It may be noted with regret, however, that an
electric railway now runs over the Bernina Pass.

The Maloja.

As with the Bernina so with the Maloja; the pass is practically in Switzerland, but constitutes a direct route from the Lake of Como to the Upper Engadine. It is picturesque from end to end, and there was never the slightest reason why motorists should not have been free to travel over it if they wished. The following is the itinerary:—

Place.	Altitude. (Feet.)	Intermediate Distances. (Kils.)	Progressive Totals. (Kils.)
Chiavenna - -	1,083	—	—
Piuro - - -	—	4	4
S. Croce - - -	1,588	1	5
Villa di Chiavenna -	2,051	3	8
Castasegna(Italian and Swiss Customs) -	2,297	2	10
Promontogno - -	—	4	14
Stampa - - -	3,281	3	17
Borgonuovo - -	3,442	1	18
Vicosoprano - -	3,543	1	19
Asarina - - -	4,429	5	24
Casaccia - - -	4,790	2½	26½
Maloja Kulm - -	*5,942*	5	31½
Hotel Kursaal - -	—	1½	33
Sils - - -	5,905	6	39
Silvaplana (entrance to Julier Pass) -	5,964	4	43
Campfer - - -	6,000	3	46
St. Moritz Dorf -	6,089	3½	49½
Cresta - - -	—	3	52½
Celerina - - -	5,656	½	53
Samaden (Fork to Bernina Pass) -	5,669	3	56

(*Hotels at nearly every stage.*)

The pass may be said to begin at Chiavenna, "the key to Italy," from which the Splügen route also diverges. Up to Vicosoprano there is nothing steeper than 7½ per cent., while the average is considerably lower, but a stage of

8½ per cent. follows to a point a kilometre beyond Asarina, whence the road is level to Casaccia.
The last stage, however, of five miles to the
summit is very steep, the gradient averaging
10 per cent., and the road winding upwards in
twelve zigzags.

The chief charms of the Maloja Pass are,
firstly, the way in which the road passes from
valley to valley, six in all; the fine view of the
Albigna group of peaks as seen from below
Casaccia; and the remarkably impetuous way in
which the Ordlegna and Maira rivers hurl themselves over their rocky beds, in close proximity
to the road. Much of the road, ·by the way, is
of fair surface, but some of it is bad, and there
are many transverse gullies.

I have included in the itinerary the road
from the summit to Samaden in order to link it
with the Julier and Bernina Passes. It is only
necessary to mention that this section, constituting as it does the major portion of the Upper
Engadine valley, is one of the most attractive
highways in Switzerland, and only needs to be
thrown open to motor-cars, and to be put in a
better state of repair, to reduce, at all events,
the tide of motoring traffic to the Tyrol, which is
almost daily increasing in volume.

The Splügen.

A wonderful pass is the Splügen, with a
type of picturesqueness all its own. While the
major portion of the route, however, is on Italian
territory the motoring tourist for the present
must needs come to a dead stop at the Swiss

Custom-house, instead of continuing to Thusis or returning over the S. Bernardino. The complete itinerary, however, is as follows :—

Place.	Altitude. (Feet.)	Intermediate Distances. (Kils.)	Progressive Totals. (Kils.)
Chiavenna - -	1,083	—	—
S. Giacomo - -	1,726	4	4
Mescolana - -	2,133	2	6
Gallivaggio - -	2,592	2	8
Lirone - - -	2,799	1	9
Prestone - - -	3,517	3	12
Campodolcino - -	3,533	1	13
Corte - - -	3,570	1	14
Pianazzo - -	4,573	4	18
Teggiate Refuge -	5,423	3	21
Stuetta Refuge -	6,155	$3\frac{1}{2}$	$24\frac{1}{2}$
Italian Custom house	6,260	$2\frac{1}{2}$	27
Summit - - -	*6,945*	3	30
Splügen (Swiss Customs)	4,790	$9\frac{3}{4}$	$39\frac{3}{4}$
Thusis - - -	2,349	26	$65\frac{3}{4}$

(*Hotels at Chiavenna, Campodolcino, Splügen and Thusis; inns at Pianazza and Teggiate.*)

A glance at the foregoing figures will show that the average gradient is relatively high, the journey involving an ascent of 5,862 feet, in 30 kilometres; and, as there are one or two interruptions to the continuous rise, the gradient is fully 200 feet per kilometre, or 333 feet per mile. It is true that this only represents an average gradient of 1 in 16; but in reality the ascent is more formidable than would seem to be the case, as it is practically continuous collarwork over a long distance. The corners, moreover, are acute, and the pass is only to be attempted by cars with particularly good locks. For such the task is perfectly feasible; but at the same time it should be understood that the pass is not to be regarded as one to be taken in the ordinary way of touring, but rather as a sporting feat.

From that point of view, however, the journey is well worth the effort, as the pass has many striking features. In the first place the construction of the road, which was completed by the Austrian Government in 1821, is magnificent as an engineering undertaking. In boldness it excels in some respects even the Stelvio itself, though, of course, it does not reach anything like so great a height; it passes, too, through scenery of grim wildness that is perhaps unequalled elsewhere. On the lower stages it is bounded by innumerable boulders, some of colossal size, and looking as if they had been thrown there by a race of Titans. Secondly, the rock tunnels and winter galleries on the route are numerous and impressive, the route being particularly exposed to avalanches.

But the thing for which above all others the road is worth visiting is the wonderful fall made by the river Madesimo at Pianazzo; there is nothing like it elsewhere in the Alps. The river sweeps down from the right, and then drops into space for no less than 650 feet without a single check. From a platform conveniently extended from the roadside one may view this stupendous drop to singular advantage, and, though the fall has not the width and volume of the Handegg on the Grimsel Pass, the effect created on the mind by the appalling depth which it reaches before it strikes *terra firma* is not to be expressed in words. Personally, I had seen both the Falls of the Rhine and the Handegg Fall before I came into close quarters with the Madesimo; but though the first-named has great width, and the second some amount of width and some amount of height, they neither of them convey the same idea of uniqueness as the fall of Pianazzo. The ascent from Campodolcino will already have exhausted a good

A CAR ENTERING A WINTER GALLERY ON THE SPLÜGEN PASS.

many of the tourist's superlatives; but the sight of the fall will leave him speechless.

The descent from the summit to Splügen village is by way of a series of *lacets*, and at the village there is the option of recrossing the range by means of the S. Bernardino Pass or descending to Thusis. The lower stage of the latter route leads through the Via Mala defile, which in character is somewhat akin to the

A a

Schyn road. The precipices tower higher above the road, but the latter is nearer the stream level than in the case of the Schyn.

The Grand St. Bernard.

For many years the road from Martigny to the Grand St. Bernard summit and back was a tourist-ridden haunt owing to the fame of the Hospice and its dogs. There was no carriage-road on the Italian side, and, unless mules were

THE GRAND ST. BERNARD LAKE AND HOSPICE.

taken to St. Rhémy, the return to Martigny was inevitable. A new road has been constructed, however, on the Italian side; but as a through route for motor-cars the Great St. Bernard Pass is impossible save under a restriction too ridiculous to be tolerated. The Swiss magnanimously allow the motor-car to ascend from Martigny provided it be drawn by a horse! The only case in which this monumentally foolish proviso has been with-drawn is that of ex-Queen Margherita of Italy, who obtained special leave to cross the pass in a legitimate manner in 1908.

In the circumstances it cannot be said that the route offers any inducement to the motorist. It is one of the least picturesque of the high Alpine passes, and, but for the romance of its dogs and its historical associations, its reputation would have been inconsiderable.

In case anyone be tempted, however, to make the journey under the conditions above named, or after the Swiss have adopted a Federal law releasing motorists from nonsensical restraints, I append the itinerary as follows :—

Place.	Altitude. (Feet.)	Intermediate Distance. (Kils.)	Progressive Totals. (Kils.)
Martigny - - -	1,558	—	—
Bourg Combe - -	- -	1½	1½
La Croix - -	—	½	2
Le Brocard - -	—	1½	3½
Les Valettes - -	2,280	2½	6
Bovernier - -	—	1	7
Sambrancher - -	—	5	12
La Douay - -	—	3½	15½
Orsières - - -	2,920	2½	18
Fontaine - - -	—	4½	22½
Rive Haute - -	—	1	23½
Liddes - - -	4,429	2½	26
Bourg St. Pierre (Swiss Customs) -	5,348	5½	31½
Cantine de Proz -	5,905	4½	36
Chalet - - -	—	2	38
Pas de Marengo -	6,430	1	39
Pont Nudrit - -	7,185	2½	41½
Hospice and *Summit* -	8,110	3	44½
Frontier - - -	—	½	45
Cantine (Italian Customs) - -	—	3½	48½
St. Rhémy - -	5,315	8	56½
Etroubles - - -	4,150	6	62½

Place.	Altitude. (Feet.)	Intermediate Distances. (Kils.)	Progressive Totals. (Kils.)
Echevenoz - -	4,035	2	68
Condemine - -	3,707	4	72
Gignod - - -	3,297	$2\frac{1}{2}$	$74\frac{1}{2}$
Variney - - -	—	$2\frac{1}{2}$	77
Aosta - - -	1,919.	4	81

(*Hotels at Martigny, Sembrancher, Orsières, Liddes, Bourg St. Pierre, St. Rhémy, Etroubles and Aosta, with sundry inns. To all intents and purposes, also, the Hospice may be regarded as an hotel.*)

The ascent is decidedly steep, and at one point, namely Liddes, touches 12 per cent. There is a Swiss custom-house at Bourg St. Pierre, although the actual frontier is not attained until a short distance beyond the summit. The last eight kilometres of the ascent have gradients ranging from 7 to 10 per cent. To expatiate upon the attractions or associations of the Hospice would be a work of supererogation; they may be found described in any guide-book to Switzerland.

After passing a small lake the new road descends in windings to St. Rhémy, an unpicturesque village, where the Italian custom-house is situated. Down to Gignod the scenery is uninteresting, but then assumes the usual pleasing aspect of the average Italian valley, and the descent to Aosta is distinctly attractive.

The Col de Sestrières.

In Chapter VII we have seen how the Mont Genévre road may be linked with the Mont Cenis Pass by a cross route between Césanne and Susa. The Col de Sestrières, however, provides an alternative connection with Turin. In the following itinerary the route is detailed westwards for the benefit of those who may have taken the cross journey already described, and may desire to return by way of Fenestrelle:—

Place.	Altitude. (Feet.)	Intermediate Distances. (Kils.)	Progressive Totals. (Kils.)
Turin - - -	771	—	—
Michelino - - -	751	$5\frac{1}{2}$	$5\frac{1}{2}$
Candiolo - - -	778	$5\frac{1}{2}$	11
None - - -	804	$5\frac{1}{2}$	$16\frac{1}{2}$
Airasca - - -	853	5	$21\frac{1}{2}$
Riva - - -	1,060	8	$29\frac{1}{2}$
Pinerolo - - -	1,234	$4\frac{1}{2}$	34
Abbadia Alpina -	1,332	2	36
Riaglietto - -	1,329	1	37
Porte - - -	1,401	$2\frac{1}{2}$	$39\frac{1}{2}$
Pinasca - - -	1,837	$8\frac{1}{2}$	48
Perosa Argentina -	2,014	3	51
Roure - - -	3,051	9	60
Mentoulles - -	3,412	3	63
Fenestrelle - -	3,773	$3\frac{1}{2}$	$66\frac{1}{2}$
Pragelato - -	5,000	11	$77\frac{1}{2}$
Summit - - -	*6,660*	11	$88\frac{1}{2}$
Champlas du Col -	5,807	4	$92\frac{1}{2}$
Césanne - - -	4,429	$7\frac{1}{2}$	100

The road was built by Napoleon for strategical purposes, but is now, of course, entirely in the possession of Italy; at the same time it may be mentioned that French is still normally spoken over the major portion of the pass—all the way, in fact, from Césanne to Fenestrelle. The road is well engineered, with few zigzags, and for the most part is of good width; in places, however, it is stony.

The gradients are moderate all the way from Turin to within a kilometre of Fenestrelle, to which town there is a rise of from 6 to 8 per cent. Beyond the town there is another rise of the same gradient over three kilometres, followed by a very slight rise to Pragelato, after which the gradient to the summit averages from 6 to 8 per cent. On the descent to Césanne there are two brief stages of 7 to 9 per cent., but the average gradient is less steep.

The pass has been the scene of many historic struggles, and is still strongly fortified. It is picturesque throughout, and the views from the summit are particularly ample. As compared, therefore, with the alternative route from Césanne to Susa, and thence to Turin by the Mont Cenis route, the Col de Sestrières offers more beauty and a better highway, but involves a climb of 6,660 feet, whereas the other road is at no point higher than Césanne itself.

CHAPTER XXIV.

THE APENNINES.

THAT the Alps extend into Italy from France, Switzerland, and the Tyrol alike has already been sufficiently demonstrated. The vast plains of Lombardy and Piedmont lie at their feet; and southwards we come anew to rising ground, and the Apennines run as a continuous ridge right through the heart of the peninsula.

To what extent, the tourist may ask, do the Apennines offer obstacles or otherwise to automobile locomotion, incentives to sporting driving, or summits and scenes of grandeur and charm? The question does not come strictly within the main scope of this volume, but, as I happen to be in a position to answer it, I have thought fit to devote a brief chapter thereto. In addition to having made several visits to northern Italy, both by motor-car and other means, I travelled all round the country in 1906 on a 40-h.p. 6-cylinder Napier, by an itinerary which was only just short of 4,000 kilometres. Going as far south as Naples by one route and back by another, I crossed the Apennines several times in the course of the following comprehensive route :—

Place.	Kilometres.	Place.	Kilometres.
Milan	- - —	Padua	- - 50
Brescia	- - 103	Rovigo	- - 44
Verona	- - 67	Ferrara	- - 34
Vicenza	- - 52	Bologna	- - 83

Place.	Kilometres.	Place.	Kilometres.
Forli - -	- 65	Alessandria	- 99
Arezzo -	- 131	Turin -	- 89
Perugia -	- 83	Ivrea -	- 59
Rome -	173	Gravellona -	- 103
Terracina -	- 118	Novara -	- 64
Capua -	- 99	Milan -	- 45
Naples -	- 32	Cremona -	- 90
Frosinone -	- 145	Mantua -	68
Rome -	- 82	Verona -	- 42
Siena - -	- 226	Mestre -	- 123
Arezzo -	- 63	Treviso -	- 20
Florence -	- 87	Udine -	- 126
Pistoia -	- 41	Ampezzo de Carnia 75	
Modena -	- 148	Belluno -	- 98
Parma -	- 53	Vicenza -	- 116
Piacenza -	- 58	Brescia -	- 117
Genoa -	- 141	Milan -	- 160
Sestri Levante	- 59		
Parma -	- 147	Total	- 3,936 kils.
Piacenza -	- 58		

As a result of this experience I may say, in a
word, that the Apennines present nothing really
formidable in the way of pass-climbing by car.
The highest road is that of the Passo dell' Abetone,
between Pistoia and Modena, but its altitude is
only 4,553 feet. Next comes the Passo dei Man-
drioli, between Forli and Arezzo, with an altitude
of 3,848 feet. The Passo di Cento Croci, between
Varese (Liguria) and Borgotaro, is the next in importance, with 3,445 feet, while the road over
Monte Cimino, between Rome and Viterbo, attains
a height of 2,828 feet. The Pass of Póggio
Berceto, between Parma and Borgatoro, attains
a height of 3,116 feet, while the road between
Viterbo and Siena rises at Radicofani to a height
of 2,510 feet. It will be noticed that the itinerary above detailed passes through Udine and
Ampezzo, and therefore crosses the Della Mauria;

but this, of course, is not in the Apennines but in the Carnian Alps.

On all these roads the grading is good, the *lacets* are well designed, and the surface is excellent; as a matter of fact the mountain roads are better in this respect than those of the plains, which are appallingly dusty in dry weather and very muddy in wet. So far, therefore, from entertaining the least fear of the Apennines the automobilist should rather court them to the utmost degree possible, if only to free himself of the dust of the plains and the often intolerable heat.

Naturally the scenery of the passes lacks the rugged grandeur of the Alps, but commands many fine prospects, none the less, of charming lakes and rolling hills. The lower stages, too, are amazingly verdant. One is accustomed, of course, to think of Italy in connection with the classic and artistic associations with which the cities themselves are so liberally endowed; but, provided the tour be taken in April or May, a road journey from Milan to Bologna, Perugia, Rome, Naples, Florence, and Genoa will afford a most enjoyable experience.

CHAPTER XXV.

THE IDEAL TOUR.

TO a greater or less degree we have now reviewed in passing some hundred or more
mountain roads. To what extent is it
feasible to include these in a single tour, if time
be no object? And failing this, what is the best
selection that can conveniently be made with the
minimum of doubling on one's tracks, and the
smallest sacrifice of passes which one should aspire
to see?

Each problem is full of difficulties. In the
first place, even if time were no object, it would
be practically impossible to cover everything in
one journey without enormous detours and the
doubling of routes; and this, of course, is a much
more serious matter in respect of time and effort
than if flat roads only had to be considered. Then,
again, the time of year has an important bearing
on the question; one may be too early for the
higher passes or too late for the lower ones to be
endurable.

The two extremes in this last respect are represented on the one hand by the Stelvio and other
lofty passes, and on the other by the numerous
cols in the south of France between Grenoble and
the Riviera. The high passes will not be found
free from snow before the beginning of June, and
the Stelvio not for a fortnight later, while the
southern *cols* of France should only be attempted
in spring or autumn.

It is true that one may withstand a great deal more heat when travelling by car than by any other means; but there are limits even for the motorist. I have known the heat so great when cruising about southern France that the upholstery and bodywork of the car could not be touched with the hand. There is also the practical consideration, moreover, that the hotels on the Côte d'Azur are mostly of the " season " order, and closed in summer accordingly.

The matter is further complicated by the consideration of whether the tourist is free to make pass-storming his prime object, or whether the Continent to him is as yet virgin ground, and he desires accordingly to see some of the stock showplaces such as are ordinarily visited by rail. There are big towns in plenty which may be avoided in the former case, but which otherwise it seems a pity to ignore in a journey covering France, Switzerland, Italy and the Tyrol.

Then, too, there is the item of the car itself. It is by no means necessary to own a highpowered vehicle for the sake of climbing the passes; one could ascend them all—save a few of the minor routes of the second class, with stiff gradients and bad surfaces—in a London taxicab. But when mileage has to be amassed on the flat roads between the mountains, and the motor-car is to be used instead of the train, a good degree of power, if not essential, is at least desirable.

Premising, however, that the planning of a route is capable of infinite variation according to the time and tastes of the individual, and the amount of his existing knowledge of the Continent, I venture to put forward a working scheme for a single journey, with a view to the inclusion of what should least readily be missed. Some amount of heat, some amount of loss of picturesqueness in the way of unvisited routes, and some amount of circumlocution, are inevitable; but each of these factors I have endeavoured to reduce to the irreducible minimum.

I would suggest that, starting about the beginning of June, the motorist should proceed from Boulogne to Rheims, Troyes, and Dijon, and then cross the Col de la Savine and the Col de la Faucille to Geneva. From there he should go to Annecy, Chambéry and Grenoble, by way of the Cols de Mont Sion, du Frène (Grande Chartreuse), du Cucheron, de Porte, and de Vence. As long a stay as possible should be made at Grenoble, in order to make daily out-and-home runs in the vicinity. He may then embark upon a through journey over the Col du Lautaret, Mont Genèvre, and the Col de Sestrières to Turin, but make Briançon a centre for daily excursions. as at Grenoble, for a few days.

From Turin the Mont Cenis Pass should be climbed, and descended as far as Pont Royal, and from there the Petit St. Bernard route should be taken as far as Albertville; whence, if there be not time to run up to the summit and back, the car should be headed for Chamonix, if only to show what glorious treasures the French Alps possess in the Mont Blanc range. Geneva should next be aimed for, by way of the Col des Aravis and Bonneville. More of the French

Passes than this itinerary involves it would be difficult to include, though one admits it with regret; to do them thoroughly one should return by road, after wintering on the Riviera, and tackle the high ones as soon as they are clear of snow.

Switzerland must now be crossed by way of Berne and Lucerne to Sargans or Ragatz; so long as one touches the country at all Lucerne cannot well be ignored, for there more than anywhere else is the motor-car in evidence and welcomed, the great hotels being full of touring motorists from all parts of the world. The Palace and Schweizerhof hotels have their own garages, and there is one just opposite the National, the amiable proprietor of which hotel, by the way, Colonel Hans Pfyffer, is Vice-President of the Swiss Automobile Club. Even in the neighbourhood of Lucerne, however, the vote of the peasant has sufficient power to work mischief, and the road round the lakeside to Küssnacht, on the direct route to Fluelen, has been closed to cars, although all on the flat, and a big detour has therefore to be made through Zug.

By way of the Walen Lake and Sargans the good road to Feldkirch may next be followed and the Arlberg Pass crossed to Landeck, where, if time allows, a run may be made to Hoch-Finstermünz and the Reschen-Scheideck summit, returning, however, to Landeck, as a journey over the Stelvio at this juncture would complicate the remainder of the itinerary. From Landeck it is a level journey to Innsbruck, and from there the Brenner should be crossed to Bozen. Here superfluous luggage may be left for a time, as the town will be passed through at a later stage. The road to Verona should then be followed as far as Trient, where a turn eastwards should be made for Roncegno, in order to cross the new road over the Broccon and Gobera Passes, and thus avoid crossing the Italian frontier. The delightful trio of the Rolle, Pordoi, and Falzarego Passes may then be followed to Cortina. From there the tourist may usefully proceed northwards to Toblach, and thence back to Bozen by way of the Pusterthal. As the Stelvio has yet to be crossed it is impossible to go over the interesting chain of the Mendel, Tonale and Aprica Passes; but by all manner of means a run should be made to the Mendel summit and back to Bozen.

The valley route should then be followed to Meran and Neu Spondinig, whence the Stelvio may be crossed; but, if the Reschen-Scheideck has not been visited from Landeck, it is certainly worth while to run up to the summit and return to Neu Spondinig.

The crossing of the Stelvio, the goal of the motorist's aspirations, may now be undertaken, and the long descent into Italy will bring him to Tirano. Here it would not be amiss to run up to the Belvidere Inn on the Aprica Pass, and, better still, to continue to Edolo, cross the Tonale, and descend as far as the Strino fort, in order to view the beautiful Presanella peaks and glaciers; but there is no option but to return by the same route.

Flat, but glorious, running may be enjoyed to Colico, then along the east bank of Lake Como, and across to Como town, Gallarate and Arona, and thence along the shores of Lake Maggiore to Stresa and Gravellona. If the Lugano Lake be as yet unknown to the tourist he may run out and home to Lugano town from Como. From Gravellona the level road should be followed to Domo d'Ossola, whence the Simplon may be crossed, and, with a quick run along the Rhone Valley, Lausanne or Geneva may soon be reached. For variety's sake the Col de St. Cergues may be crossed from Nyon, or the Col de la Faucille route be taken a second time. Instead of crossing France by way of Dijon, however, Pontarlier and Besançon may be aimed for, and the road to Rheims and Boulogne be joined at Vitry.

Much beautiful territory will of necessity be missed by this itinerary, but it is the best that can be devised for a single tour, and certainly includes the cream of mountain travel by road. Without the slightest hesitation, however, I may say that the other passes described in this volume, save in the special cases which are mentioned as more or less undesirable, are well worth visiting as opportunity allows, and personally I should be glad to retrace my wheel-tracks not once but many times.

It is not suggested that this volume should enable the tourist to dispense with the use of ordinary maps and guides where lowland territory is concerned; there is information enough and to spare in that respect already in existence, whereas details of the mountain routes, especially as to gradients, surfaces and corners, are painfully lacking. But it may be found a convenience, in order to show the length of journey involved by my "ideal tour," if I bridge the connecting links between the passes: and I give below the kilometre distances from end to end:—

	Kils.
Boulogne	—
Rheims	308
Dijon	304
Poligny	102
Geneva (*v. p.* 258)	111
Grenoble (*v. p.* 263)	164
Col du Lautaret to Briançon (*v. p.* 54)	119
Mont Genèvre (*v. p.* 66)	20
Col de Sestrières to Turin (*v. p.* 357)	100
Mont Cenis Pass to Pont Royal (*v. p.* 76)	189
Albertville (*v. p.* 94)	21
Chamonix	69
Col des Aravis (*v. p.* 276)	70
Bonneval	22
Geneva	26
Lausanne	55
Berne (by Fribourg)	93
Lucerne	91
Sargans	118½
Feldkirch	31
Arlberg Pass (*v. p.* 124)	97½
Innsbruck	72
Brenner Pass (*v. p.* 134) to Bozen	123
Trient (*v. pp.* 140–1)	61
Broccon and Gobera Passes (*v. p.* 251)	107½
Rolle Pass (*v. p.* 188)	43

	Kils.
Pordoi and Falzarego Passes (*v. p.* 152 and 168)	88
Toblach (*v. p.* 176)	31
Franzensfeste (*v. p.* 175)	58
Bozen (*v. p.* 134)	48
Mendel summit and back (*v. p.* 198)	30
Meran (*v. p.* 220)	29
Neu Spondinig (*v. p.* 220)	47
Reschen-Scheideck Pass and back (*v. p.* 243)	59
Stelvio Pass (*v. p.* 222)	89½
Tirano to Fort Strino and back (*v. pp.* 207 and 214)	147
Colico	68¾
Lecco	41¾
Como	30¾
Gallarate	38½
Arona	25¾
Domo d'Ossola	57¼
Simplon Pass (*v. p.* 108)	63
Aigle	112
Col du Pillon (*v. p.* 315)	97½
Berne	26
Boulogne	789
Total	4,494¾

To this total must be added such excursions ·as may be made from Grenoble and Briançon respectively, and any extensions which may be found possible if a stay of any length be made in the beautiful Tyrol.

CHAPTER XXVI.

THE GRANDE ROUTE DES ALPES.

NO book on Alpine roads would be complete without a reference to the scheme which the excellent Touring Club de France is endeavouring to carry through under the name of the "Grande Route des Alpes." This project, in fact, is designed to form a continuous mountain high-road from Thonon, on Lac Léman, to Nice in the Alpes Maritimes, without traversing a yard of Swiss or Italian ground. It is estimated that the cost will amount to four million francs. The French Government, which has given its approval to the proposal, decided to apportion the cost among the different districts concerned; but it was found that the Département des Hautes Alpes was not wealthy enough to contribute its share, amounting to 376,000 francs. In the circumstances, therefore, the Touring Club de France has generously offered to provide half this sum itself, and there is little doubt as to the ultimate realisation of the scheme.

A reference to the accompanying map will show that the route passes over the Col des Gets, the Col de Chatillon and the Col de Mégève, and then over a portion of the Petit St. Bernard route to Séez. It then crosses the Col de l'Iséran in order to join the Mont Cenis route at Lanslebourg, descending thence to Modane, and, after crossing the Col de Galibier, descends the Col

B b

du Lautaret route to Briançon. From there it follows the main road to Guillestre, crosses the Col de Vars to Barcelonnette, and then by the Col de la Cayolle to Guillaumes, and into Puget-Théniers and Nice.

All, therefore, that requires to be done is to improve the Galibier and de Vars routes, especially the latter, and the approaches on either side of the Col de l'Iséran, and, last but not least, build a new road over the summit of the last-named mountain. This, as will readily be realised, is a formidable undertaking, as the altitude of the *col* is 9,088 feet. The " Grande Route," therefore, will not only provide a continuous highway from north to south on French soil, but will have the distinction of including what will ultimately be the highest road in Europe, as it will exceed the Stelvio by 47 feet. The new section of road will be 25 kilometres in length, and will take five years to construct.

It is true that, in one sense, the Col de l'Iséran development is the least necessary item of the scheme as a whole, inasmuch as it is already possible to descend from Albertville to Modane on the west side instead of the east; where the through route question is concerned, the important considerations are the improvement of the Galibier and de Vars routes. To the inhabitants of Savoy, however, the construction of the road over the Col de l'Iséran will be an enormous benefit; for at the present moment, though the actual distance between the Val d'Isère and Bonneval is only 18 kilometres, anyone wishing to pass from the one place to the other by carriage must make a detour

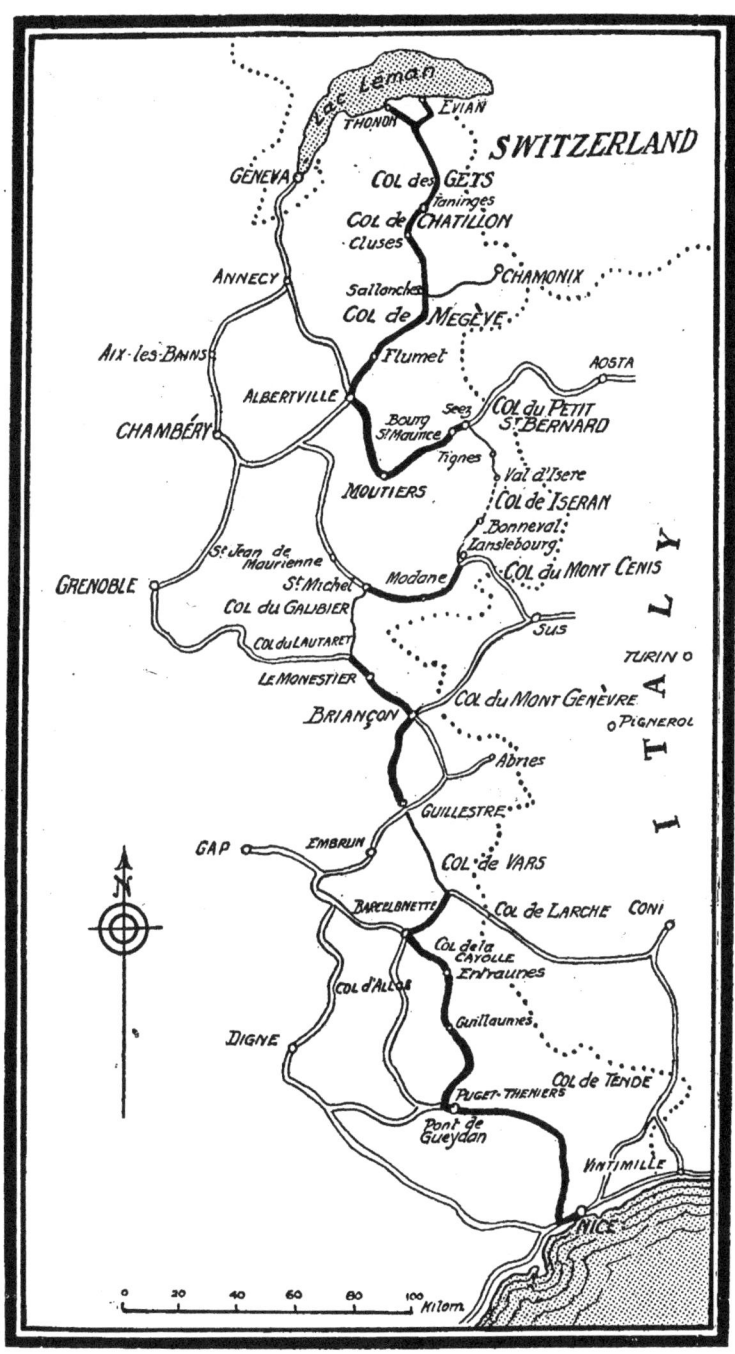

THE GRANDE ROUTE DES ALPES.

of 226 kilometres on the French side and 355 kilometres on the Italian side!

No one can have read Chapter XXI of this volume, on "The Minor French Passes," without realising that the French Alps are exceptionally well provided with means of inter-communication; but this one example to the contrary still remains, and is the more remarkable in consequence. The French are justifiably proud of their road system, and it may be taken for granted that they will not rest until the "Grande Route des Alpes" is an accomplished fact.

CHAPTER XXVII

PASSING THE CUSTOMS.

CRUISING among the Alps by road to any appreciable extent inevitably involves the crossing and re-crossing of frontier lines, and in the course of my own continental wanderings I have experienced the equivocal delights of passing the Customs on several hundred occasions. Where motor-cars are concerned, of course, the matter is more serious and complex than the process of hustling through with one's impedimenta on an ordinary journey by rail.

In these days of triptyques, however, matters are greatly simplified, especially as so many motor-cars now cross the Alpine Passes each summer that the routine is perfectly understood by all the officials concerned. The automobilist who takes his car abroad is almost sure to belong to one or other of the various motoring organisations, and will be able to obtain his triptyques before leaving his own country.

My reason for broaching this subject, however, is merely to give some practical advice on one or two points. The tourist who travels abroad by road for the first time may not unnaturally conclude that the Customs barriers will be only too effective, and that, so far from his needing to look out for them, his progress will be stopped only too often. He will find, however, that in certain cases it is quite a simple matter to over-run a frontier, so far as his exit is concerned; and it is often possible at times, though less likely, to do so at the point of entry as well.

Now the very essence of the triptyque system is that one's papers should be stamped each time one leaves the particular country concerned; otherwise the document is valueless from the point of view of being an indemnity against payment. The holder, it is true, escapes the consequences, but the Government will ultimately come down upon the organisation which issued the triptyque to the tourist, and demand payment accordingly. Naturally the custom-house officials are more keenly on the look-out for people entering than leaving, and the responsibility of obtaining the official stamp at the point of exit is vested entirely with the tourist; and nothing is easier for him than to fix his mind upon the question of passing the Customs of the country he is about to enter, and forget all about the mere formality of making a becoming exit from the one he is about to leave.

Even more important is the question of final exit from any country in respect of a long tour in which France, Italy, and Austria may be entered and re-entered several times. The holder of the triptyque cannot be too careful in seeing that the official who handles his papers at any intermediate frontier does not stamp the document in the wrong place. On most of the triptyques several spaces are provided for these preliminary stampings, while at the foot there is a separate and final one which cancels the document for good and all.

Now the average custom-house official invariably takes it for granted that when you cross his frontier line you are leaving the country for good, and will promptly affix his stamp at the bottom of the sheet. At the very outset, therefore, of the proceedings inside the custom-house the tourist must be meticulously careful to explain that he intends to re-enter the country. " *Pas définitive* " he must exclaim with all the emphasis at his command; otherwise he may have to write home for another triptyque, send an additional cheque to his club or association as deposit, and wait until the document arrives, unless he is prepared to pay cash down the next time he crosses the line.

There is one minor contingency which may occur, however, which can generally be got over. We will suppose that the traveller has left France or Switzerland with the intention of returning again on the same tour, and has had his triptyque stamped accordingly without the final cancellation. Circumstances may then arise which prevent him completing the line of tour which he had mapped out, and he does not return to that particular country. When he arrives home, therefore, although his triptyque shows readily enough that he actually cleared the customs at his last point of exit, the document is nevertheless of no official value so long as it lacks the final stamping.

He will be able, however, to secure this provided he writes a civil letter to the chief of the custom-house which he last visited, enclosing the triptyque, and, after explaining the circumstances, requesting the official to affix the final stamp. To ensure attention it is necessary to enclose a *coupon-réponse international* ; otherwise the official will have to pay the postage out of his own pocket.

Matters, of course, are greatly facilitated at the various custom-houses if the tourist be a fluent linguist; at the same time, always provided he can make clear the matter of definite exit or otherwise, the negotiations are of a routine character, and involve no conversation other than the exchange of commonplace civilities.

Another hint which may be given concerns the engine and chassis numbers, which are duly inscribed in advance on the triptyques. The holder must know exactly where the numbers are stamped on the car, and be able to point to them at once on lifting the bonnet or footboard. At some custom-houses the officials are content merely to note the registration figures on the number-plates, and do not trouble themselves about the maker's numbers; but in other cases the particulars on the triptyque are compared with the car down to the minutest detail.

There is yet another way in which the tourist may unwittingly find himself at a disadvantage, and through no fault of his own. On the last road journey I made abroad I found at Boulogue that, owing to the carelessness of the issuing clerk in London, the engine numbers had been wrongly inscribed on the triptyque, and only by the kindness of the customs official concerned was I able to have the document amended on the spot. He would have been quite within his rights, however, had he refused to accept the triptyque as corresponding to the particular car.

Even more serious was an error of which I was near to being the victim on a tour twelve months earlier. My triptyques had been obtained through a Paris organisation, and I had crossed the Col du Lautaret and Mont Genèvre to Turin, and returned to Chambéry over the Mont Cenis Pass, without any trouble at either the French or Italian frontiers. I then set off for Italy anew by the Petit St. Bernard route, and, on arrival at the French custom-house at Séez, presented my French triptyque for stamping as having left the country for the time being.

To my entire surprise the *douanier* exclaimed that the triptyque was "*annullé.*" For the moment I thought he wished to imply that it had been cancelled at the previous point of exit, and I duly pointed out, therefore, that the space for the *définitive* stamp was still blank. He reiterated his statement, however, that the triptyque was useless, and pointed to the date. Triptyques are available for twelve months, but by an act of thoughtlessness the individual who had issued mine had put in the figures for the current year in the space reserved for the date of expiry one year later.

In the end I was able to convince the *douanier*, by producing my Italian and Austrian triptyques, which had been issued at the same time, that the error was purely clerical, and after much persuasion induced him to accept the document; otherwise I should have had to deposit over £40 in cash before proceeding on my way over the Pass. It will thus be seen that on two successive journeys—namely in July, 1908, and

August, 1909—my triptyques contained formal errors of detail which might have resulted in serious inconvenience; and I can only, therefore, warn all tourists, in addition to being alive to their individual responsibilities at the frontiers, to take special care before leaving home that other people have already done their part efficiently, and that the triptyques are made out correctly.

Until a comparatively recent date there have been other matters for the touring automobilist to negotiate at the frontiers besides that of the Customs—the registering of his car and the obtaining of licences to drive. The formalities have varied according to the country concerned, and in every case there has been the initial necessity of obtaining French number-plates, and a *permis de circulation* after the driving examination, immediately upon landing in France. If the tour has been continued as far as the Tyrol there has been the additional necessity of obtaining special number-plates at the Austrian frontier. On a number of photographic illustrations in this volume, for example, a square plate may be seen both at the front and back of the car, with the inscription " ZWI 437," which was obtained at Buchs, before entering on the Arlberg Pass, and resigned at the summit of the Tonale.

Fortunately, however, matters are now very much improved in respect of registration and driving licences alike. All the chief foreign countries have agreed to accept the imprimatur of the country of origin, whichever that may be; that is to say, the driver whose car is duly registered in his own country, and who himself possesses a driving licence, may pass muster in any other country after conforming to certain formalities before leaving home. In other words, the English tourist must obtain from the Local Government Board an "international travelling pass"; and, so far as number-plates are concerned, all that is necessary is for him to affix above his county council number-plates a small plate bearing the letters "G. B." to indicate that he has come from the United Kingdom. He will still have to discharge the requirements of the Customs as heretofore, either by presentation of a triptyque or payment of actual cash; but obligations as to number-plates and licences are a thing of the past, save such as are necessary before he leaves his own home.

FINIS.

INDEX.

EYRE AND SPOTTISWOODE, LTD., EAST HARDING STREET, E.C.

WS - #0081 - 121224 - CO - 229/152/24 - PB - 9781333874919 - Gloss Lamination